Offender Rehabilitation and Therapeutic Communities

Offender rehabilitation has become increasingly and almost exclusively associated with structured cognitive-behavioural programmes. For fifty years, however, a small number of English prisons have promoted an alternative method of rehabilitation: the democratic therapeutic community (TC). These prisons offer long-term prisoners convicted of serious offences the opportunity to undertake group psychotherapy within an overtly supportive and esteem-enhancing living environment.

Drawing upon original research conducted with 'residents' (prisoners) and staff at three TC prisons, *Offender Rehabilitation and Therapeutic Communities* provides a uniquely evocative and engaging portrayal of the TC regime. Individual chapters focus on residents' adaptation to 'the TC way' of rehabilitation and imprisonment; the development of caring relationships between community members; residents' contributions towards the safe and efficient running of their community; and the greater assimilation of sexual offenders within TCs for men, made possible in part by a lessening in hypermasculinity.

By analysing residents' own accounts of 'desistance in process' in the TC, this book argues that TCs help offenders to change by enabling positive developments to their personal identity and self-narratives: to the ways in which they see themselves and their life. The radically 'different' penal environment allows its residents to become someone 'different'. *Offender Rehabilitation and Therapeutic Communities* brings a fresh, resident-centred perspective on and insight into the valuable work of forensic therapeutic communities and will be of interest to all researchers, students, practitioners, and policy makers concerned with prisons, offender rehabilitation, and desistance from crime.

Alisa Stevens is a Lecturer in Criminal Justice Studies at the University of Kent, UK. Her main areas of research interest are the correctional services (prisons and probation), offender rehabilitation, and desistance from crime.

International Series on Desistance and Rehabilitation

1. The Dynamics of Desistance
Charting pathways through change
Deidre Healy

2. Criminal Behaviour in Context
Space, place and desistance from crime
Nick Flynn

3. Cultures of Desistance
Rehabilitation, reintegration and ethnic minorities
Adam Calverley

4. Offender Rehabilitation and Therapeutic Communities
Enabling change the TC way
Alisa Stevens

Offender Rehabilitation and Therapeutic Communities

Enabling change the TC way

Alisa Stevens

LONDON AND NEW YORK

First published 2013
by Routledge
2 Park Square, Milton Park, Abingdon, Oxfordshire, OX14 4RN

Simultaneously published in the USA and Canada
by Routledge
711 Third Avenue, New York, NY 10017

First issued in paperback 2014

Routledge is an imprint of the Taylor & Francis Group, an informa company

British Library Cataloguing in Publication Data
A catalogue record for this book is available from the British Library

Library of Congress Cataloging-in-Publication Data
Stevens, Alisa.
Offender rehabilitation and therapeutic communities : enabling change the TC way.
p. cm. -- (International series on desistance and rehabilitation)
Includes bibliographical references and index.
1. Therapeutic communities. 2. Criminals--Rehabilitation. 3. Group psychoanalysis. 4. HM Prison Grendon. 5. Prisoners--Mental health services--England. I. Title.
RC489.T67S74 2012
616.89′14--dc23
2012013625

ISBN 13: 978-0-415-67018-0 (hbk)
ISBN 13: 978-0-415-63527-1 (pbk)

Typeset in Times New Roman
by Taylor & Francis Books

Every heart has its secret sorrows which the world knows not,
and oftentimes we call a man cold, when he is only sad.

Longfellow, *Hyperion*

History, despite its wrenching pain, cannot be unlived
but if faced with courage, need not be lived again.

Maya Angelou, *On the Pulse of Morning*

Contents

Series editor's foreword

The International Series on Desistance and Rehabilitation aims to provide a forum for critical debate and discussion surrounding the topics of why people stop offending and how they can be more effectively reintegrated into the communities and societies from which they came. The books published in the series will be international in outlook, but tightly focused on the unique, specific contexts and processes associated with desistance, rehabilitation and reform. Each book in the series will stand as an attempt to advance knowledge or theorising about the topics at hand, rather than being merely an extended report of a specific research project. As such, it is anticipated that some of the books included in the series will be primarily theoretical, whilst others will be more tightly focused on the sorts of initiatives which could be employed to encourage desistance. It is not our intention that books published in the series be limited to the contemporary period, as good studies of desistance, rehabilitation and reform undertaken by historians of crime are also welcome. In terms of authorship, we would welcome excellent PhD work, as well as contributions from more established academics and research teams. Most books are expected to be monographs, but edited collections are also encouraged.

Alisa Stevens's book is another very welcome and stimulating addition to the series. In *Offender Rehabilitation and Therapeutic Communities* – based on fieldwork in three prison-based therapeutic communities – Alisa argues that 'what helps' to promote positive change is the development of a more adaptive and prospective self-narrative. This, combined with an improved concept of 'oneself' (which is no longer compatible with serious offending), is what mattered for those prisoners featured in this research. Their resulting 'identity reconstruction' was possible, Alisa found, because of the ways in which therapeutic communities provide opportunities for their 'residents' to live within a community which reinforces different moral codes (of conduct, values, and culture) and which allowed for the emergence of 'a new me'. The new identity is accepted and validated by their peers, and as such helps to internalise, reinforce, and reaffirm the possibility and 'achievability' of change. Residents in therapeutic communities therefore enjoy a shared social identity; namely members of a superior 'penal club' who are consciously and actively, to varying degrees, trying to change. Using numerous approaches and insights developed by those studying desistance from crime, Alisa is able to demonstrate that therapeutic communities encourage and foster positive, desistance-focused identity reconstruction. Whilst this has yet to be explicitly explored within the wider literature on therapeutic communities, this approach is supported by wider theories of desistance (especially those which have relied on qualitative data and which support the idea of change being a process which unfolds over time). Such theories are to be found amongst the testimonies of those interviewed for this research. Beyond the concerns with fostering desistance, those familiar with research on the moral performance of prisons and the need to treat people in prison decently will find themes here that resonate with that literature. Alisa's book therefore offers a new understanding of the work and process of change which become possible within prison-based therapeutic communities.

Stephen Farrall
Sheffield
April 2012

Preface

Long Lartin high-security prison rises up incongruously in the south Worcestershire countryside; a concrete grey fortress enclosed by verdant fields. Its size and solemn purpose is best appreciated at night, when the orange glow of the vertiginously tall lights illuminate the surrounding area, like some strange, static fireball. As a child, periodically passing by the prison from the comfort of a car or train, I always enjoyed this luminous spectacle, which my parents had told me was a prison for 'very naughty people'. Sometimes the local newspaper would carry a short story about an 'incident' at the prison, a stabbing, or a small wing fire, and the Prison Service would issue a curt one-sentence response in which the details remained as impenetrable as the prison walls. Over the years, such journalistic sketches or occasional sightings of the prison increasingly made me wonder who lived there, what they had done, and why, and what it must be like to reside within this visible yet secret, public yet private, citadel.

I began reading about prisons in general, but the more I sought to understand, the more questions emerged to which I could find no satisfactory answers. The explosion of media coverage that accompanied the mesmerizing 25-day spectacle of the 1990 Strangeways riot, in particular, made me reflect even more upon what happened in prisons, in the name of public protection, retribution, deterrence, and rehabilitation. The rooftop protesters were evidently extremely angry about something, and the physically and psychologically injurious conditions that the subsequent Woolf Report described did not seem to me, as a matter of common sense, likely to be helpful for those in need of a 'good and useful life'. Yet, I also kept encountering brief references to a prison where, apparently, things were done differently and to greater effect: Grendon, a therapeutic community prison, whatever that was. Prisons, surely, were places like Long Lartin or Strangeways – 'built with bricks of shame' in which 'men their brothers maim' according to Oscar Wilde, a former prisoner himself – so it was intriguing to me how anywhere as warmly suggestive as a community, let alone one therapeutically literate, could also be a prison.

This curiosity ultimately led me to undertake this research. Its focus is the democratic therapeutic communities (TCs) at Her Majesty's Prisons (HMPs)

Gartree, Grendon, and Send, in which men and women engage in psychodynamic psychotherapy intended to help them understand, and so reduce, their offending behaviours. Its method is qualitative, semi-ethnographic, and exploratory, designed to capture, what I came to call, the TC way: my abbreviated expression for the many comments people made about their general TC experience, in which, for example, 'the way we do things here' was regularly contrasted, implicitly or explicitly, with 'normal' 'system' imprisonment. This experience is of an often tentative and always demanding inner journey, departing from the criminogenic customs and codes of mainstream imprisonment, travelling through 'therapeutization', the provision of care, acquisition of collective and self-responsibility, and acceptance of vulnerability, and on towards a new destination in which a desistance-focused 'new me' may finally be located. In analysing this experience, this book reveals what a proudly counter-culture, distinctively rehabilitative regime can do to help 'very naughty people' become less so, and thus contributes towards answering at least some of those perplexing questions about prisons and prisoners, which originated for me from an early, and enduring, fascination with grey walls and orange lights.

Acknowledgements

This book began as doctoral research at the Centre for Criminology, University of Oxford. The successful completion of that doctorate owes much to my inspirational and ever-loving mother, Dorrie Baker, and to my superlative former doctoral supervisor and continuing cherished friend and mentor, Ros Burnett. Both carefully read and astutely commented upon numerous drafts of chapters and have remained tirelessly supportive of my academic endeavours. I also remain most grateful for the financial assistance I received during my doctoral studies. I am indebted to the British Federation of Women Graduates for the award of their Centenary Scholarship; to the Law Faculty, University of Oxford, for successive awards; and to Oriel College, University of Oxford, and the Open University's Crowther Fund, for help with fieldwork expenses.

My thanks also go to Mary Bosworth and Ben Crewe who diligently examined my doctoral thesis and whose constructive suggestions for improvement greatly informed the preparation of this book's manuscript. Insightful comments on chapter drafts, or answers to factual queries, were also provided by Geraldine Akerman, Catherine Appleton, Roxana Bratu, Catherine Nichols, Guy Shefer, Richard Shuker, Alex Stevens, Elizabeth Sullivan, Sarah Taylor, and Kirk Turner. The realization of this book, meanwhile, has only been possible because of the enthusiasm of the series editor, Stephen Farrall, the anonymous reviewers, and the commissioning editor, Tom Sutton, and the skilled work of the editorial and production teams at Routledge.

Finally, but most importantly, I would have had nothing to write about without the support and cooperation of research facilitators and participants throughout the duration of my fieldwork at the therapeutic communities at HMPs Gartree, Grendon, and Send during 2006 and 2007. My greatest thanks therefore go to Peter Bennett, Judy Mackenzie, and Karen Pinder, who welcomed me into 'their' TCs; and to the residents and members of staff, across all three establishments, who gave so generously of their time and thoughts, in interviews and informal conversations, and often with such wisdom, candour, and good humour. The testimonies of TC residents in particular have given this book its evocative richness. I hope they will feel that their trust in me to relate and make sense of their experiences, accurately and compassionately, has proven well founded. Wherever they may now be, I send them my heartfelt gratitude, and my warmest wishes for a contented and peaceful future.

List of abbreviations

ACTRAG	Advisory Committee on the therapeutic regime at Grendon
BSU	Barlinnie Special Unit
CJS	criminal justice system
CSAP	Correctional Services Accreditation Panel
CSCP	Cognitive Self-Change Programme
DSM-IV	*Diagnostic and Statistical Manual of Mental Disorders* (4th edition)
ESOTP	Extended Sex Offender Treatment Programme
ETS	Enhanced Thinking Skills
GTC	Gartree Therapeutic Community
HMP	Her Majesty's Prison
IEP	incentives and earned privileges
MDT	mandatory drug test
MQPL	Measuring the Quality of Prison Life
NHS	National Health Service
NOMS	National Offender Management Service
OASys	Offender Assessment System
OBP	offending behaviour programme
PCL-R	Psychopathy Checklist (Revised)
PED	parole eligibility date
PIPE	psychologically informed planned environment
ROTL	release on temporary licence
RTU'd	returned to unit
SOTP	Sex Offender Treatment Programme
TC	therapeutic community
VPU	Vulnerable Prisoners' Unit

Introduction

Offender rehabilitation and therapeutic communities

> *Has prison ever felt like rehabilitation to you before?*
>
> Please! Let me tell you, when I first came away, a prison would have two or maybe three psychologists and just look at how many they have now – and they've got to do something to justify their wage packets, haven't they? Psychologists aren't about helping people to change; they only care about risk assessment. TCs *are* about change – really helping people to change. You think nodding your head through one of them courses is going to change you? No, if you want to change, you've got to come somewhere like here.
>
> (Ross, GTC)

After a long and chequered history, and some confusion about what it encompasses and entails, offender rehabilitation is back in fashion. The moral conviction that even people who have committed the most serious of crimes can, and do, 'change *for the better*' (Robinson and Crow 2009:3, emphasis preserved) has found empirical validation in criminological studies of desistance – the 'giving up' of crime – and in a body of forensic psychological research into correctional interventions.

When offenders in prison and in the community, and the correctional staff tasked with working with them, talk about rehabilitation, they are generally referring not just to 'going straight' but the ways in which that notoriously tricky aspiration is to be achieved. Chief amongst the proposed methods in contemporary corrections is the provision of a suite of structured, cognitive-behavioural, group-work based offending behaviour programmes (OBPs). These programmes, which may address general criminal behaviour, substance misuse, or violent and sexually violent offending, derive from a series of Canadian and North American meta-analytic (statistically aggregated) studies which identified key variables associated with the reduction or elimination of criminal recidivism. The resulting literature, collectively known as 'what works', rescued rehabilitation, as a legitimate and feasible function of punishment, from the pessimism of the 'nothing works' era, unwittingly unleashed by the unfortunate Martinson (1974); provided a coherent meta-theoretical framework by which to understand 'the psychology of criminal conduct'

(Andrews and Bonta 1994) and to devise and conduct rehabilitative work with offenders in accordance with principles of 'human service' (Andrews 1995) and 'effective intervention' (McGuire 1995, 2002); and produced some encouraging – though also some unsupportive or ambiguous – evaluations of the ability of OBPs to reduce reconviction moderately (for meta-analytic reviews and discussions of key findings, see Andrews *et al.* 1990; Lipsey 1992; Lösel 1995; Redondo *et al.* 1999; Harper and Chitty 2005; MacKenzie 2006).

As the term suggests, forensic cognitive-behavioural programmes are based on positivistic assumptions that rational individuals have the capability to monitor and modify their 'faulty' thinking in order to change their criminogenic (crime producing or supporting) patterns of behaviour. The programmes accordingly focus upon replacing rigid, dysfunctional thinking and schemas, hostile interpretations of others' actions, and anti-social behaviours, with creative, abstract, and consequential thinking, interpersonal problem-solving skills, and social perspective-taking. Offenders, generally working in groups of eight to twelve, work through a schedule of treatment 'blocks', targeting specific risk factors or 'criminogenic needs', and which require participation in discussions, games, presentations, and role-play scenarios, and the completion of written exercises and in-cell 'homework'. The programmes are facilitated by specially trained staff in accordance with a detailed, structured, programme-specific treatment manual, and last for a predetermined number of sessions, of less than one year.

This 'new rehabilitationism' has had the unfortunate side-effect, however, of promoting the de facto coronation of cognitive-behavioural interventions as *the* 'best' way by which to conduct rehabilitative work with offenders; notwithstanding attempts by some scholars to highlight their limitations, especially if one is interested not only in desisting from crime or managing one's risk but leading a more holistically satisfying 'good life' (Ward and Brown 2004; Thomas-Peter 2006; Ward and Maruna 2007). Indeed, cognitive-behavioural OBPs have now become so central to understandings of what the attainment of offender rehabilitation requires that the National Offender Management Service (NOMS) – which, in England and Wales, is responsible for commissioning and delivering all adult offender management services in prisons and the community[1] – sets and monitors 'key performance targets' for the number of OBP completions. In consequence, 43 OBPs are currently accredited for use[2] (Ministry of Justice 2010a), and over 31,000[3] programme completions, across almost every prison category and probation region, were recorded during the reporting year 2010–11 (Ministry of Justice 2011a).

Included in the list of Anglo-Welsh accredited interventions, however, is the democratic therapeutic community. A therapeutic community – habitually abbreviated to TC – uses the social milieu and various forms of psychotherapy[4] to help troubled people recognize and re-experience, in real time and within the real-life laboratory of a stable social community, the aspects of their personality and ways of thinking and behaving that have damaged them and, certainly in relation to offenders, led to their infliction of damage on others.

Unlike cognitive-behaviouralism, the TC developed organically without transparent reliance upon or reference to a particular clinical doctrine or theoretical approach (Kennard 1998), other than the psychoanalytic and psychotherapeutic orientation of its pioneers (see Chapter 1). In its prison incarnation, however, the TC is informed by psychodynamic[5] theory and principles and by social learning: learning from observing, imitating, and interacting with others. In contrast to the many and varied criminological theories that seek to explain why people commit crime by reference, for example, to biological variables, or perceived relative deprivation, or estrangement from or rejection of society and its norms, or a lack of self-control combined with a tempting and seemingly low-risk opportunity, or, of course, 'deficient' thinking, forensic TC clinicians argue that fundamentally 'offences happen when an individual falls out of relationship', with oneself, others, and wider society (Cullen and Mackenzie 2011:228). The role of the TC is accordingly to provide the 'secure base' (Bowlby 1988) within which the work of healing and restoring those relationships can be achieved, in the belief that once one is fully aware of one's value as a human being, and one's essential similarity and connectedness to other valuable human beings, then it becomes impossible to do anything that will harm or diminish that shared, equally felt and equally cherished, humanity.

The prison-based TC rehabilitative method, then, combines 'slow, open'[6] psychotherapy groups of up to eight prisoners – or, in the preferred terminology of TCs, 'residents' – with community meetings and a range of community-based activities. Three mornings a week, residents punctually assemble in their allocated group room and sit in a circle for ease of visibility and communication. In a largely nondirective and unstructured manner, and facilitated by staff members who may be qualified group analysts, psychologists, or uniformed prison officers, residents collectively explore, clarify, interpret, challenge, and reconstruct over time the entire personal and offending history and internal world of each group member. Residents must be willing to examine in unflinching detail the crime(s) they committed, and critically 'unpack' the disastrous (for their victims and themselves) thought processes, emotional states, and inner conflicts that preceded, and were enacted through, their offending. They also reflect upon their own and others' experiences of and emotions evoked by daily life in the TC, with members 'bringing to the group' in particular any aspect of an individual's observable behaviour and attitude and the 'issues' they contain – a much-favoured TC word, encompassing anything that might be identified as problematic or potentially indicative of a problem – which they think should be therapeutically investigated. Within the psychodynamic tradition of psychic determinism, all the individual's conscious and unconscious thoughts, feelings, behaviours, and motivations, and social experiences, interactions, and relationships have meaning and so are diagnostically and therapeutically informative (Yalom 1980). Accordingly, everything that happens in the TC – apparently inconsequential incidents or dramatic crises alike – has to be thoroughly dissected, if residents are to acquire insight into, and in particular, make connections between, their problematic past experiences and ongoing dysfunctional behaviours, and between what has been done to the offender and what the offender has done to his or her victims.

In contrast to forensic cognitive-behavioural OBPs' tight focus upon generic and readily identifiable cognitive deficits and criminogenic needs, then, the TC approach emphasizes unearthing and understanding the historical *causes* of the individual's difficulties – often to be found in 'hidden' (unconscious) emotional meanings, motivations, and fears, dating back to early traumatic experiences – which are thought to be central to treating and overcoming the present-day *symptoms* of pathological and challenging behaviour, which include but are not restricted to offending. The social learning about and modification of behaviours is evocative rather than didactic (Downie 2004), arising from the search for 'truth' and understanding that emerges from the therapeutic explorations of the small group and a community of peers, rather than from expert instructors.

On the remaining two mornings, all residents and available staff are expected to attend their wing's community meeting, presided over by an elected resident. All members' chairs are placed against and around the walls, so that everyone can see everyone else, and staff and residents sit together in no particular (status-indicative) or consistent pattern. In these meetings, members examine, debate and, when necessary, vote upon by show of hands, any issues of interest and concern to the entire community. This may include residents' therapeutic progress (or otherwise) and difficulties between members, or arrangements for the regular and highly prized family, children's, and lifer days (extended visits from friends and family, held either on the community or in the visits room), and other social events. Notably, any resident who has broken one of the TC's cardinal rules of abstinence – no violence, no drink or drugs, no sex – or, in the judgement of his or her peers or staff, has repeatedly 'pushed boundaries' or in any other way behaved unacceptably, may face a commitment vote, in which members indicate to staff their opinion on whether that person's TC residency should continue. Less dramatically, residents must also seek in this public forum their community's opinion of, and preferably support for, applications for recategorization or release on temporary licence (ROTL) and, more routinely, their preferred choice from the range of (mandatory) paid work options and unpaid 'rep[resentative] jobs' available to residents, and perhaps, their (voluntary) participation in education and skills training and complementary therapeutic activities such as art therapy or psychodrama.

After each small group session, and in order to advance cohesion and connection across the groups, the whole community reconvenes for a feedback meeting, in which group members précis the content of their discussion and highlight any particularly traumatic or sensitive issues which have arisen and of which the community needs to be aware. Additionally, any resident can call, at any time during 'unlock', a group or wing 'special' for any personal issue, interpersonal conflict, or rule violation which cannot be deferred for discussion until the next scheduled group or community meeting. In contrast to the strictly respected time boundaries of groups and community meetings, where latecomers are refused admittance and discussions end promptly at the appointed time, 'specials' can last for as long as it takes to resolve satisfactorily the difficulty; or at least until a temporary, tolerable solution is found which will ensure the safety of both the individual and the community.

The contribution of this entirely atypical '(24/7)' rehabilitative programme is easily overlooked, since just five English secure prisons – Blundeston, Dovegate, Gartree, and Grendon for men and Send for women – currently offer TC treatment, amounting to a mere 538 places or less than 1 per cent of the present prison population. Yet, the TC programme pre-dates the rehabilitative rise of cognitive-behaviouralism, with the establishment in 1962 of Her Majesty's Prison (HMP) Grendon as an 'experimental psychiatric prison', modelled upon the therapeutic community (Pickering 1970). Grendon's early championing of rehabilitation for even the most 'damaged, disturbed and dangerous' of offenders (Shine and Newton 2000) earned it the accolade of the 'jewel in the crown' in the Anglo-Welsh Prison Service (Genders and Player 1995:202) and the admiration of criminologists internationally. Grendon remains the only prison in England to operate entirely as a TC, with places for 235 men across five distinct, semi-autonomous communities and one assessment wing. The other four prisons offer a TC 'unit' which is located within, but physically, and to varying degrees, operationally, distinct from the host establishment; albeit Dovegate TC, with 200 places across four communities and an assessment unit, provides a very similar offering to Grendon.

Outline of the book

Based on fieldwork and qualitative interviewing in three prison-based TCs, this book offers a unique sociological portrayal and new criminological understanding of residents' progression towards change. It differs from previous works which have largely evaluated *whether* (and for whom) TCs 'work', by introducing a supplementary and complementary explanation of *how* TCs may 'work' to enable enduring psychological and behavioural change, based upon residents' accounts of their TC experiences. Surprisingly for an avowedly egalitarian treatment model, this 'bottom-up' perspective has routinely and comprehensively been excluded from much of the prison-based TC's self-description to date. Furthermore, most books on TCs have focused solely upon Grendon, notably Genders and Player's (1995) ground-breaking study of Grendon, conducted during the 1980s. For the first time, however, this book privileges residents' experiences of the TCs at Gartree (known as GTC) and Send, as well as Grendon, in order to provide a detailed and engaging depiction of the contemporary TC regime and culture. Although this research discusses the English prison-based democratic TC experience, the core themes expounded here should resonate with other similarly principled and prison-based European social therapeutic environments and the addictions (hierarchical or concept) TC model favoured especially, but by no means exclusively, in the United States, and with those committed to identifying and promoting humane prison regimes (for example, Toch 1997; Liebling, assisted by Arnold 2004; Jones 2006).

This book is therefore about the experience and enablement of change in TC prisons. It neither attempts to uncover the process of change as specifically facilitated by group psychotherapy (for example, Yalom 1995); nor is it concerned with the stages of behavioural change (Prochaska and DiClemente 1984) or offender rehabilitation more generally (for which see, inter alia, Raynor and Robinson 2005; Robinson and Crow 2009). Rather, its central argument is that the prison-based TC socially enables, produces, and reinforces identity reconstruction and narrative reframing, so that a 'new' and 'better' person emerges for whom long-term desistance from crime is a feasible, meaningful, and personally desirable achievement. This requires immediate clarification of two concepts: desistance and identity.

Desistance research normally considers what happens to offenders who are trying to 'go straight' once released from a period of imprisonment and/or community punishment. Notwithstanding the considerable personal achievement that curtailing one's offending *within* prison (against other prisoners, staff, or prison rules, or through the continuing 'management' of illegal activities 'on the out') may involve, desistance 'behind bars' is clearly something of an imposed virtue and not what criminologists normally envisage when discussing giving up crime. Declarations of desistance require observable 'significant crime-free gaps' (Bottoms *et al.* 2004:370) in the 'free world', and one could argue that desistance can only ever truly be determined retrospectively, after the offender's death (Maruna 2001). If one understands desistance, however, as a causal process which begins prior to, and continues after, the 'outcome' of termination (Laub and Sampson 2001:11), and which, after Lemert (1951), includes a 'secondary desistance' in which the would-be ex-offender assumes 'the role or identity of a "changed person"' (Maruna *et al.* 2004:274; Maruna and Farrall 2004), then it is appropriate to acknowledge residents' recognition of change in the present and progression towards sustained change in the future. Identifying, exploring, and understanding this experience of *desistance in process* – of people in the process or course of change – in the prison-based TC is the focus of this book.

Traditionally, desistance theories have stressed the importance of, and 'interplay' (Farrall and Bowling 1999) between, 'maturational reform' (Glueck and Glueck 1940) and the acquisition of a 'stake in conformity' (Hirschi 1969) in conventional society: a valuable social bond and legitimate routine activities, which prompt a re-evaluation of one's past actions, present priorities, and likely legacy (Sampson and Laub 1993; Graham and Bowling 1995; Farrall 2002; Laub and Sampson 2003; Healy 2010). More recent theoretical developments, however, have additionally highlighted the subjective, purposive changes successful desisters make to their personal identity and self-narrative, which result in the creation of a 'new, improved' self-concept which no longer cognitively or emotionally coheres with the expressive and sensual attractions and 'sneaky thrills' (Katz 1988) of offending (inter alia, Shover 1985, 1996; Burnett 1992, 2004; Leibrich 1993; Sampson and Laub 1993; Maruna 2001; Farrall 2002; Giordano *et al.* 2002; Laub and Sampson 2003; Gadd and Farrall 2004; Rumgay 2004; Farrall and Calverley 2006; Veysey *et al.* 2009). This enlarged, interactionist perspective accordingly suggests that 'desistance resides somewhere in the interfaces between developing personal maturity, changing social bonds ... *and* the individual subjective narrative constructions which offenders build around these key events and changes' (McNeill 2006:47, emphasis added; see also Bottoms *et al.* 2004; Farrall *et al.* 2011).

This relatively new emphasis upon identity and self-narratives follows the fine criminological tradition of eliciting offenders' own stories about why they began to commit crime, continued to do so (despite the best efforts of the criminal justice system to punish and rehabilitate them), and eventually, in most cases, renounced crime (Bennett 1981; Presser 2008, 2009). Such tales of offending and desistance reflect contemporary conceptualizations of identity as essentially consisting of 'the stories we live by' (McAdams 1993, 2006) and (metaphorically and literally) tell ourselves and others about who we are. In preference, then, to conceptualizing personal identity as a categorical or trait-based core self which remains largely fixed throughout life, identity is increasingly understood as an inherently fluid and fragile, actively and selectively constructed and repeatedly reconstructed, dramaturgically performed and achieved 'storied self' (McAdams 1996), the believability and coherence of which rests in 'the capacity *to keep a particular narrative going*' (Giddens 1991:54, emphasis preserved).

Scholars interested in the narrative study of lives (Josselson and Lieblich 1993) accordingly suggest that everyone continuously creates and consciously internalizes a self-narrative or life story which provides unity and purpose and conjoins, in a personally (and ideally socially) acceptable and plausible way, the disparate elements of one's past and present life into one meaningful whole. To enable this narrative to 'keep going', one may have to refine certain aspects of it in the light of new plot developments or arrival of new characters, or rhetorically accentuate or minimize, interpret, and revise key autobiographical events and themes, achievements and failures, satisfactions and regrets, in order to craft a consistent and temporally logical storyline ('emplotment') and so justify 'why it was necessary (*not* causally, but morally, socially, psychologically) that the life had gone a particular way' (Bruner 1990:121; emphasis preserved). To this extent, then, the strict historical accuracy of the narrative matters less than its psychological truth and emotional veracity to the story teller, as both narrative theorists and psychotherapists accept (McAdams 1993; Cordess and Williams 1996). Yet of course, that narrative and the identity it supports has to be credible to others and continually negotiated with others; it can never be claimed unilaterally. Neither can one's personal sense of self be disentangled from the social self, for one's identity, as a 'looking glass' or 'empirical self' (Cooley 1902), is always dependent upon the mirrored reflections, acceptance, and endorsement of (significant) others. Moreover, the elements of one's identity and the aspects of the stories one chooses to tell about oneself will change, depending on the audience and the audience's willingness to acquiesce and engage in the performance. Identity therefore emerges conditionally and reflexively from the synthesis of internally derived self-concepts and externally derived definitions and validations, and our relationships, of similarity and of difference, with others and the social structure (Goffman 1959; Giddens 1991; Hall 2000; Elliott 2001; Jenkins 2004; and see further Stevens 2012).

For would-be desisters, this means that they must, first, make sense of and forgive themselves for their offending past and, second, be able to identify changes in their inner selves and daily life that not only make desistance possible but render offending irrelevant to their now preferred self-concept and prospective life story. They must, in other words, be able to create, develop, and internalize a self-narrative which explicates and reinforces the nature of the changes they have undertaken and explains why offending no longer logically 'fits' into their life and the future plotlines they are scripting for themselves. A 'better' (non-offending) and personally more satisfying sense of self will then emerge, which continues to mould and guide one's behaviour in the future, in order to 'keep going' one's story of desistance.

Two seminal works illustrate this facet of desistance theory particularly well. Shadd Maruna (2001) compared and contrasted the life stories of 65 convicted offenders. The 30 people who were desisting from crime had created for themselves a coherent and credible 'prototypical reform story'. They portrayed their former offending self as a false identity, or a 'non starter' (Burnett 1992), not representative of their true self. For some, this involved emphatically 'knifing off' their criminal past by denying that it was ever the 'real me'. For others, their offending was not to be exiled from their life history but embraced in 'redemption' and 'generative' scripts, in which the sorrows and indignities they had endured during their criminal careers were now positively reinterpreted as the necessary prelude to their triumphant transformation into older and wiser survivors. 'Wounded healers', for example, who had typically endured addictions to alcohol or drugs, were now inspired by their recovery to help others who continued to suffer and struggle, as they once had. Conversely, those who lived by a 'condemnation script' believed themselves to be 'doomed to deviance' whereby, as much as they might like the idea of rehabilitation, they were perpetually defeated by their personal failings and the structural barriers to resettlement.

Peggy Giordano and her colleagues (2002) drew from 180 life history narratives of offenders to theorize desistance as occurring through a four-stage agentic process of 'cognitive transformation'. The potential desister's 'cognitive openness to change' had to be matched by an opportunity or 'hook for change' which made change possible, though certainly not inevitable: the difference between desisters and persisters was the willingness and ability of the former to recognize, connect with, and capitalize upon this 'hook'. This in turn required the development of a 'replacement self': a consciously refashioned 'better' version of oneself, through which all decisions could be filtered, and all actions assessed, for their consistency with this new identity. The final stage in the change process occurred when the desister repeatedly chose to behave in a way which was relevant to and reaffirmed the 'new' (pro-social) identity, whilst actively deprecating and rendering redundant the 'old' (anti-social) behaviours associated with the 'old' self.

This book begins with a concise definition of the democratic TC and how it differs to and is distinguished from other TC variants. It explores the psychiatric origins of the TC, and explains how something as unlikely sounding as a 'democratic therapeutic community' came to be imported into the British prison system, and modified and evolved its regime to survive for five decades. The chapter concludes by considering quantitative research upon the effectiveness of TC treatment in reducing re-offending and improving psychological functioning. Chapter 1 therefore sets the scene for all that follows: the prison-based TC is such a strange correctional entity that the reader needs to understand very clearly what it is (and opposes) in order to make sense of the experiences detailed and arguments propounded in this monograph.

Chapter 2 marries concise methodological explanation of the qualitative research design the author employed with a reflexive 'natural history' account of the research experience. The personal tone of this chapter allows readers to appreciate both how the research was conducted and how the research process itself contributes to the final research 'product'. Conducting research in prisons is an experience I characterize as a tightrope walk, requiring constant commitment and attention to 'emotion work' (Hochschild 1983), because of the (gendered) difficulties of retaining one's perceived impartiality, of bridging the divide between 'authenticity' and 'distance' (Pearson 1993), and of managing one's feelings in a profoundly and peculiarly affecting environment.

The empirical findings and analysis garnered by the research method are explored in Chapters 3 to 6, in which the common theme is the incremental development of a strengths-based, desistance-supporting self-concept and self-narrative. To begin to change, let alone to 'come good', an offender needs 'not only motive but also method' (Leibrich 1993:51). Chapter 3 accordingly explores why people applied to enter the TC and engage with its method of treatment, how 'persisters' adapted to it and overcame episodic ambivalence about the therapeutic process, and so found, within a 'different' penal environment and mode of correctional rehabilitation, the impetus to 'do *everything* differently' and to strive to become someone 'different'. This chapter also initiates a theme that flows through the remainder of the book: that the TC represents a radical penal counter-culture, discussion of which therefore contradicts the portrayal of prison life depicted in the 'standard' sociology of imprisonment literature (for stellar examples of which, see Sykes 1958; Morris and Morris 1963; Cohen and Taylor 1972; King and Elliott 1977; Jacobs 1977; Sparks *et al.* 1996; Owen 1998; Crewe 2009). Interviewees' accounts routinely contrasted their experiences of the TC way (or 'the way we do things here') of imprisonment and offender rehabilitation with 'the system' ('mainstream' or 'normal' imprisonment), and this overwhelmingly resulted, particularly at Grendon, in trenchant criticism of the latter. This should not be read, however, as an attempt to promote some facile equation to the effect of 'system nick' = bad; TC = good, but rather as reflective of residents' concern to convey unambiguously the ways in which the two institutions of incarceration dramatically diverge.

Attachment theory informs the premise of Chapter 4 that, through the experience of bidirectional care, emotional support, and trust, and in the sharing of experiential knowledge and enactment of the 'helper-therapy principle' (Riessman 1965, 1990), people residing within the TC can usefully redefine their self-concept and reappraise their expectations of personal relationships. The care that emanates from staff members and resident peers, and is enabled through TC-specific institutional structures, allows residents to form genuine, empathetic and, crucially, desistance-supportive and reparative attachments (in prison), and to discover that their often trauma-inducing life experiences are not unique, and their trauma-inflicting cognitions and behaviours are not beyond modification and amelioration.

Chapter 5 details how residents are consulted upon and contribute to the democratized, mutually beneficial, and optimal operation of their community through community meetings and rep jobs, and how they progress their own and other residents' therapy, sense of responsibility, accountability, and pro-social self-management through feedback and challenge. Residents are entrusted by staff, for example, to perform key communal tasks and to police, prosecute, and provisionally judge any 'naughty stuff' which threatens the therapeutic progress of individuals and/or the safety and cohesion of the community. Such a 'social-plus' model of crime prevention, the chapter suggests, inculcates normative acceptance of the TC way and '*our* rules', and thus helps account for the TC's safe (and, against comparable prisons, much safer) and well-ordered environment. Moreover, the uncommon penal experience of '*real* responsibility' allows residents to enhance their sense of self-efficacy and improve their estimation of their capabilities, so strengthening their realization of 'better' 'possible selves' (Oyserman and Markus 1990).

The central theme of Chapter 6 is the related emergence of vulnerability and contraction of hypermasculinity. This chapter revisits some of the themes of Chapters 4 and 5, as specifically applied to the desistance in process amongst male residents. It argues that the TC's 'deflationary' culture encourages self-proclaimed 'hard' men to learn to tolerate vulnerability, in both themselves and others; to revise their internalized, essentialist, and often criminogenic notions about 'being a man'; and hence over time to free themselves from the imprisoning strictures of gender and the 'macho masks' habitually worn in men's secure prisons. The chapter continues by showing how Grendon atypically enables the integration of sexual and sexually motivated offenders into the daily life of the prison and therapeutic regime. Such 'de-othering', amongst men now emboldened by more empathetic and emotionally assured identities, fosters the re-evaluation of the hierarchy of offending – that is, the traditional penal caste system by which all offences are ranked and classified for acceptability and excusableness – and the reassessment of masculine characteristics and values which deserve respect. This acquired combination of being able 'to be who *you really are*' in the TC, and cultural permission to see all residents as 'who they really are', regardless of offence status, further distances the 'new me' resident and would-be desister from the 'old-style' 'con' and prisoner.

The book concludes by distilling the key themes from this research to elucidate succinctly how it is that the prison-based TC can enable pro-social change amongst its residents and bestow upon its residents evidence-based hope for desistance from crime in the future. Residents' self-evaluations of their prospects are reported, and the importance of 'difference' to the rehabilitative power of the TC is explained.

Offender Rehabilitation and Therapeutic Communities, then, does not tell a triumphant tale of desistance completed, but rather the story of desistance in process. Of the many aspects of the TC way one could choose to highlight, this book, as part of the International Series on Desistance and Rehabilitation, focuses upon the thematic and conceptual similarities between the findings this research elicited and existing elements of the desistance literature, and so hopes to advance a new understanding of 'what helps' (Ward and Maruna 2007:12) people to change in the prison-based TC.

1 Therapeutic communities and prisons

> Grendon is about changing mindsets: changing your attitudes, beliefs, and values, so that you can be the best person you can be.
>
> (Johnny, Grendon)

A democratic therapeutic community (TC) is surprisingly difficult to define. At its most general, the term refers to a psychosocial method and programme of treatment which is intended to help troubled people, residing in or regularly attending a carefully designed and maintained social community, understand and, as far as possible, lessen or overcome their psychological, social, and emotional problems. This is achieved in two ways: first, through residents' active participation in group (or occasionally, individual) psychotherapy, in order to unearth, examine, and work through the often unconscious motives, unresolved conflicts, and learned maladaptive self-protective behaviours that can result from traumatic or abusive formative experiences (Malan 1979; Cordess and Williams 1996; Campling 2001); and second, through residents' contribution to the daily nurturance of an interdependent, cohesive, pro-social environment, including involvement in specific activities of therapeutic benefit to the individual and of practical or domestic benefit to other community members.

A well-functioning community serves as 'the primary therapeutic instrument' (Roberts 1997a:4). It provides daily 'living-learning experiences' (Jones 1968:106) and opportunities for self-disçovery and 'two way communication of content and feeling, listening, interaction, and problem solving, leading to learning' (Jones 1980:35) which, over time, enable residents to recognize, reflect upon, and understand their problems and work towards change. The general 'feel' of the TC should be of a dynamic 'culture of enquiry … into personal and interpersonal and intersystem problems' (Main 1946, cited in Dolan 1998:410), where every incident and every interaction is potentially subject to therapeutic scrutiny. Each member of the community should be able to participate equally in administrative decision making and contribute meaningfully to other residents' therapy. The former allows residents to acquire a profound sense of investment in, ownership of, and responsibility for their community's decisions, their implications and implementation, and the safe and effective functioning of the community. The latter ensures that the community's 'total resources ... are self-consciously pooled in furthering treatment' (Jones 1968:85) and promotes a sense of egalitarianism between residents and staff. Amenities and domestic arrangements are shared, and informality and the 'freeing' of communication encouraged. Residents' 'deviancy' and 'mistakes' are accepted rather than condemned, but this tolerance is tempered by the imparting of constructive 'therapeutic feedback', in which community members relate the impact such behaviour has upon them and instigate discussion upon the 'issues' they consider this raises for the resident (Rapoport 1960; Haigh 1999).

Another way to understand what a TC is, is to understand what it opposes. In psychiatry, from whence the TC originates, it denotes an approach to care that avoided the medical model, with its reliance on diagnostic categories and pharmacological remedies, and rejected the autonomy-sapping and power-abusing characteristics of 'total institution' mental hospitals. Here, paternalistic medics preoccupied themselves with the maintenance of control, hierarchy, and routine and slavish adherence to a myriad of, often bizarre, bureaucratic rules (Stanton and Schwartz 1954; Belknap 1956; Caudill 1958; Goffman 1961); whilst no more was expected (or desired) from patients than they played an apathetic 'sick role' (Parsons 1951). In prisons, the environment with which this book is concerned, the TC represents a counter-culture way of imprisonment and offender rehabilitation. For prisoners, this means the TC seeks to resist the 'criminalistic ideology' (Clemmer 1958:300) of the inmate code and reverse the counterproductive effects that prevent imprisonment from being 'a constructively painful experience' (Johnson 1996:xi). For prisons, the TC way demands that the institution relinquishes some decision making to prisoners, empowers them to take more responsibility for themselves, and loosens, within limits, its automatic over-reliance upon, and at times in secure prisons, obsessive fetishism about, security, as the meta-narrative of the prison's purpose. As a method of offender rehabilitation, the TC extends beyond current penological preoccupations with minimizing or managing risk of harm and re-offending, to offer help to the prisoner as a whole person, with complex, multi-dimensional needs and frequently, low self-esteem and minimal aspirations for and expectations of a productive and peaceable life after prison. In both psychiatric and penal settings, the TC's ultimate aim is to ensure that the community member can enjoy a 'stable life in a real role in the real world' (Main 1996:80) that awaits beyond the TC. As a result, the living experience within the community needs to be as 'normal' as possible, and to offer daily opportunities to acquire and practise 'normal' ways of being, behaving, and relating to and interacting with others.

Part of the reason for the definitional vagueness that still afflicts therapeutic communities comes from the adoption of TC principles in various similar-but-different institutions internationally. Specifically in relation to penal or forensic establishments, these include variations on social therapeutic regimes in Europe, and addictions TCs in the United States and elsewhere.

Notably, Denmark's renowned Treatment Institute at Herstedvester prison in Copenhagen was the first European institution to forge a TC 'approach' (Clark 1965)[1] with its establishment in 1935 – almost three decades before Grendon – to provide intensive psychiatrist-led, individualized psychodynamic therapy. Indeed, Grendon's first governor, Dr William Gray, travelled to Herstedvester in 1967 to consult with its medical director, Dr Georg Stürup, then considered to be 'the high priest of prison psychiatry, and his institute the mecca' (Royal College of Psychiatrists 1986:125). Herstedvester provides a national resource for male and (since 1987) female, often personality disordered,[2] sometimes psychotic,[3] serious offenders, and has gained an enviable reputation for working successfully with recidivist, sadistic sexual offenders by combining psychotherapy with chemical castration (Stürup 1968; Hansen and Lykke-Olesen 1997; Mollerup *et al.* 2005). Germany, meanwhile, has developed an extensive network of social therapeutic prisons, either as independent institutions wholly devoted to social therapy or as part of a 'regular' prison (Dünkel and Johnson 1980; Lösel and Egg 1997; Ortmann 2000). Switzerland boasts an 11-bed 'centre for sociotherapy', La Pâquerette, at Champ-Dollon prison,[4] near Geneva (de Montmollin *et al.* 1986; Bernheim and de Montmollin 1990; Federal Department of Justice and Police 2011); and the Netherlands offers a secure forensic psychiatric hospital, the Van der Hoeven Kliniek, in Utrecht (Feldbrugge 1990; de Ruiter and Trestman 2007; de Boer-van Schaik and Derks 2010). Like their English democratic TC counterparts, these institutions work with serious violent and sexually violent, (severely) personality disordered offenders, whilst the Van der Hoeven Kliniek additionally works with people with major mental illness.

By contrast, addictions (also known as hierarchical, concept, or drug-free) prison-based TCs are specifically for offenders with problematic drug use. Many offenders in democratic (sometimes known as psychoanalytic, milieu, or Maxwell Jones) TCs will also have had substance abuse problems, but the addictions model targets offenders where their main 'issue' is drugs, rather than personality disorder. Scholars disagree about whether addictions TCs are, in ideology and practice, predominantly similar to (Sugarman 1984; Vandevelde *et al.* 2004; Shefer 2010a) or significantly different from (Glaser 1983; Lipton 1998, 2010) their democratic cousin, but certainly they share an encouragement of residents' active involvement in, and responsibility for, the day-to-day running of the TC; a respect for the social learning and behavioural reinforcement that occurs naturally in the course of communal living; and a distrust of the medical model of addiction (Jones 1980; Wexler 1997). Conversely, residents are expected to conform to an overtly hierarchical regime, with disciplined adherence to the community's rules, engagement in a structured day, the incremental earning of (and potentially loss of) privileges, and progression through clearly defined stages of treatment.

The addictions model's history, international expansion, and underpinning principles are beyond the scope of this book (but for which, see de Leon 1997,

2000; Lipton 1998; Kooyman 2001; Broekaert *et al.* 2006). In brief, though, this model originates with the creation of Synanon[5] in Santa Monica, California, in 1958, and Daytop Village and Phoenix House in New York, in 1964 and 1967 respectively. These promoted a form of community-based treatment based on the self-help 12-step cognitive-behavioural programme established by Alcoholics Anonymous, and adhered to a set of explicit values or concepts consistent with 'right living' and the psychological causes of (alcohol and drug) addiction and its treatment. Daytop Village and Phoenix House subsequently developed into very successful, non-profit making global organizations, offering a variety of treatment programmes for people with substance abuse problems across community, residential, and custodial settings. From the late 1980s in America, federal training, support, and funding for hierarchical TCs in prisons ensured that these programmes became well established (Wexler 1997). Following a plethora of consistently positive outcome evaluations (inter alia, Wexler *et al.* 1990; Schwartz *et al.* 1996; Pearson and Lipton 1999; Wexler *et al.* 1999; Lees *et al.* 2004; Mitchell *et al.* 2007; cf. Zhang *et al.* 2011), especially when multi-stage (with aftercare) TC treatment is provided (inter alia, Knight *et al.* 1997; Inciardi *et al.* 1997; Hiller *et al.* 1999; Martin *et al.* 1999; Inciardi *et al.* 2004; Prendergast *et al.* 2004), the hierarchical TC can now claim to be 'the treatment of choice in American prisons' (Wexler 1997:161) for offenders with drug problems. The success of these programmes in America in turn encouraged the Prison Service in England and Wales (and elsewhere) to introduce hierarchical TC treatment in 1996, as part of its reinvigorated drug treatment and rehabilitation strategy (Mason *et al.* 2001). Programme specification, development, and delivery was contracted to external providers. As with democratic TC units, discussed shortly, establishing, nurturing, and expanding addictions TCs has proven difficult. Five units (three of which were for women) survived only briefly (Shefer 2010a), but the renamed Phoenix Futures currently delivers addictions TC treatment in four units within men's English prisons (Phoenix Futures 2012).

The term therapeutic community therefore has to be used with some care and caution, since it can mean different things to different people, given its diversity of practice and breadth of clientele. The sole focus of this book, however, is the *democratic* model of TC treatment for *prisoners*, and reference to TCs in the chapters to come implies only this democratic model in prisons, though the research findings will doubtlessly resonate with practitioners and residents of other TC 'types'. In this chapter,[6] after outlining the origins, expansion, then contraction in use of democratic TCs in psychiatry, I proceed to explain why and how, via a meandering and uncertain pathway, TCs came to be adopted by a limited number of English prisons, with varying degrees of long-term success. The chapter concludes by summarizing existing research on the forensic TC's evidence base, and thus the potential it holds to help the serious imprisoned offender become 'the best person you can be'.

A short history of therapeutic communities

The origins of therapeutic communities can be traced to the earliest attempts of providers of psychiatric care to offer 'moral treatment'[7] (Kennard 2004; Whiteley 2004), but most clearly developed from the creation during World War II of specialist units to treat traumatized military personnel presenting with acute dissociative, neurotic, and hysterical disorders. The regime in these units was, separately but within a short space of time, devised by a handful of, often Tavistock Clinic-trained,[8] British psychiatrists and psychoanalysts, who were inspired by psychoanalytic, psychological, and social scientific theorizing about small group processes, interpersonal relations, and social environments (inter alia, Freud 1922; Adler 1924; Mead 1934; Lewin 1935), and were informed by their determination not to replicate the punitive and disabling mistreatment which Great War shell-shocked[9] soldiers had encountered. It seemed to them that the authoritarian, oppressive, and dependency-inducing culture of the secure psychiatric hospital only exacerbated self-damaging behaviours, so that their patients were, in effect, prevented from getting well because their 'treatment' was taking place within an anti-therapeutic environment. Conversely, they thought, a more humane, tolerant, and empowering milieu, which provided for a flexible, egalitarian organizational structure and collaborative, group-based interaction, might relieve more effectively their patients' symptoms of distress (Manning 1976; Kennard 1998).

The initial, modest attempt at innovation occurred in the unlikely setting of a temporarily converted public school at Mill Hill, north London, to which psychiatric patients from Maudsley Hospital were evacuated in 1940. Maxwell Jones, a psychiatrist researching effort syndrome,[10] decided to share the findings with his patients through regular didactic lectures. He soon realized, however, that his patients understood more, and their morale and self-esteem consequently improved, if he involved them in interactive group discussions. These small groups fostered social learning, encouraged greater sociological contextualizing of the challenges that treatment posed, and began to affect the social structure of the ward by promoting a flattened hierarchy between staff and patients, which allowed for some decision making by consensus and more open communication (Jones 1952, 1968; Whiteley 2004).

Wilfred Bion, meanwhile, was appointed director of the Training Wing of Birmingham's Northfield military psychiatric hospital and charged with rehabilitating men who, although psychologically disturbed, were considered capable of returning to military service. Together with his colleague John Rickman, Bion decided to confront his patients' disruptive behaviour by redefining disciplinary problems, in suitably combative terms, as the 'common enemy', and by attending proactively to the therapeutic climate of the treatment setting. For six weeks in 1943, they introduced discussion groups and communal activities, designed to replace the fractured social bonds of war with the mutual support of a peer community and, hence, 'to treat socially the social elements of the patients' neuroses' (Roberts 1997b:14). The insubordination and subversion of military discipline this (what has been retrospectively called) 'first Northfield experiment' represented, however, proved intolerable to their superiors and Bion and Rickman were transferred. Undeterred, over the next three years Siegmund Foulkes and Harold Bridger, amongst others, implemented gradually a 'second Northfield experiment' – but crucially, this time with the approval of a new, more supportive, commanding officer – which again advocated the use of group analysis, regular meetings, creative pursuits, and social activities involving the whole community (Kennard and Roberts 1983; Harrison 1999; Whiteley 2004).

In 1945, Northfield acquired a new hospital director, Tom Main, who sought to incorporate techniques from both psychiatry and psychoanalysis to construct a psychodynamic and interpretative exploration of his patients' objective difficulties through their subjectively felt interpersonal frustrations and conflicts. In an article published in May 1946, Main argued that the neurotic individual with disturbed social relationships needed 'a framework of social reality which can provide him with opportunities for attaining fuller social insight and for expressing and modifying his emotional drives according to the demands of real life' (Main 1996:77). He rallied his colleagues to replace the 'social refuge' of the hospital with an internal community, and the role of the expert 'superintendent' psychiatrist *of* patients with a humble 'technician' *among* patients, whose daily task was to study and facilitate the therapeutic potential of and communication within the community and the effective social integration and personal development of its patients (ibid.:79). Several commentators have since timed the appearance of Main's 'stirring and inspirational' paper as the 'date of birth' of the democratic therapeutic community (Kennard 1996:71).

Somewhat by accident then, a dispersed cluster of innovators discovered that small group discussion could constitute a therapeutic tool and encourage members to become more involved in the daily management of their environment and more invested in self-managing their problems. Many TC pioneers went on to develop illustrious careers. Foulkes (1948, 1975) and Bion (1961, 1970), for example, became world-renowned authorities upon group psychoanalytic psychotherapy. Main further developed the TC model during his tenure as medical director of Cassel Hospital, in Richmond, Surrey, establishing both his reputation as an 'outstanding' psychodynamic psychiatrist and the Cassel as an internationally known centre for psychodynamic psychotherapy (British Medical Journal 1990:1718). The concept and contemporary practices of the TC are most associated, though, with Maxwell Jones, whose efforts to treat complex personality and psychopathic disorders at the Social Rehabilitation Unit at Henderson Hospital,[11] in Sutton, Surrey, prolific stream of writings (inter alia, Jones 1952, 1953, 1968, 1976, 1982), and international evangelizing of social psychiatry[12] secured for him the reputation of the 'father' of the TC movement (Manning 1976). While Main and his Northfield colleagues can therefore claim the creation of the TC *philosophy*, it was Jones at Mill Hill who devised the *method* (Whiteley 2004), and most conspicuously disseminated its development.

During the 1960s and 1970s, the number of British TCs, both in the National Health Service (NHS) and independent non-statutory sectors, continued to grow, and acceptance of its ideals to flourish within psychiatry. More liberal, 'open-door' psychiatric hospitals became the norm, as mental health professionals recognized the importance of the emotional and social atmosphere of the treatment setting, and society became more understanding and accepting of mental illness. The loosely organized anti-psychiatry movement[13] – comprising, amongst others, the existentialist and radical psychiatrists Ronald Laing (1960, 1961, 1966); Thomas Szasz (1961); and David Cooper (1967, 1980) – also mobilized critical thinking about the social role and bio-medical basis of psychiatry, and facilitated the opening of a number of TCs, most famously the experimental community at Kingsley Hall (see Barnes and Berke 1971; Burston 1996) and Villa 21 (Cooper 1967).

Yet, some of these (ultimately, short-lived) regimes attracted considerable controversy and, with it, criticism of the TC concept more fundamentally. Notably, Sharp's (1975) study of a TC for former psychiatric patients contrasted the TC's claims of flattened hierarchy with the reality of dictatorial decision making and control. The clinical staff's selective and manipulative 'nihilation' (a term taken from Berger and Luckmann 1967) of residents' verbalizations and behaviours, he argued, allowed them to reinterpret any attempts at dissent from residents as evidence of their psychopathology, and thus tyrannically to impose their beliefs about and solutions to residents' problems. An equally damning assessment was made by Baron (1987), in her portrayal of the anti-psychiatry-inspired TC at Paddington Day Hospital. Baron's account was subsequently challenged by Spandler (2006), while Bloor's (1986) appraisal of a similar TC to that studied by Sharp argued that whilst staff's interpretative work did sometimes serve a social control function – perhaps to ensure the efficient organization of the community or to avert (verbal or physical) confrontation between residents – staff also orchestrated and provoked dissent and disruption for therapeutic ends. The critiques raised by Sharp, Baron, and others, however, continue to serve as a warning to mental health professionals of the potential for misuse of power and corruption of purpose within 'egalitarian' and 'permissive' TCs, and, hence, critical criminologists would assert, for the reassertion of Foucauldian discipline, deftly disguised as therapeutic concern.

The 1980s marked the beginning of a gradual but continuing decline in the influence and popularity of psychiatric TCs as a treatment modality. The advent of 'community care'[14] – the relocation of mental health provision from institutions to community settings and, preferably, the family – combined with the concomitant greater needs of the fewer long-stay patients, and changes to the management structure and funding of psychiatric services, progressively reduced NHS interest in and support for TCs (Clark 1999). The most high-profile casualty to date is the Henderson Hospital, which closed in

2008 after the withdrawal of national funding resulted in a sharp decline in referrals. It is the story of the TC's development, tentative growth, and surely surprising endurance in the unlikely environment of the prison to which I now turn.

'A penal institution of a special kind': the prison-based TC

The original impetus to create a therapeutic community in prison owed more to governmental concern about recidivism than ideological commitment to rehabilitation. In 1931, nine years prior to the innovative work of Jones and his peers with traumatized military personnel, the Home Office appointed a departmental committee to inquire into existing methods of dealing with persistent offenders. Its resulting report argued that 'a certain amount of persistent crime ... is due to abnormal mental factors' and thus 'certain delinquents may be amenable to psychological treatment' (Home Office 1932:46, para. 116). Given the then paucity of scientific knowledge about crime, criminals, and offender rehabilitation, however, both the Committee and, separately, the Medical Commissioner and Committee member Sir (William) Norwood East, recommended that an experiment be instituted with 'willing' offenders by which the value of psychological treatment could be assessed (East 1932; Home Office 1932:48, paras. 120–22).

This experiment was duly conducted between 1934 and 1938 with selected prisoners at Wormwood Scrubs, under the auspices of the medical psychologist and psychotherapist William Hubert, and subsequently formed the basis of doctors East and Hubert's (1939) *The Psychological Treatment of Crime*. Although they did not attempt to establish whether, in fact, levels of recidivism had been reduced, based upon their clinical judgements of behavioural improvement, they unequivocally concluded that 'the most satisfactory method of dealing with abnormal and unusual types of criminal would be by the creation of a penal institution of a special kind' (East and Hubert 1939:159, para. 172).

Although East and Hubert's recommendation was welcomed, the outbreak of World War II and prolonged bureaucratic procrastination ensured that two decades passed before building work commenced on the envisaged category B (medium-security)[15] 'experimental psychiatric prison': HMP Grendon, situated on the outskirts of a small Buckinghamshire village, 20 miles north from the world-famous university town of Oxford. When it finally opened in September 1962, Grendon – or, as it was initially called, the East-Hubert Institution (Gray 1973a) – was tasked with caring for up to 250 men, 25 women, and 50 'borstal boys'[16] who were, in East's phrase, 'non-sane non-insane' (cited in Gunn *et al.* 1978:18): neither suffering from psychosis nor legally insane (and hence not responsible for their actions), but who might have 'mental disorders generally recognised as responsive to treatment' (Commissioners of Prisons 1963, cited in Genders and Player 1995:6), including potentially psychopathy.[17]

From the outset, Grendon married its psychiatric orientation with a keen identification with the TC regime (Pickering 1970), and distanced itself from 'normal' Prison Service practices. Instead of being managed by a Prison Service governor, an experienced forensic psychiatrist, Dr William Gray, was employed as Grendon's first 'medical superintendent'; while Grendonites – the traditional term for Grendon's residents – were prescribed as necessary psychotropic (mind or mood altering) medication. By 1973, Grendon's clinical staff comprised seven psychiatrists, four psychologists, one psychiatric social worker, and four welfare officers (Gray 1973a). To modern-day sensibilities, this level of psychiatric expertise seems unnecessary given that most residents in 1973 were recidivist property offenders: 57 per cent of Grendonites had been imprisoned for property offences, but only 17 per cent were serving sentences for violence, 8 per cent for robbery or its attempt, and 7 per cent for sexual offences (Cullen 1997).

This early focus on recidivism rather than offence seriousness contributed to the perception that by the mid 1980s, Grendon had become unacceptably 'apart': out of touch, both with the political (and public) mood and with the Prison Service. Grendon had been built in the optimistic era of penal welfarism when a political consensus existed that the offender's personal, interpersonal, and/or psychological problems could be addressed through professional expertise, and social deprivation and disadvantage alleviated by welfare provision. With the apparent failure of correctional interventions to rehabilitate (Martinson 1974), however, and the tougher mood advanced by a new, overtly politicized 'law and order' debate, fanned by the chilly winds of global economic recession, the notion that 'the rhetoric of "treatment and training" has had its day and should be replaced' (May 1979:67, para. 4.27) now appeared more persuasive than seemingly fanciful faith in the 'rehabilitative ideal' (Allen 1981). Moreover, Grendon was increasingly criticized from within the Prison Service as an aloof, inflexible establishment, overly selective in its clientele, and uncomprehending of or unresponsive to the needs of a penal estate struggling to manage increasing numbers of 'heavy end' and 'control problem' prisoners (Cullen 1998). Grendon's unashamed pursuit of holistic and humane rehabilitation, which was not *primarily* intended to reduce re-offending but 'to facilitate and promote the welfare of each individual inmate' (Genders and Player 1995:12), now began to appear obstinately anachronistic.

This was the potentially hazardous context in which the Home Secretary decided to establish an Advisory Committee on the therapeutic regime at Grendon (ACTRAG), in order to review the prison's future. The resulting report (Home Office 1985) contained no fewer than 29 recommendations, fundamentally and irrevocably changing its referral and management practices. Grendon was henceforth to concentrate upon providing therapeutic community treatment for 'sociopaths',[18] men convicted of sexual offences, and the long-term (and particularly, life-sentenced) prison population (Faulk 1990). Symbolically, the post of medical superintendent was abolished and replaced with a generalist (non-medically qualified) governing governor, allied to the traditional Prison Service management structure and accountable through the conventional channels (Newell and Healey 2007). Responsibility for therapy remained with an experienced clinician, however, and a 28-bed psychiatric rescue unit was established for men suffering acute mental breakdown or prison-induced crisis, thereby preserving some continuity with Grendon's original objectives. Led by a psychiatrist, this unit offered individual psychotherapy and continued to prescribe psychotropic medication, which otherwise was now abandoned as inimical to the emotional reconnection therapy must induce (Selby 1991).

Neither of these measures panned out quite as ACTRAG intended, however. ACTRAG had envisaged a dual-management structure, but after wide-reaching reforms to Prison Service management structures, working practices, and conditions of service were introduced in 1987 (the 'Fresh Start' initiative), the primacy of the governor was confirmed, to whom the senior medical officer (now, the director of therapy) reported. Furthermore, over time, the rescue unit unintentionally morphed into a chronic long-stay refuge, with a high proportion of suicidal prisoners, and as a result it was closed in 1993 (Cullen 1998).

The implementation of ACTRAG's recommendations, combined with the emergence in the early 1990s of quantitative evidence of reduced re-offending amongst Grendon 'graduates' (discussed presently), was to prove decisive in reviving the prison's flagging fortunes. In the years that followed, the prison successfully repositioned itself as a national resource and centre of excellence for the TC treatment of the most serious and clinically challenging offenders. In contrast to the property offenders of the 1970s, nearly all (95 per cent) of contemporary Grendonites have been imprisoned for (sometimes, fatally) violent or sexually violent offences, and nine out of ten (91 per cent) are serving indeterminate sentences (HM Chief Inspector of Prisons 2011). Amongst the national adult male sentenced prison population, by comparison, 55 per cent have been convicted of violent or sexually violent offences and 16 per cent are serving indeterminate sentences (Ministry of Justice 2011b).

The seriousness of Grendonites' offences and sentences are reflected in the seriousness of the psychological disturbance with which Grendonites typically present. On the DSM-IV version of the Personality Diagnostic Questionnaire (Hyler 1994), Birtchnell and Shine (2000) found that 88 per cent of men received at Grendon met the criteria for at least one personality disorder, while the mean number of disorders per person was 4.02. Using the Hare Psychopathy Checklist (Revised) (PCL-R) (Hare 1991), Hobson and Shine (1998) found 26 per cent of 104 new arrivals obtained a PCL-R score of 30 or above, indicative of prototypical psychopathy, and Grendonites' mean PCL-R score, at 24, surpassed that (at 22) of high-security prisoners (Clark 1998, cited in Shine and Newton 2000). When a lower cut-off score of 25 was applied – then recommended for British offenders as metrically equivalent to a score of 30 in North America (Cooke and Michie 1999)[19] – 47 per cent of

78 newly admitted residents were found to be psychopathic (Gray *et al.* 2002), with PCL-R scores ranging from 5 to 39, with a mean of 22.

For fifty years, then, Grendon has doggedly endured: rebranded, redefined, but continuously committed to being 'a special kind' of prison for 'a special kind' of prisoner. It has not, however, been entirely alone in its distinctive approach to offender rehabilitation during this time.

The development, and varied fortunes, of TC units

Beginning in the 1970s, Grendon's success inspired the development of, and provided the template for, a small number of discrete TC units located within – what TC residents uniformly and rather ominously refer to as – 'mainstream' or 'system' prisons. Whilst none of these units now survive, a modest expansion in the use of TC units has occurred this millennium, in response to expert evaluations of the extent of unmet psychiatric need amongst sentenced prisoners. Forensic psychiatrists from the Institute of Psychiatry analysed the prison files of, and conducted semi-structured interviews with, a 5 per cent cross-sectional random sample of sentenced male adult and young offenders (Gunn *et al.* 1991), and then additionally 25 per cent of women inmates (Maden *et al.* 1994), from 16 prisons in England and Wales. They assessed for any psychiatric disorder and determined, from five options, the most appropriate treatment modality. They concluded that 5 per cent of male and 8 per cent of female prisoners would benefit from TC treatment, 47 per cent of whom (in total) were diagnosed with a personality disorder. The authors suggested that this provided a rough guide to the level of need nationally and justified the development of an additional TC prison. This recommendation was strengthened by the Prison Service Directorate of Health Care Task Force's 1994 estimate that TC treatment would be advantageous for at least 2,392 prisoners by 2001 (Genders 2003); and a separate 1998 feasibility study which suggested between 6 and 7.5 per cent of women prisoners would be suitable for and could benefit from a TC (Kennedy 1998, cited in Stewart and Parker 2007).

These findings provided the rationale to build, as part of a new private sector prison in Staffordshire, a 200-bed, entirely self-contained TC unit for category B male prisoners. HMP Dovegate's TC duly opened in 2001,[20] and two years later, a 40-bed unit for category C men was established at HMP Blundeston in Suffolk. These communities joined the longest surviving TC unit – HMP Gartree in Leicestershire – which, since 1993, has offered therapeutic community treatment for 23 men, all recruited from within this prison's exclusively indeterminate sentenced category B population. Residents at GTC, as Gartree TC is known, are in the earlier years of their sentence, and a distinguishing aim of this TC is to help lifers come to terms with, and find ways to profit developmentally from, their sentence (Mackenzie 2007).

The therapeutic needs of women were belatedly addressed in 2003 by the provision of a TC unit at Winchester West Hill prison. Within a year, however, this prison reverted to the male estate, requiring the TC to relocate to the closed women's prison, Send, in Surrey – with predictably disruptive consequences for the nascent community (Stewart and Parker 2007). Unlike the other units, Send TC does not presently offer an entirely separate unit because it has not yet attracted enough women to fill its envisaged maximum potential occupancy of 40 places. The residential accommodation is therefore shared with 'regular prisoners' on A-wing, though the TC's community and therapy rooms are housed in a separate block adjacent to A-wing. The difficulty Send TC has encountered in recruiting women arises from the requirement, in common with the men's TCs, that potential applicants commit to a minimum residency of 18 months, but two-thirds of all adult women prisoners are serving sentences of a year or less (Ministry of Justice 2011b), so the potential pool of applicants is inherently constrained. Initially, Send TC was also poorly advertised within the female estate, leading HM Chief Inspector of Prisons (2006:71, para. 8.52) to recommend 'national action and responsibility' to facilitate resident recruitment. Whilst the TC now enjoys a higher profile and is 'flagged' as a possible intervention for (particularly life-sentenced) women arriving at Send, the regime continues to be undermined by staff shortages and its shared accommodation with mainstream women (HM Chief Inspector of Prisons 2008, 2010). Neither the problem of shared accommodation nor the lingering uncertainty surrounding Send TC's long-term viability will be overcome until it is able to recruit and retain sufficient numbers of women to fill an entire wing.

Indeed, all TC units are keenly aware that some prominent communities have 'failed', for reasons which are not always clear but in which the problems, pressures, and preoccupations of the *host* prison sometimes appear to be implicated (see, for example, Fowler 1997 and Mackenzie 1997). As Lewis (1997:8) wisely warned, 'A small unit can be likened to a foreign body, or transplant, in the human body, and is subject to the same process of "rejection"'. Three separate facilities for young offenders have closed: at Glen Parva, Leicestershire (1979 to 1996); Feltham, Middlesex (1989 to 1997); and Aylesbury, Buckinghamshire (1997 to 2006). Judy Mackenzie, a former Glen Parva therapist and continuing TC champion, attributes the closure of all three TCs to 'administratively expedient and short-sighted reasons … [and] local managerial decision-making based primarily on budget comparisons rather than merit or wider value' (Cullen and Mackenzie 2011:94). Additionally, the Max Glatt Centre (originally known as the Annexe, but renamed after its founder, a distinguished psychiatrist who specialized in addictions) at HMP Wormwood Scrubs, London, operated as a TC from 1975 to 2002. During this time, like Grendon, it successfully transformed its target clientele to reflect its evolving remit, from adult male prisoners with addictive and compulsive behaviours to violent and personality disordered offenders (Glatt 1985; Jones 1997). Maintaining programme integrity and dedicated staffing levels, however, proved persistently challenging (Woodward 1999). Ultimately, the TC's need for a stable and secure community, committed to therapy, could no longer be reconciled with the operational exigencies of this overcrowded local prison,[21] and which, moreover, at the time of its mooted closure, was beset by 'dysfunctional' management and a 'corrosive' situation following shocking allegations of widespread staff brutality (HM Chief Inspector of Prisons 2001:7).

Most (in)famously, the Barlinnie Special Unit (BSU) in Glasgow achieved astonishing rehabilitative success with 36 of the most 'difficult' and 'dangerous' men in the Scottish prison system (Cooke 1989, 1991). The 10-bed[22] BSU opened in February 1973 exclusively for the treatment of long-term and known or potentially violent prisoners (Scottish Home and Health Department 1971, cited in Scottish Prison Service 1994), for whom it offered a last resort alternative to indefinite detention in Carstairs state mental hospital or isolation in Scotland's then notorious 'cages' and 'diggers' (segregation units) (Light 1985; Sparks 1994). The BSU was largely allowed to develop its own ethos and whilst it never identified itself as a democratic therapeutic community, its 'social community' (Whatmore 1987:251) drew explicitly on TC principles and practices. Residents could choose, for example, to attend weekly 'informal meetings ... to discuss issues in general as well as individual and group behaviour' (Stephen 1988:135) with psychiatrists, psychologists, and social workers, and its culture emphasized individual support and accountability, collective governance and solidarity, and informal and collaborative staff–resident relationships. The regime was otherwise unstructured though, and residents enjoyed hitherto unknown freedom to personalize their cells, follow creative pursuits, and enjoy unlimited and largely unsupervised visits (Coyle 1987; Bottomley *et al.* 1994; Cooke 1997; and for ex-residents' autobiographies, see Boyle 1977, 1984; Collins 1997; Steele 2002).

The BSU is now remembered by criminologists almost as much for its controversial end, as for the imaginative and enlightened penological approach to 'disruptive' prisoners it pioneered. Opinions still differ as to whether its closure, in January 1995, was inevitable after becoming 'stagnant and fossilised' (Scottish Prison Service 1994:17), with radical practices made routine, negative behaviour ignored, and non-involvement normalized (Cooke 1997); or whether the – perhaps only temporary – problems it was experiencing were merely an expedient excuse to close a unit whose empathetic and tolerant treatment philosophy unacceptably challenged and politically embarrassed a neo-liberal penal system more concerned with retribution and punishment than genuine rehabilitation (Collins 1997; Sim 2009). Certainly, it is difficult to reconcile the overwhelmingly supportive evaluation by Bottomley *et al.* (1994), who anticipated the correction of the problems they observed and confidently dismissed the option to close the unit, with the catastrophic 'regime "slippage"' highlighted by the Scottish Prison Service (1994:17) in its internal working party's report partly *informed by* the findings of these distinguished scholars. The fate of the BSU therefore reminds all researchers of the dangers of others' selective reading and interpretation; and, as Sparks (2002) described in his exquisitely poignant memorial to the BSU, of the intricate difficulties and game playing that can result from contentious policy-relevant research.

Evidence of effectiveness

Outcome research of British penal democratic therapeutic communities – which largely means, given its longevity, research into Grendon – has predominantly concentrated upon two discrete areas. Post-imprisonment reconviction studies have quantified known re-offending among ex-residents during a specified follow-up period and from that assessed the crime control effectiveness or otherwise of the regime. In-treatment studies have measured improvements in behaviour and psychological functioning and well-being during therapy.

Longitudinal reconviction studies are inherently problematic: they offer only a proxy measure of re-offending, since just 3 per cent of crimes result in conviction or caution (Lloyd *et al.* 1994); methodologically valid control groups can be hard to establish; and the probable existence of intervening variables makes the proclamation of a causal mechanism problematic, and thus a specific treatment effect difficult to isolate. This is especially so when prisoners have (sometimes considerable and indefinite) time still to serve in other prisons. Nor does reconviction data necessarily tell the whole story: the reconviction may be for an offence that represents an important decrease in severity or extent of offending, and so indicates that whilst an offender is clearly not 'rehabilitated', he or she is encouragingly progressing towards giving up crime permanently. (The converse could also, of course, apply.) In short, then, 'recidivism is an unreliable measure of programme effectiveness … [which] rarely presents an accurate picture and is often too far removed from the specific intervention itself to have direct relevance' (Matthews and Pitts 2000:136).

Nevertheless, reconviction rates have always been, and remain, the preferred measure of effectiveness by which correctional interventions are judged. The first reconviction studies of adult Grendon graduates were published in the 1970s and were wholly discouraging. Newton (1971, 1973, discussed in Cullen 1997) successively compared the reconviction rates, after one to five years, of men who left Grendon between 1964 and 1966, with men with a seemingly similar offending profile who had received psychiatric treatment at HMP Wormwood Scrubs, or no treatment at HMP Oxford, and found no meaningful difference in their rate of reconviction. Gunn *et al.* (1978) found that 70 per cent of men admitted to Grendon between 1971 and 1972 were reconvicted after two years, compared to 62 per cent of their control group; whilst further disappointment came with the results of a 10-year follow-up (using official records) of the same cohort, with a staggeringly high 92 per cent of ex-Grendonites now reconvicted, compared to 85 per cent of the control group (Robertson and Gunn 1987).

No further reconviction studies were undertaken until Cullen (1993). In an update to this research, Newton and Thornton (1994, reported in Cullen

1994) were able to determine that 19 per cent of 150 determinate sentenced men who spent 19 months or longer at Grendon between the years 1984 to 1989 were reconvicted within two years, compared to 50 per cent who spent 18 months or less. Of those paroled directly from Grendon after more than 19 months in therapy, 10 per cent were reconvicted, as opposed to 39 per cent of men whose stay at Grendon had been shorter.

These two studies confirmed George's (1971, discussed in Gray 1973b) finding of the existence of a time in treatment or dosage effect: that duration of therapy is related to reconviction, so that those who stay longer are reconvicted less. His follow-up of men discharged between 1967 and 1968 had discovered that of men who stayed at Grendon for more than one year, 39 per cent were reconvicted, compared to 66 per cent for those residing less than 12 months. This positive correlation between dosage and reconviction was further illuminated by Genders and Player's (1995) qualitative evaluation of residents' achievements in therapy and proposal of a sequential five-stage 'therapeutic career model' of change. Genders and Player found that successful progression through the stages of problem recognition, motivation to change, understanding of and insight into how to overcome one's problems, and testing out new ways of coping was highly correlated with the length of time spent in therapy, with the critical threshold for treatment effectiveness again occurring at or after 18 months.

It is, however, the reconviction studies undertaken by Marshall (1997) and Taylor (2000) that have since become the most widely quoted (and still most recent) evidence of Grendon's 'success'; although as Shuker (2010) notes, neither were published in peer-reviewed academic journals, and some of their findings did not attain the generally accepted criterion for statistical significance (that is, that the results were unlikely to have occurred by chance). In the first study, Marshall (1997) examined the reconviction data of 702 former Grendonites who were in therapy between 1984 and 1989 and were serving neither life nor very long sentences. For the first time, he compared this 'admitted group' with a satisfactory control group: a 'waiting list' of 142 prisoners who matched admitted prisoners on all important characteristics and were selected as suitable for Grendon, but who did not proceed to therapy for reasons such as lack of space, a medical condition, or insufficient time left to serve in which to enter and complete therapy. Marshall then further compared these groups with a 'general prison' control group of approximately 1,400 male offenders, of similar age, offence type, and sentence length to those admitted to Grendon, and who had been released from prison in 1987. Four years after release, the admitted group had a lower overall reconviction rate (58 per cent) than the waiting list control group (66 per cent). They were also less likely to be reconvicted of violence and sentenced to further imprisonment. Interestingly, both the admitted group and the waiting list group were substantially more likely to be reconvicted than the general prison population control group, indicating that the type of prisoner selected as suitable for Grendon (whether subsequently admitted or not) had a higher prior risk of reconviction. This therefore suggested that the unpromising 1970s reconviction studies, which compared Grendon graduates with other prisoners on the basis of similar age, offence, and sentence, were nevertheless methodologically flawed because they did not compare 'like with like' for risk; a failing which Gunn *et al.* (1978) had acknowledged in their criticisms, and hence dismissal, of their own reconviction findings.

The time in treatment effect was also replicated in Marshall's study. After differences in risk and mode of leaving had been taken into account, Marshall found that those who spent more than 18 months in therapy had reduced their rate of re-offending, as measured by reconviction within four years, by around one-fifth to one-quarter. He further found evidence of a treatment effect for older offenders (aged 30 or over) with two or more previous convictions for violence. Amongst these men, 28 per cent were reconvicted within four years, compared to 49 per cent of older offenders in the waiting list group. (It was as a result of these successive findings about optimal treatment dosage that 18 months became the required minimum period of time to which would-be residents must commit.)

Using the same method, Taylor (2000) re-examined Marshall's sample, now seven years post-release from Grendon. Again, substantially more men from the waiting list were reconvicted for any offence, reconvicted for violence, and imprisoned than the general prison control group, confirming that people selected for Grendon are more high risk than 'regular' prisoners. The admitted group recorded a significantly lower reconviction rate (66 per cent), and reconviction for violence (30 per cent), than the waiting list group (73 per cent and 37 per cent respectively); they were also less likely to be re-imprisoned (36 per cent compared to 42 per cent). Taylor cautioned, however, that, on average, the waiting list group's criminal antecedents and youth increased their risk of reconviction and when the findings were adjusted to reflect this, the difference in reconviction became more marginal. Marshall's finding that reconviction was related to time in therapy, however, was again confirmed, with general reconviction rates of 71 per cent for residents who resided for less than six months, compared to 62 per cent for those staying over 18 months. These 'long-stayers' also significantly reduced their involvement in violent offences and were less likely to be imprisoned. Taylor also examined reconviction rates for 73 released lifers and again reported a positive finding: 8 per cent of Grendonites were convicted of another offence, compared with 12 per cent for all life-sentenced licensees discharged in 1987. Furthermore, given the more serious antecedents and relative youth of Grendon's released lifers, Taylor calculated their expected reconviction rate to be 24 per cent at four years, three times greater than their actual reconviction rate.

In contrast to the insubstantial and inconclusive reconviction evidence, in-treatment studies have consistently reported statistically reliable and clinically significant improvements in psychological functioning. Especially for men who stay in therapy for at least one year, TC treatment has been found to result in lower levels of psychoticism and neuroticism, including reduced anxiety and depression; reduced levels of hostility and negatively relating to others and improved attitudes towards authority; reduced impulsivity and increased acceptance of internal locus of control;[23] higher levels of extroversion and improved self-esteem and self-confidence; enhanced perspective-taking skills; and improved mental well-being (inter alia, Newton 1973, 1997, 1998, 2000; Gunn *et al.* 1978; Miller 1982; Lees *et al.* 1999; Shuker and Newton 2008; Birtchnell *et al.* 2009; Niven *et al.* 2010). Such changes translate into additional, more imaginative, measures of Grendon's effectiveness, when compared with other category B prisons: 'remarkably low' rates of suicide and self-harm (Rivlin 2010), and much improved behaviour (discussed further in Chapter 5), as evidenced through significantly reduced rates of offending against prison rules both at *and after* Grendon, when ex-residents transfer back to mainstream prisons (Cullen 1994; Newton 2006, 2010).

Finally, Grendon has long been recognized as providing an exceptionally physically safe, emotionally secure, humane environment (Genders and Player 1995; Bennett 2006). The creation by Liebling and her colleagues at the Cambridge Institute of Criminology of the 'Measuring the Quality of Prison Life' (MQPL) survey, however, has made it possible to conceptualize, assess, and compare between prisons, quantitatively and systematically, what collectively amounts to their 'moral performance': 'those aspects of a prisoner's mainly *interpersonal* and material treatment that render a term of imprisonment more or less dehumanizing and/or painful' (Liebling, assisted by Arnold 2004:473, emphasis preserved). These, more elusive, moral and emotional dimensions of prison life include decency, fairness, rehabilitation, relationships with staff, safety, and well-being and 'matter because they matter, and not (just) because they might "work"' (ibid.:166). Whilst some might question the legitimacy of measuring a prison's achievement in terms of its provision of humane treatment (in addition to, not instead of, reconviction outcomes), the adoption of the MQPL survey by the Prison Service Standards Audit Unit in 2002 as an integral part of its biannual audit process represents institutional recognition of the importance of the moral context and therapeutic climate in which imprisonment and rehabilitation is experienced. The quality of life at Grendon during the period of time in which this research was conducted can be ascertained from the 2005–6 and 2006–7 surveys, in which Grendon recorded the highest mean score for each dimension compared to eight other equivalent (category B training) prisons, with only one open (category D) prison scoring higher. When Grendon's scores were compared to the best scores recorded for each of the dimensions in any of the 87 secure men's prisons surveyed in 2005–7, for all but three dimensions, Grendon's score was higher than the highest score gained by the other prisons. Furthermore, when prisoners were asked to rate their overall quality of life in prison on a scale of one (poor) to ten (high), Grendon's score, at 6.99, was the highest of all 97 surveyed male adult prisons, across security categories, and only one of three prisons in which the score exceeded six (Newton 2006; Shefer 2010b).

TC units research

The very limited amount of research conducted on TC units has also supported the effectiveness of the regime in reducing rates of reconviction and positively influencing behaviour. Most notably, Cooke's (1989, 1991, 1997) progressive evaluations of the BSU provided impressive evidence – although the numbers involved were extremely small. Of the 25 men who had been or were resident at the time of his first survey, all had at least one conviction for violence (the mean was 6.8), 64 per cent had been convicted of murder, 80 per cent were category A prisoners, 76 per cent had 'psychopathic traits', and 68 per cent had received additional sentences for offences against prison discipline (Cooke 1989). Extrapolating from these most unpromising antecedents, Cooke (1989) devised a formula to calculate the expected rate of assaults. Of the 105 anticipated assaults during these residents' stay, only two occurred; of the 73 expected post-release, only ten were recorded. Similarly, of an expected frequency in the BSU of 154 disruptive incidents, the actual number was 9. Furthermore, this improvement was maintained when the men returned to mainstream prisons, with 99 episodes predicted but only 17 occurring. Additionally, 12 residents had been released and Cooke calculated an expected frequency of reconviction within two years at 8.31, yet the observed frequency of actual reconvictions was 4.0.

Further evidence of the TC's reformatory potential was offered by the reconviction study of 122 former Max Glatt Centre treatment residents. This found that 55 per cent of those who completed treatment were reconvicted within two years, compared to 82 per cent for those who left the TC prematurely (Jones 1988, reported in Healey 2000). The rate of reconviction was therefore once again significantly related to length of stay (Jones 1997).

Equally consistent with research at Grendon, an early evaluation of GTC found that the average number of disciplinary proceedings incurred by its residents declined threefold, from 0.18 per month before admission to 0.06 per cent per month after leaving (Woodward and Hodkin 1996). Additionally, amongst Glen Parva TC's young offenders, only four assaults were recorded during its 17-year history, notwithstanding the severity of their offences and the high levels of psychological disturbance and distress prior to admission (Mackenzie 1997).

Finally, Surrey University's Psychology Department undertook a longitudinal, mixed method evaluation of treatment outcomes at Dovegate TC between 2003 and 2008 as part of the research contract it held with the prison. Again, echoing successive studies at Grendon, researchers found an increase in residents' functional (pro-social) behaviours (such as asking for advice, accepting feedback, and giving emotional support to others) and a decrease in dysfunctional behaviours (such as giving inappropriate advice and feedback, disrupting therapy groups, and displaying hostility and anger towards staff) (Neville *et al.* 2007). Moreover, the existence of a treatment dosage effect was again seemingly reaffirmed. Of 94 former residents who had been released from prison by May 2008, 45 (48 per cent) had been reconvicted; just over 70 per cent of whom had stayed for 17 months or less (Miller and Brown 2010). This research is not directly comparable with the Grendon reconviction studies, however, since the reconvicted and non-reconvicted ex-Dovegate residents had on average only been at liberty in the community (and hence had had the opportunity to re-offend) for 19 and 18 months respectively.

In summary, then, the evidence of effectiveness for democratic TCs is nowhere near as robust, in quantity or quality, as for addictions TCs, and there has not been as much evaluative research of Grendon's effectiveness over the years as one would have expected and preferred (Lees *et al.* 1999, 2004). Moreover, the meagreness of research on reconviction rates seems likely to continue: as the number of penal TC units has increased, the prospects for devising a suitable waiting list control group have waned, while the omnipresence of cognitive-behavioural OBPs in mainstream prisons renders it unlikely that a valid control group of genuinely 'untreated', comparable prisoners could now be found. 'Gold standard' randomized controlled trials are, for democratic TCs, fraught with methodological and ethical obstacles (Campbell 2003; Lees *et al.* 2004), which to date have not been overcome and, debatably, will prove to be insurmountable. Measurements of the prison-based TC's effectiveness, or otherwise, will therefore continue to rely heavily on indications of psychological change.

Yet, there exists compelling evidence that the prison-based TC ameliorates psychological functioning and behaviour, and treatment is clearly most effective, reconviction-wise, amongst older, serious offenders who remain in therapy for at least 18 months. Moreover, any assessment of the effectiveness of prison-based TCs should be contextualized by attention to the 'special kind' of prisoners Grendonites in particular tend to be, and by acknowledgement of the abject failure of *mainstream* regimes to rehabilitate: in England and Wales, 55 per cent of offenders are reconvicted within two years of release from prison, rising to 74 per cent within nine years (Ministry of Justice 2010b). In other words, prisons in general do not 'work' to reduce re-offending (as measured by reconviction rates), but prison-based TCs, and more specifically, Grendon, can claim to 'work' somewhat better than most, with some of the prison population's most high-risk, 'damaged, disturbed and dangerous' men (Shine and Newton 2000), and to 'work' very well at improving residents' psychological health.

2 Conducting research in prisons

Tightrope walks and emotion work

Grendon prison officer: So, are you a spy?

Alisa: No, I'm doing research.

Officer: Same thing.

Discussion of social research methods in monographs is sometimes exiled to an appendix. Such material may seem boring to those who (wish to) know little about research methodologies and processes, and really boring to those who understand them well. In what follows then, my intention is not to test the patience of the reader anxious to proceed to 'the main event', but to explain the context in which the research findings were gained. Some audit trail of the methods employed is always necessary for the instillation of reader confidence in the validity and reliability of the findings presented. When, however, as here, the researcher is the research instrument, some personalization of and reflexivity about the 'doing' of the research is desirable in order to illuminate precisely how the resulting data were obtained, notwithstanding the personal investment and emotional entanglement that research has required and occasioned. When, moreover, the principal informants are prisoners, trust in whom to provide credible and truthful (even if, as with all self-narratives, inevitably partial) evidence some would consider naive, a 'natural history' account of the negotiation and production of data can reassuringly explain how the, sometimes surprising, disclosures the researcher elicited were situated within the sincerity of the research relationship and the intensity of the shared research moment.

This chapter, then, succinctly describes the qualitative research methods employed in this study, in the assumption that those who want or need to understand methodology, theoretical perspectives, and research ethics better will consult the many excellent textbooks available on these topics. In line with contemporary understandings of the role of emotion in, and the value of reflection upon, fieldwork (inter alia, Stanley and Wise 1983; Kleinman and Copp 1993; Coffey 1999; Widdowfield 2000; Hubbard *et al.* 2001; Jewkes 2012), though, I also reflect critically upon my researcher role and the felt experience of conducting fieldwork in prisons; an experience I characterize as a tightrope walk, made ever more perilous by the burden of carrying, in Hochschild's (1983) apt phrase, 'emotion work'.

Research rationale, methods, and settings

> What's a posh bird like you doing in a dump like this? Why would you choose to put yourself through this *misery*? [laughing]
>
> (Robbie, Grendon)

Prison-based democratic TCs, especially Grendon, have attracted sustained academic and practitioner research interest. Given the necessity for all correctional interventions to demonstrate their effectiveness, much of this research (as discussed in the previous chapter) has focused upon outcomes, evaluating whether, for whom and, to a lesser extent, how TCs 'work' to reduce re-offending or improve psychological functioning and behaviour. Other studies have sought to explicate the particular issues surrounding TC practice in prisons and the management of programme implementation and integrity, and sometimes this has allowed for the presentation of 'service user' experiences through therapists' or psychologists' depiction of clinical vignettes and case studies, or for a closer examination of the effect of TC work on prison staff (inter alia, Cullen *et al.* 1997; Williams Saunders 2001; Morris 2004a; Jones 2004a; Parker 2007; McManus 2007; Shefer 2010a; Shuker and Sullivan 2010; Cullen and Mackenzie 2011). Minimal attention, however, has been paid explicitly to detailing the processes and culture of the TC, as seen through the perspectives and experiences of serving or former residents (cf. Smartt 2001; Wilson and McCabe 2002; Miller *et al.* 2006).

The relative invisibility of men and women prisoners residing in TCs in the literature (as indeed in prisons sociology more generally) is surprising, given that in prisons research 'arguably the most valuable source of information is the inmates concerned' (Liebling 1992:104). Prisoners' lived experience of imprisonment will always be more vivid than that produced by even the most dedicated of 'academic tourists' (Reuss 2000:26), and the deliberate foregrounding of residents' accounts of their TC experiences in this 'bottom-up' research was therefore both an ethical and methodological decision. In this sense, this book, with its generous use of direct quotations from residents, does intend to give residents and their subjective understandings of 'what helps' (Ward and Maruna 2007:12) (or hinders) them to progress towards change in the TC a 'voice'. As the researcher, author, and hence 'gatekeeper to the truth' (Morgan 1999:330), however, I have necessarily reduced, filtered, interpreted, analysed, and reframed these raw data into a coherent, academic text, in which I trust participants[1] will still recognize their 'voices' but for which, in its theoretical and empirical emphases and omissions, I bear full responsibility. The aim has thus been to produce, as Goodey (2000:482) puts it, 'a balanced assessment of subject-led revelation and researcher-based interpretation'.

In its deliberate, appreciative focus upon and phenomenological approach towards residents' perspectives, the research draws upon the well-established qualitative research traditions of exploratory ethnography – or, more accurately in prisons, semi-ethnography[2] – and in-depth one-to-one semi-structured interviewing, triangulated by some use of descriptive data from official prison records (including initial and periodic therapy targets and progress reports), databases, and literature. The fieldwork was accomplished in three distinct phases. The bulk of the work was conducted over five months at Grendon during the summer of 2006, followed by shorter spells at the TC units at Send and Gartree, in the spring and autumn of 2007 respectively. As a dedicated TC prison, Grendon has all the facilities it requires for prisoners on one site. GTC is located in a small, two-storey building, separate from the rest of the prison. It benefits from its own ground-floor kitchen and dining room and a small courtyard (and prized sun trap) with raised flower beds and aviary, both maintained by residents. The community room, wing and therapy offices, and residential accommodation are all on the first floor. GTC residents access the gym, education, and other opportunities for 'purposeful activity' in the mainstream prison. Send TC, as already noted, shares its accommodation with other women on A-wing, with only the community room and therapy rooms and office located in a discrete unit by, but not attached to, A-wing. Apart from one association room reserved for TC women on A-wing, all other activities, including dining, take place within the main prison. These differences were reflected in the fieldwork experience. Whereas I could spend the entire prison day at Grendon and GTC, from 08.00 'unlock' to 20.00 'bang up', at Send, I was required to leave the prison at 17.00, with the clinical staff, and my opportunities for observation were therefore mostly restricted to the daytime community meetings and social gatherings.

As is usual ethnographic practice, I wrote a private fieldwork journal in brief during each day 'inside' and punctiliously in full once at home, usually the same evening and always within 24 hours. This journal constitutes a factual, chronological record about what I had seen and done – observations, conversations, activities, and events – in which the anthropological strangeness of the TC prison emerges through the pedestrian detailing of its regime. It also, however, provided me with a constructive medium for reflexivity; a repository into which to consign and contain the frustrations, fears, and sorrows the fieldwork sometimes provoked.

Both the transcripts of interviews and fieldwork notes were thematically coded and systematically analysed in accordance with the principles of liberal grounded theory (Strauss 1987; Corbin and Strauss 2008). This method and product of enquiry seeks to derive or refine theory solely from empirical data but allows for the use of literature, before and after data collection, 'to enhance, rather than constrain, theory development' (Strauss and Corbin 1998:49). The process of transcribing, disaggregation, coding, and analysis (the 'old fashioned' way, without recourse to qualitative data analysis software) began immediately after the first Grendon interview and was continued on days away from the TCs, but most of this time and labour-intensive, creative and cognitive work was conducted in concerted periods after each period of fieldwork.

Access, observation, and 'hanging out'

> Observation? Just a posh word for doing naff all!
>
> (Callum, Grendon)

Research access is physical, social, and psychological. To 'get in' to prison in England and Wales, one must petition and gain the support of individual establishments and, for multi-site investigations, regional or national research committees to conduct the research. The would-be researcher must be able to convince these institutional guardians of the research's academic merits and policy relevance. Permission is far from assured, for there are many more reasons – both pragmatic and protectionist – to say no rather than yes. When one is fortunate enough to 'get in', however, one must then 'get on' with building a trusting rapport with potential research participants. It is their acceptance of the researcher, and consent to the research, as much as the institution's, that effectively determines the scope, duration, and quality of the fieldwork and hence of the final research 'product'.

I began by attending community meetings on each wing. After the ever surreal experience of sitting in an extended circle, swiftly introducing ourselves – 'Tom, rape'; 'Dick, armed robbery'; 'Harry, murder'; 'Alisa, Oxford University'[3] – I was allocated a few minutes to 'sell' my research and, in effect, to ask for permission to observe their community. Chiefly at Grendon, a period of sustained observation then followed, though the techniques – if that is not too grand a term – employed were replicated in compressed form at Send and GTC. I introduced myself and my research repeatedly; answered far more questions (about criminology and university life) than I asked (about the prison); listened to residents' personal disclosures or potentially controversial views and did not repeat them; seized any opportunity to engage, or be engaged, in conversation; watched the 'comings and goings' of the prison day; and tried to absorb everything and evaluate nothing. Some residents talked freely to me and showed real interest in my research, but others did not, and in my nervousness about being able to 'get on', it was easy to mistake such indifference for dislike (Shaffir 1991). As I subsequently came to realize, however, many residents were simply biding their time, monitoring my character and conduct with the same intense scrutiny that I noted theirs. They were, as Hammersley and Atkinson (1995:83) predict, 'more concerned with what kind of person the researcher is than with the research itself'; with one's personal, rather than academic, credentials. As one participant later told me:

> You're all right, Alisa. With you being from *Oxford University*, I thought you might be a bit stuck up, but no, I've seen you about the place and

> you talk to everyone, you don't judge the guys in here; you're a lovely lady. So I thought yeah, I'll do this interview of yours.
>
> (Winston, Grendon)

My attempts to 'get on' at Grendon were further complicated by its non-negotiable instruction to draw keys.[4] This, I was to discover, conferred on me the significant advantage of independence of movement, and hence a certain invisibility, around the prison, which greatly aided ethnographic observation. The not unreasonable assumption this possession of keys created amongst some residents, however, was that I must be, if not a member of staff, allied with staff: 'You've got keys, so you're one of them', one discontented resident informed me. Carrying keys also sometimes placed me in the uneasy and identity-compromising position of not knowing whether I should or should not unlock the gate for residents wanting to leave or enter the community, and I was sometimes asked by busy officers, 'as you're going that way', to 'escort' a resident from one part of the prison to another (fieldnotes). For the 'outsider', the possession of keys can therefore induce confusion about one's role and risks diluting the desirable impression and important principle 'that one is in but not of the prison' (King 2000:305). In practice, however, I found that the majority of Grendonites were wholly unperturbed by my status as a key holder. It was I who felt self-conscious and angst-ridden about the power keys afforded me.

As I became better known to and, on some level, trusted by residents, I started to garner volunteers for interviews. The 'pure' observation stage now gave way to the hybrid research method of 'reserved participation' (Bottoms, cited in Liebling 1999:160) in prison life, with the many opportunities for spontaneous, casual 'chats' this allows, and regular interviewing. I was much more comfortable in, and less anxious about, my role once I committed to a task as tangibly productive as interviews: observation looks very much like inactivity ('doing naff all') and this invites suspicion of one's true purpose. At best, one appears to be the stereotypical academic 'obsessional boffin' (King 2000:300) who, despite eccentrically volunteering to spend time in a prison and with 'no proper job' that staff or prisoners could discern (Sparks *et al.* 1996:348), is considered harmless enough to be tolerated. At worst, overtly hostile prison officers[5] repeatedly questioned the 'real' function of my research and legitimacy of my presence – specifically, whether I was from or working for Prison Service Headquarters or NOMS, conducting perhaps a covert time and motion study – and struggled to comprehend, quite understandably, one might think, how 'chatting' and 'hanging about' were genuine research activities. In particular, they became mistrustful of my on-going conversations and 'friendliness' with residents whom I had already interviewed,[6] when they were more used to researchers coming on to the community to administer a quantitative survey or interview a resident just once. My own inability in the early stages of the research to define exactly what I was looking for, and my failure to appreciate the necessity of explaining, repeatedly and proactively, what I was doing and why, doubtlessly fuelled some staff's fears that I was indeed 'a spy' and caused me some wholly unnecessary difficulties.

Throughout the interview 'stages', I continued to attend community meetings, residents' therapy assessment and progress meetings, and staff-only business and feedback meetings; accepted any and all invites to social events, including at Grendon the weekly and ever popular inter-wing chapel drop-in (with free tea and biscuits!) hosted by the prison's dynamic chaplains; and consciously tried to ensure that, whilst 'hanging out', I observed – and was *seen to be* observing – both residents and staff if not equally, at least equitably. I did not, however, attend small groups, nor did I ask participants to divulge what they discussed in therapy, although some interviewees chose to volunteer this information. The highly sensitive and emotive nature of therapy and finely tuned dynamics of small groups (in recent years, always) precludes the occasional and non-contributory attendance of 'visitors' and was in any case unnecessary for this research: I wanted to acquire a criminological understanding of residents' experiences of the TC regime, not the clinical processes or confidential content of forensic psychotherapy.

My efforts to become a 'marginal native' (Freilich 1970) were most profitably advanced, however, in the relaxed, informal recreational atmosphere of evening association at Grendon and GTC, where I could socialize regularly with certain residents, most but not all of whom were formally interviewed. One can view this as developing a 'cadre of "favourites"' (Genders and Player 1995:44), with all the attendant dangers this implies both methodologically and, more acutely in my experience, because of concerns about conditioning and making oneself vulnerable to breaching security. Alternatively, one can, as I did, perceive such regulars as key informants who could be relied upon to keep me up to date with developments, to promote my research to others, and to assist with what a genuine spy might term infiltration. It was within these professional boundaries that I developed trusting and mutually supportive relationships that approximated friendship, coming to know some residents as both individuals, with all the irreducibility and intricacy of human experience this entails, and as members of a community. As Crewe (2009:488) poetically described, the prison has a tendency to create 'iceberg identities whose appearances are deceptive and whose depths are submerged'. It was this discovery of residents' less obvious identities, and the informal conversations we shared, that I enjoyed most throughout the fieldwork and which, more instrumentally, beneficially mediated my understanding of residents' experiences.

The value of fieldwork is thus neatly encapsulated by this quotation from the key participant of one famous sociological study: 'If people accept you, you can just hang around, and you'll learn the answers in the long run without even having to ask the questions' (Doc, in Whyte 1981:303). In situ observation ensures the researcher's knowledge and understanding is tethered to and evolves directly from her participants' perspectives, expressed in discourse and other symbolic constructions (Vidich 1955); and, by remaining open to the contingency of naturally occurring interaction, allows her to profit from 'the advantage of serendipity' (Whyte 1984:27). Such 'empathetic ethnography' bestows upon the researcher the opportunity to acquire an emic understanding or Weberian *Verstehen* of how micro-societies are enabled to exist (Smircich 1983), and, from Rapoport (1960) onwards, has had particular value in TCs, where residents' everyday life and social world have to be understood in order to appreciate and illuminate fully the complexity yet coherence of the TC way. The dissociated, theoretically acquired knowledge I had attained prior to commencing fieldwork therefore acquired real resonance and meaning through my naturalistic observations, which in turn enhanced my ability to formulate culturally appropriate and meaningful interview schedules and to discuss issues from a position of (within obvious limits) shared experience and frames of reference.

Finally, one must also acknowledge that the observer/participant does not just collect data, but to some extent, through her attendance and relationships with others, creates and distorts data. The observer is also observed. By becoming part of the communities – however provisionally – I inevitably impacted upon them and cannot fully know to what extent what I saw and experienced was manufactured or moderated for my benefit. The more obvious reactive or Hawthorne effects my presence induced at the beginning of fieldwork, however, did abate. The senior officer who was complaining animatedly to a colleague on the telephone before stopping mid-sentence because 'there's a researcher here so I'd better shut up', for example, or the Grendonite who ineptly reprimanded another for exclaiming 'fuck' in my presence with the words, 'Watch your fucking mouth in front of a fucking lady!' (fieldnotes), tended to speak more freely and behave more naturally without (so much) concern for 'the spy' in their midst, once I became well established 'about the place'.

Interviews and conversations

> I done one of them tick box questionnaires before but it weren't no cop.[7] It didn't say what *I* wanted to say.
>
> (Colin, Grendon)

Social researchers and journalists alike have come to rely upon the face-to-face, qualitative interview as the predominant means of data collection (Atkinson and Silverman 1997). Survey questionnaires or rigidly adhered to protocols can ascertain how participants respond to the researcher's interests. Semi-structured and unstructured interviews, however, give the interviewee considerable autonomy to respond flexibly and spontaneously to open-ended questions, and thus potentially to go beyond the researcher's concerns to reveal or prioritize issues of real or symbolic value to the interviewee (Holstein and Gubrium 2004; Lofland *et al.* 2006). Such co-construction of knowledge can result in highly rewarding and unanticipated discourses: indeed, my 'best' interviews were those that took this form of 'conversational partnership' (Rubin and Rubin 2005:79) about our mutual (if differently motivated) interest in TCs which, as noted above, with some participants was extensively previewed and advanced further in informal discussions before and after the actual interview 'event'.

The key component of this research was therefore the semi-structured, in-depth interviews I conducted with 80 residents and staff at the three establishments. In keeping with the TC ethos of voluntariness and self-determination, I asked people to put themselves forward to be interviewed. I also considered it ethically preferable that interviewees did not feel under any pressure or expectation to participate because *I* had selected *them*, not least since the questions I wanted to ask of residents demanded a relatively high level of candid self-disclosure about their offending and intra-individual prison experiences. The only exclusion criterion, in order to ensure interviewees had a reasonable amount of TC experience, was that they had resided or worked in the TC for at least three months. Some 43 residents at Grendon, 10 from Send, and seven from GTC volunteered to be interviewed. Most came forward independently, in response to my intermittent 'sales pitches' or as a result of talking to me when I was 'hanging out', but I also benefited from a significant element of snowball sampling, when those whom I had already interviewed encouraged their friends to participate. Of this combined resident sample, 55 per cent were serving an indeterminate sentence, 58 per cent had been sentenced primarily for violence, 17 per cent for robbery, and 15 per cent for sexual offences. At the time of interview, residents' length of stay varied from four months to five years, but averaged 20 months at GTC, 17 months at Grendon, and 12 months at Send.

Twenty disciplinary, managerial, and clinical[8] staff, all but five of whom worked at Grendon, either volunteered to be interviewed or, in the case of Grendon's governing governor and some clinical staff, accepted my request for an interview. The staff interviews, although smaller in number and infrequently referred to in this book, proved very instructive in informing, challenging, and/or confirming my resident- and observation-derived data, and in greatly enhancing my theoretical understanding of forensic psychotherapy.

I chose, then, not to employ a random or purposive sample. The cohort was one of self-selection – people who wanted to discuss their TC experience – and who, as it unintentionally transpired amongst the residents, were often well advanced in their treatment. In effect, then, so-called 'senior' residents who had committed to therapy and had progressed over time towards and become aware of change were overrepresented in this non-random sample; a limitation of the research that may well be reflected in residents' almost universally glowing evaluations of the regime and their rehabilitative experiences within it. Clearly, a researcher who seeks volunteers cannot know what those people who did not choose to participate would have said, and how this might have affected the findings. Nothing in my informal interactions with residents who did not volunteer themselves for interview, however, caused me to believe that they were unusually 'anti-TC' or would have described a radically divergent, more critical version of rehabilitation and imprisonment in the TC. Moreover, the positive experiences interviewees overwhelmingly recounted did not preclude or deter them, most especially at Grendon, from simultaneously decrying deleterious regime changes necessitated by the need to reduce costs, nor worrying about the durability of a regime from which they were convinced they had benefited. In other words, I found my informants to be 'biased' only in the sense that they had definite opinions they wished to share with me, and when these opinions were critical, they related, without exception, to the operational execution, ideological support, and financial sustenance of therapeutic communities in prison, and not the fundamental principles, clinical practice, or rehabilitative value of the TC way.

All interviews were conducted in private, in 'free periods' (that is, outside of group and community meetings), and within the participant's community, with the exceptions of Grendon prison officers, who were interviewed in the psychology department, and Grendon's governing governor, who was interviewed in his office. Participants were asked by what name they would like to be known when quoted. In attributing quotes, however, great care has been taken not to associate interviewees' names with any details which might reveal their identity to readers once known to them and this has therefore meant not citing the TC location of staff interviewees, and occasionally not providing a resident's name or substituting a pseudonym for the participant's preferred (actual) name. On average, the interviews lasted around two hours, though this ranged from slightly under one hour to over six hours, conducted over four sessions.

In order to ensure accuracy, permission was sought (from the prison and each interviewee) to tape record the interviews and they were fully transcribed to facilitate the thematic analysis.[9] Although transcription has an entirely deserved reputation as a tedious and excessively time-consuming activity, listening repeatedly to interviews effectively imprinted participants' voices and stories in my memory and ensured that, when 'writing up', I could literally 'hear' my data and their emotional context. In the reproduction of participants' testimonies, I have retained the exact wording used, including solecisms, swearing, local dialects, and prison slang.[10] Whilst I hope such faithful transcription will not cause offence, if one is to claim authentic representation of participants' experiences, they must be expressed verbatim and not filtered through the 'translation' of the academic's sensibilities. The nickname of 'posh bird' I acquired amongst some residents partly derived from our contrasting speech patterns and my lack of a regional accent, the reciprocated acceptance of which, incidentally, caused much mutual amusement and affectionate teasing.

Four Grendonites agreed to pilot interviews: two residents who were due to leave within days and two assessment wing residents who met the minimum residence criterion of three months. These and other early interviews prompted me to amend the schedule slightly. I clarified some evidently ambiguous questions, discarded questions of lesser interest or consequence to my informants, and conversely added questions on aspects of the regime whose significance I had not at first fully appreciated, as the multiple intricacies and subtleties of, and the matrix of meanings contained within, the TC way emerged.

The interviews, then, began with some 'warm up' questions about the interviewee's decision to apply to live or work in a TC. These answers frequently elicited considerable autobiographical information which, for residents, included their motivation for therapy and, often, attitudes towards their offending and sentence. A series of generative questions within six distinct areas then followed, all intended to facilitate a lengthy conversation about the TC experience, how this differs from mainstream regimes, and its perceived benefits and problems. These comprised a mixture of descriptive questions which participants could answer with ease and authoritative fluency, and more challenging, evaluative questions upon which many participants had to ponder before answering.

As the interview progressed, participants would often return to earlier questions and elaborate upon their original answer with greater candour, clarity, and analytical depth; or I would revisit generalized responses if I sensed that the rapport we had developed might now be rewarded with more explicit detail. Other times, it was interviewees who would actively redirect my enquiries towards issues more reflective of their opinions and anxieties, sometimes touching upon surprisingly intimate and sensitive topics with disarming frankness. This indicated, I felt, more than a desire for conversational mutuality or even a conscious assertion of agency, but rather illustrated further how the role one seeks for oneself can be rejected and reinterpreted by others and, specifically, may be mediated through the lens of gender. Self-evidently, one's gender can enhance or impede rapport, and make it more or less likely that certain topics will be freely discussed. The cultural, if essentialist, expectation that women are 'good listeners', for example, sometimes converted into an assumption that I would be an appropriate and, moreover, safe person with whom to discuss personal problems and concerns. I was therefore assigned by some resident interviewees a stereotypically gendered role more befitting a counsellor or confidante than a researcher; a role I did not resist because it facilitated my acceptance (see also, Gelsthorpe 1990) and accomplished my desire to offer some reciprocity which, in prisons, can only be achieved through an exchange of time, knowledge, and interest (Patenaude 2004).

Accordingly, my experience was that – despite not asking explicit life history questions – the vast majority of resident interviewees told me something of their personal biographies and/or the details of their index offence(s), and discussed the realities of 'doing time' and the undeniable 'pains of imprisonment'. In particular, our interviews would sometimes digress into deeply moving admissions of personal traumas and private troubles. When interviewees were visibly upset, my natural inclination towards tactility meant I wanted to reach out to hold their hands – but of course, this is not 'allowed' in prisons. What would represent only an instinctive act of kindness 'on the out', would expose the researcher in prison to the danger of sexualized misinterpretation of motive and had to be resisted, leaving the interviewee with only a cathartic opportunity to cry and 'offload', and me with an intense sense of my own impotence when directly confronted with others' unprocessed pain. In these circumstances, I would unconsciously but explicitly re-identify with the counsellor role, by gently asking some quasi-therapeutic questions until the resident signalled his or her willingness to return to the concerns of the interview schedule. Listening attentively and offering whatever soothing or supportive words I could, though, hardly felt an adequate response.

Other interviews were disturbing for less sympathetic reasons. One Grendonite, for example, stared transfixed at my breasts for most of our two hour interview, rather than make eye contact. He somehow managed to answer many of my questions with reference to the joys of pornography, the agonies of enforced celibacy, and his 'very high sex drive', no matter how hard I tried to forestall these ruminations, redirect the conversation, and encourage him to engage with me as a person and not just someone possessed of two mammary glands. Another interview was unnerving because the respondent repeatedly told me how he 'had no time for women' given their 'natural inferiority to men … and trivial nature. I'm a man of *very* superior intelligence, you see.' He noted with some pride that his therapeutic progress was such that he was now able to communicate with 'quite a few females; I've learned to tolerate them better at Grendon'; for which, presumably, he expected me to be grateful. In both instances, I chose neither to comment upon nor challenge these interviewees' conduct or statements. Partly this was due to my embarrassment: it was easier to attempt to circumvent the sexual preoccupation and ignore the misogyny. Partly, however, I clung to my stated objective of listening and trying to appreciate their opinions, regardless of how personally distastefully I experienced them.

More happily, most participants remarked that they found the interview an interesting and enjoyable experience which allowed them, however transiently and nominally, to be known and to have me acknowledge their situated difficulties and superior experiential understanding. Most prison interviews are for the purposes of legal consultations, risk assessments, or progression reports. The empowering opportunity that semi-structured research interviews offer prisoners to construct, and to seek support for, an alternative, preferred version of the self which their subordinated moral status does not normally allow (Presser 2004; Crewe and Maruna 2006), accordingly seemed to be warmly appreciated:

> I can talk to you, *really* talk. I feel like you understand me. Me and you could be chatting anywhere now; I don't feel like I'm in prison sat talking to you … We can *converse*, like two equals, like two adults.
>
> (Robbie, Grendon)

> I'm surprised that a posh bird like you is interested in what us cons have to say, but it's nice that you are! [laughs] It's good to be taken seriously, you know? Most people think we're all thickos or something and don't know nothing, but we're the ones doing the time, aren't we? *We* know about that, don't we?
>
> (Francis, GTC)

Other participants recognized that volunteering to be interviewed represented a welcome improvement in their self-knowledge and self-confidence and verbal and interpersonal skills:

> Sitting here being able to speak to you is a big, big step. I've always been a person that won't speak about my feelings and to be able to talk about them with you, well, it's been like a one-to-one therapy session, hasn't it? [laughs] But I wouldn't have put myself forward to be interviewed before. That's the TC for you, it gives you a new confidence!
>
> (Ben, GTC)

> I am now so different from the shy person I used to be. I think even last year, if you had come then, I wouldn't have been able to do this. I wouldn't have no confidence to speak to someone like you … I do speak up now; I don't put myself down no longer.
>
> (Josephine, Send)

> Before here, I couldn't communicate with people. I was a paranoid mess. I wouldn't have been able to do this before, sitting in here talking with you for this long, without going absolutely mad and running out the room! [laughs]
>
> (Don, Grendon)

The valuable opportunity to reflect upon their TC experiences was also much commented upon, or as one participant joked:

> I've never thought so much in my life as today! You've certainly given my brain a right old kicking!
>
> (Richard, Grendon)

The fieldwork experience

> You're getting in deep here! You're right serious about this, ain't you?
>
> (Nick, Grendon)

So much of what contributes to the experience of fieldwork in prisons, although hugely influential at the time and poignantly memorable long after its completion, is difficult to recapture adequately within the conventions of academic discourse. Without some discussion of the difficulties encountered, however, a sterile version of serenely accomplished fieldwork is portrayed, every bit as false as the 'chronological lie which is at the heart of most research' (Cohen and Taylor 1972:32). Qualitative research, particularly of the ethnographic variety, does not tend to follow the neat, relentlessly logical research trajectory some accounts would suggest, and neither is it without sporadic bouts of awkwardness, loneliness, anguish, and loss of self-confidence.

Two themes, then, most succinctly yet completely summarize my experience of prisons research, particularly at Grendon: the precariousness of the tightrope walk and the demands of emotion work. Neither will come as any surprise to seasoned prison ethnographers but I discuss them here in the interests of transparency, and in the hope of stimulating further frank discussion about the difficulties prison researchers can encounter.

The tightrope walk

Morris (1967:147) famously likened the experience of prisons research as akin to 'taking a moonlight walk through a minefield', in which a single misguided step could result in disaster. Not dissimilarly, I think of prisons fieldwork as a tightrope walk, in which one's progress through the two worlds of jailer and jailed is always perilous and uncertain, and successful completion is contingent upon a mercurial cocktail of skill, luck, diplomacy, and sheer nerve.

This tightrope walk largely results from a perennial criminological debate, seemingly beyond a definitive answer: on whose 'side' is the researcher? Becker (1967), who originally identified the issue, argued that since sociological researchers have personal and political values which pre-exist and remain independent of their research, and since they can 'fall into deep sympathy' with their participants (ibid.:240), it is inevitable that researchers take 'sides'. What makes those who conduct research with the marginalized and the 'deviant' particularly prone to the charge of partiality and contaminated sympathies, however, is the 'hierarchy of credibility' (ibid.:241) which differentially accords the right to be heard to the powerful. It is this that exposes penologists who prioritize prisoners' accounts to accusations that they have lost their objectivity and become, in modern parlance, 'con lovers', ripe for manipulation, and liable to produce biased and distorted findings.

The wisest stance for the researcher to take is therefore probably that of the academic solely and unreservedly committed to the research problem (King and Elliott 1977). Indeed, this became my favoured response which I recited with increasing weariness whenever required to answer the explicit accusation or implicit insinuation that if I was interested in residents' perspectives, I either could not also be interested in staff's perspectives, or could not accept both as equally valid. It was ironic that the 'them and us' of prisoners and staff played out so overtly in seeking participants for this research study at the same time as the communities sought to dismantle this dichotomy in their attachment relationships (see Chapter 4). The researcher simply wants to gather the best – most accurate, most detailed, most thought-provoking – data she can, from whomever she can. Given the purpose of this research, the information I required was mostly to be gained from residents – so in that limited sense, I was more 'on the side' of residents than staff because they were the more 'useful' informants. This did not prevent me from also being 'on the side' of staff when interviewing or conversing with staff. I therefore arrived at the position – more through practice than considered principle – that it is entirely possible to be on both 'sides' *but not at the same time.* One has to attend consciously to the perceptions of the person one is with at that moment, and be able to bear the emotional dissonance and moral disquiet that can result. Little wonder then that many researchers focus upon *either* prisoners *or* staff, and in choosing to interview both, I unwittingly compounded others' concerns about my allegiances.

Moreover, the negotiation of this tightrope is not single-handedly determined by the researcher, but can be influenced by the expectations and demands of one's participants (Emerson and Pollner 2001). The resulting disturbance makes it extraordinarily easy to falter and to take a step in which one's balance is momentarily lost, as I discovered to my cost a few times. I agreed with a resident, for example, whose complaint had been dismissed on legally incorrect grounds by a senior officer, who then made very clear his irritation at my 'unwelcome' intervention. Conversely, I sided with an officer whose accurate account of an incident I had witnessed was disbelieved by an irate resident, who then refused to acknowledge me for the remainder of my fieldwork. It also appeared that certain residents and officers sometimes deliberately tried to trip me up, in order to force me to reveal on whose 'side' I *really* was. Thus there were Grendonites who sought my support for their (evidently long-running) debates with officers about, amongst other things, property, wages, conjugal visits, and whether the occupation of prison officer should require higher educational standards and, for a TC, more extensive formal training in psychotherapy. Officers, meanwhile, dismayed me by twice luring me into discussions about sentencing tariffs for 'kiddie rape' – in front of men who had raped children – and sought my views on whether they should have the right to strike[11] (fieldnotes). To such conversational grenades, I usually offered generalized non-opinions – 'on the one hand … but on the other, it is argued … ' – in the hope that by disappointing both sides, I would alienate neither. Such attempts at impartiality, however, were often perversely reinterpreted as evidence that I favoured the opposing faction; presumably based on the Christian exhortation that she who is not with me is against me. Neutrality, then, 'is itself a role enactment … [whose meaning] to people will, most assuredly, not be neutral' (van Maanen 1991:39), and hence rarely represents a satisfactory solution to the difficulties created by perceptions of bias.

Emotion work

From her case study of the occupational socialization of flight attendants, Hochschild (1983) developed the concepts of (paid) 'emotional labor' and (unpaid) 'emotion work'; both of which entail 'the management of feeling to create a publicly observable facial and bodily display' (Hochschild 2003:7). This requires the actor consciously to induce or suppress his or her emotions in order to meet socially constructed and contextually situated feeling and display rules, which dictate how one is entitled or obliged to feel and the extent to which it is permissible to exhibit those feelings. When in opposition to how one actually feels, a process of emotional estrangement or 'emotive dissonance' results, and can ultimately corrupt one's ability to distinguish between 'feeling and feigning' (ibid.:90), genuine and manufactured responses.

Hochschild's work, then, originally emphasized how emotions can be commercially manipulated and controlled through recourse to culturally approved feeling rules. The partially accomplished emotional turn within qualitative social research, however, with its repudiation of the possibility of 'hygienic research' (Stanley and Wise 1983), has resulted in Hochschild's seminal insights being widely appropriated by social scientists to help theorize and reconcile the emotional management of fieldwork (see, for example, Young and Lee 1996) and the 'productive turmoil' (Kane 1998:140) that results from the uncomfortable collision between, and blurring of, the personal and the professional. The elaborate emotional dynamics of criminological research in general and prison semi-ethnography in particular can, as implied here, exact a heavy personal toll, but are still routinely under-reported for fear of appearing, to one's 'objective' peers, intellectually disempowered (Jewkes 2006). Yet, the writings of those (invariably, female) scholars who have felt able to acknowledge their difficulties (in particular, Gelsthorpe 1990; Bosworth 1999; Liebling 1999, 2001; Reuss 2000; Piacentini 2004; Jewkes 2012), represent neither self-pity for one's troubles nor self-congratulatory praise for one's endurance. Rather, they attest to the fact that such research *is* challenging and imprisonment *is* painful; even 'the possibility that criminology rests on human suffering … [and is therefore] a profoundly affective enterprise' (Bosworth 2001:438). In such highly charged circumstances, then, emotion work is not an optional extra: it occurs spontaneously and unavoidably and the only choice is whether one admits to, and so potentially benefits from, its epistemological significance.

I did choose, then, actively to attend to the emotion work I intuitively undertook in order to survive the empathy I felt for many of 'my' resident participants and the pervasive sadness and interminable regret some expressed at the pain they had caused, and that had been caused to them. Whilst publicly I displayed the (qualitatively and quantitatively) appropriate feeling rules and emotional connection with, and concern for, my informants, privately, there were certain individuals at all three establishments whose testimonies and problems consumed my thoughts and overwhelmed my emotions. These participants' 'data' were distressing, and in allowing them to permeate and settle within me, I could not be but distressed. As the cumulative impact of my Grendon fieldwork, in particular, increased, I began to wrestle with a growing desire to 'escape' from my 'imprisonment' within empirical research, which was not the 'exciting and enjoyable' experience the unwritten rule of fieldwork promises it will be (Kleinman 1991:193). Furthermore, the absolute necessity of immersing myself in, and acquiring meticulous knowledge of, my fieldwork notes and interview transcripts for data analysis and 'writing up' ensured that, long after I had physically left the field, the emotion work some interactions elicited stubbornly endured and with it, as Hollway and Jefferson (2000:69) describe, the disconcerting sense of being 'inhabited … in the sense that our imagination was full of him or her'.

Lest this sound like 'over-rapport' (Miller 1952), I should add that I found emotion work to be at least as taxing with those residents whose crimes were so abhorrent that I battled to banish from my mind what they had done and to concentrate instead upon who they were: sentient, often amiable and insightful, human beings. I have always believed in distinguishing between the offender and the offence; more from an elemental conviction that people cannot and should not be defined by their worst actions or characteristics, than any unconscious defensive need to 'split off' and deny to oneself the disturbing reality and appalling meaning of certain crimes (cf. Morris 2001). Tellingly, though, I found this differentiation most difficult with one of my female participants whose sexual victimization of women baffled and offended me, as a woman. I felt unjustifiably disappointed in her, as if she had betrayed 'the sisterhood'; even whilst recognizing that in so doing I was subscribing to the very 'doubly deviant' 'malestream' discourse of female offending rightly denounced by feminist criminologists (Smart 1976; Heidensohn 1985). Whilst it is clearly unrealistic to expect that one will feel equally positive about all one's research participants, I felt I had 'failed' whenever my ability to empathize deserted me and I experienced this 'failure' most acutely when it concerned another woman.

Understanding of, and emotional involvement with, prisoner participants circuitously returns the researcher to the perils of the tightrope walk, partly because of the zero-sum game played by those who confuse such appreciative criminological research with unquestioning acceptance of participants' views, or even romanticized glorification and reinforcement of criminality (Yablonsky 1965). Personally, although there were many participants to whom I could relate and some whose company I genuinely enjoyed, I never felt remotely at risk of psychologically 'going native'. In the process of an interview or research relationship one may learn something of, for example, why a man abducted and raped a woman or why he murdered his robbery target; one may comprehend it; but I was never tempted to over-identify with and excuse the perpetrator's actions as a result. As Matza (1969), in his promotion of 'appreciative studies', argued, (fortunately) one does not have to concur with respondents' social perspectives and definitions of the situation in order to be able to understand and represent them faithfully and with integrity.

Furthermore, however, because researchers have traditionally been taught 'to be objective and "extract out" emotion' (Hubbard *et al.* 2001:135) and erase 'contaminating' personal experience and feelings from the written discourse (Kleinman and Copp 1993:2), acknowledging one's emotions about, and emotional investment in, fieldwork and research participants, risks inviting criticisms of bias – of being on one 'side' over another – and hence of the validity of the research findings. For if one accepts (and of course, not all researchers do) that 'our emotions influence our research, and our research can affect us emotionally' (Campbell 2001:15), then it might appear to be, if not impossible, certainly difficult, to separate out objective reason from subjective emotion in the analysis of one's data, and thus to undermine more fundamentally the claims of qualitative social science to be recognizably 'scientific' and impartial (Kirk and Miller 1986).

Yet, I think such concerns are to disregard the analytic value of emotions and to underestimate the ability of trained, professional researchers to apply their professional research training. Provided one retains a moral and intellectual detachment from one's participants (itself aided by the geographical distance that leaving the field bestows), one can create the analytical space within which the dispassionate work of data interpretation and analysis can proceed, *notwithstanding* the emotions still associated with the production of that data. In so doing, the researcher will benefit from careful and self-critical reflection about her work, her approach to it and analysis of it, and the emotion work it demanded of her; and from triangulating her data and subjecting her observations and informants' accounts to tests of reliability (Becker 1958; Dean and Whyte 1969). I reject, however, any suggestion that emotions defile or distort data. Emotions, and 'emotionally-sensed knowledge' (Hubbard *et al.* 2001:120), provide a valuable source of data, and inform and deepen our understanding of data, but they are not so all-conquering as to render invisible or unimportant the other sources of information that the researcher accumulates, considers, and evaluates, or the other 'rational' intellectual resources on which she also draws, in creating the final research 'output'.

Ethical dilemmas

Finally, a note on research ethics. The ethical difficulties I encountered all related to the issue of limited confidentiality, and the researcher's resulting position of '*relative* independence' (Bottoms and McClintock 1973:6, emphasis preserved). NOMS imposes on researchers a duty to divulge any behaviour that is contrary to the Prison Rules and can be adjudicated against, harmful to the research participants or others, or illegal (Ministry of Justice

2010c:8); a requirement that King and Liebling (2008:446, emphasis added) – perhaps emboldened by the strength and security of their professional reputations – describe as '*impossible* to fulfil if the research touches on drug use, trade, or many other subjects'. At the very least, given that offenders, by definition, are not averse to breaking laws, rules, and regulations, it is inevitable that a trusted prisons researcher will acquire information about all manner of misconduct and will have to decide whether it is sufficiently serious and credible to require disclosure to the prison authorities. A prescriptive, institutional requirement of limited confidentiality can therefore create substantial role conflict; result in a myriad of ethical, methodological, and even legal complications; and requires researchers to 'abdicate their responsibility to make case-by-case ethical decisions *as researchers*' (Palys and Lowman 2001:264, emphasis preserved).

Certainly – and notwithstanding my successive written (on the consent form) and verbal warnings that I could only offer limited confidentiality – I sometimes found myself being given information by both residents and staff that, frankly, I did not need to know and would have preferred not to have known. Often such disclosures arose spontaneously in the course of our discussion and seemed to be offered as genuine illustrations of the realities of prison life. This sort of information I could in good conscience ignore – hearsay of dubious provenance, 'old news', or something current but about which the staff and community were already aware. I suspected that one instance of potentially 'guilty knowledge' (Polsky 1971:138) was primarily another attempt to determine whether I really was an untrustworthy spy for 'the other side' and hence the veracity (and implications) of this information was harder to assess. This alleged 'issue' also greatly offended me personally, and thus complicated my reactions to it, though I recognized that, in 'therapy speak',[12] this perhaps indicated more about *my* 'issues' than anyone else's. After consultation with more experienced colleagues, I eventually concluded that no action on my part was necessary. Such a dilemma illustrates, however, the inescapable and imperfect nature of postmodernist social research ethics, in which absolute ethical certainties have been replaced with a 'never ending, never resolved moral anxiety' (Bauman 1993:80).

Many qualitative researchers would accordingly concede that the ethical predicaments in which they find themselves are solved quietly and situationally (Punch 1986), in accordance with the demands of their own conscience and their moral duty of fidelity to their informants. Certainly, prison researchers do seem to be remarkably adept at maintaining confidences, if only through good fortune (Genders and Player 1995); or because they decided – as I did – that, for various reasons, disclosure was unnecessary (Liebling 1992); or by 'halting the flow of the conversation' to provide the interviewee with 'the opportunity to reflect' upon the consequences of specific admissions (Cowburn 2005:59); or even because the establishment concerned appeared tacitly to accept the need for researcher discretion (Crewe 2006a). Although I avoided breaking confidentiality throughout my fieldwork, *imposed* limited confidentiality can create ethical difficulties and is disquieting, not least for its potentially ill-fitting intersection with the researcher's responsibility to 'first do no harm' to her research participants.

Social research in general, and ethnography in particular, is therefore 'a messy business' (Pearson 1993:vii) from which one rarely emerges entirely unscathed or 'innocent'; I unquestionably did not. The prison ethnographer must be prepared to contend with the inherent ambiguity of the research role, in which as neither a member of prison staff nor of the prisoner community, one resides in no (wo)man's land. For prison officers, the rules on how to react, what to disclose, and where to draw the boundaries are often as black and white as the uniform. For the researcher, such rules are closer to guidelines which are only sometimes pertinent.

Moreover, 'getting on' in prisons fieldwork is an iterative process: trust and rapport must be first gained, then actively retained. Prosaic hindrances, such as the restrictions of the operational day, or sudden changes to routines due to staff shortages and security-led 'lockdowns'; more nebulous tensions resulting from misunderstood methods and the gendered dynamics of role perception; and the unfortunate own goals of an unguarded comment or erroneous assumption, virtually guarantee 'a personally challenging and sometimes fraught experience' (Sparks *et al.* 1996:337). Yet, the feeling rules of academia demand that emotion work is laboured upon in private, and resistance remains to utilizing something as subjective as emotions in objective social scientific writing (Kane 1998; Coffey 1999).

In short, then, conducting research in prisons is at once an academically important and personally satisfying, occasionally exhilarating, exotic privilege; and anxiety-filled, emotionally onerous, exhaustingly stressful work. It requires one to master the science of being on all 'sides' and on none, and the art of becoming comfortable with discomfort. The compensation for that discomfort, however, is the wealth of authentic, embedded, and nuanced data which one can amass, from which this book profits, and to which I now turn.

3 New beginnings

Commencing change the TC way

> It wasn't a difficult decision to come here because I wanted that change. I wanted to be a different person.
>
> (Danny, Grendon)

Sampson and Laub (1993) and Giordano and her colleagues (2002) respectively highlighted the importance of a perceived 'turning point' or 'hook for change' for desistance: an opportunity of some kind which opens up the possibility of meaningful change. Whether in fact this turning point was readily identifiable as such to the would-be desister at the time, or was retrospectively afforded significant status because of the emotionally charged symbolism subsequently projected on to it, mattered less than its representational value as something – a specific event or person, an either/or situation, or 'the final straw' – that made, and more importantly, continued to make over time, change achievable and durable (Ebaugh 1988; Carlsson 2012). Ebaugh's (1988) wide-ranging sociological study of 'role exit' echoes much of the desistance literature in finding that this catalyst for change might come about incrementally and gradually, after a long period of unhappiness and frustration with oneself, or more suddenly and dramatically in response to a major life event, but in all instances, the would-be 'ex' realized that the present situation was no longer sustainable and 'something' had to be done to bring about an alteration in one's circumstances.

This chapter explores the temporary 'role exit' mainstream prisoners can make by applying to participate in the TC way of imprisonment and rehabilitation, and the ability this unlocks in some to work towards a permanent role exit from 'offender' to 'better person'. It considers the reasons why interviewees wanted to transfer to a TC, and reflects upon the penological context within which they made this potentially momentous decision. Residents' exceptionally positive first impressions of their new environment are recounted, and the considerable symbolic potency they attached to prison-based TCs' promotion of the routine and reciprocal use of first names is discussed. The chapter also highlights, however, the adaptive difficulties which many new arrivals face, and not all can overcome, in their attempts to acclimatize to and negotiate the 'culture shock' of the prison-based TC.

Engaging in therapy: a typology of motivation

It is a striking characteristic of prison-based TCs that all residents must apply in writing for admission and be assessed by staff as suitable for the rigours of therapy and the TC way.[1] In contrast to the usual practice in England and Wales, entrants cannot be administratively allocated to a TC prison according to their security classification or to the TC programme according to their risk of reconviction; nor, unlike some European countries,[2] can prisoners be mandated or in other ways coerced by the courts to participate in this form of treatment.

Applying for entry of itself suggests some motivation or 'moving force' to enter into, and continue with, a specific, goal-directed behaviour or process. Assessments for motivation are therefore integral to correctional staff's determination of prisoners' suitability for particular OBPs (López-Viets *et al.* 2002; Drieschner *et al.* 2004); yet rarely has the literature recorded why offenders agreed to participate in a specific rehabilitative intervention, with most scholars more interested in the effect or importance of motivation on completion and treatment outcomes (inter alia, Terry and Mitchell 2001; McMurran and McCulloch 2007; Gideon 2010; cf. Hudson 2005). The participants in this study, however, were asked directly what had prompted their decision to apply to what is, after all, a still rarely chosen alternative method of rehabilitation. Interviewees recalled very clearly the key reason or reasons for their application. Indeed, for many, the events leading up to or their thinking behind this particular (hoped for) turning point remained particularly vivid and for some, these memories continued to be drawn upon at will to bolster their motivation to *persist* with TC treatment. In the inductive typology of motivation to participate that follows, then, the four distinct categories (two with subcategories) that emerged, and the conceptual labels I subsequently applied, reflect the primary, most powerful motivation interviewees described or implied, although in some instances, a degree of overlap between categories was discernible.

Type one: enthusiasts

> I wanted to come here because I knew it was the best place to help me address my issues.
>
> (Richard, Grendon)

Exactly half the combined sample sought TC treatment in order to understand themselves better, their index offence(s), and criminal career, and to make the necessary internal changes to improve their potential for long-term desistance from crime. These self-aware and agentic *enthusiasts* had realized that they needed to change aspects of their character, behaviour, and approach to life. They had long been unhappy with themselves and the way their life had turned out and consciously wanted to explore the reasons behind their offending. Yet, their decision to apply had often evolved only gradually, as they garnered morsels of information about TCs, chiefly through the verbal 'prison grapevine', though, more occasionally, through reading publications aimed at prisoners, such as *The Prisons Handbook* or prison newspapers. Notwithstanding any deficiencies in the detail or accuracy of this information, enthusiasts had decided that TC treatment 'sounded all good, like it would be able to help me' (Bob, Grendon). They had then proactively instigated and persistently pursued their application – with or without the approval and assistance of correctional staff – thereby making it their personal priority to address the aching discrepancy between how, and who, they were and wanted to become. Crucially, however, they were also aware that the changes they wanted to institute would be unachievable without professional help, and considered that such help would not be as forthcoming or as palatable from 'standard' (cognitive-behavioural) offending behaviour programmes (OBPs):

> I knew that my life needed some direction because it was just useless. My crime, it really weren't good. It didn't make no sense to me why I done it and I knew that I needed help with what I was feeling. I felt if I didn't get [help], then I'd get out and hurt someone again.
>
> (Don, Grendon)

> I was struggling with my prison sentence and with actually understanding myself. Some things weren't clear for me, what I done, and with knowing who I am, and wanting to be someone better. And the TC seemed like the best opportunity to find out and to grow and become more self-confident.
>
> (Theresa, Send)

> I'd done some standard courses like ETS,[3] but basically, they just made me aware of what I was doing but I didn't get no empathy from them. They're false. I was telling them what they want to hear to get parole but as soon as I left the room, I was talking to my mates about doing drug deals and what I'm going to do when I get out … But with this, I liked the way you're living in the environment every day; that it's real … I realized how much of a twat I'd been. I've been released three times. I mean, I'm nearly 30, I'm getting old! I wanted to do something *proper*.
>
> (Stewart, Grendon)

Additionally, enthusiasts viewed TC treatment as a long-term investment in themselves: the short-term sacrifices and costs they appreciated they would incur were objectively weighed against the benefits they anticipated TC residency would eventually bestow. These costs included a potential reduction in the frequency of visits from loved ones, given the geographical distance of the TC from their home area (especially for women, for whom Send, in the south-east of England, is their only option); relinquishing (relatively) well-paid employment at their existing establishment, which for those without recourse to supplementary private cash represented a substantial financial loss with all the hardship that implies; and forgoing the possibility of early release or recategorization by committing to the optimum treatment dosage. Jenny's (Send) story vividly encapsulates the institutional obstacles and erroneous assumptions some enthusiasts had to overcome, and the personal sacrifices they were prepared to make, in order to achieve admittance:

> A lot of the staff were *very* negative about TCs … My probation officer said she wouldn't recommend me because 'you haven't got psychiatric issues'. I told her TCs aren't about that but she wouldn't listen … She got quite arsey with me, wouldn't support me, and wouldn't accept that she might be ignorant. I spoke to the lifer manager and she said I needed drug issues … But I kept pushing and pushing … I deferred my PED[4] to get here which is a *huge* thing for a lifer … It was such a battle, of strength and determination, to get here and I had to fight that alone … for something that I believed was right for me. And I hadn't let [the prison], the probation officer, and the lifer manager, stop me.

Enthusiasts had often needed to bear another treatment cost: the continuing and widely held misconception in the mainstream that Grendon, in particular, and TCs generally are disproportionately colonized by, and hence suitable only for, 'nonces and grasses,[5] nutters, the weak, the vulnerable' (Paul, Grendon). Whilst a few interviewees recalled attempting to 'educate' their peers prior to their transfer, most enthusiasts had simply dismissed the pejorative labels attached to TCs, by reasoned repudiation of this reputation, especially when propounded by former residents who had been required to leave, and assertive self-determination:

> People who have failed at a process are going to have negative views of it, and they are the people you tend to meet in the system, especially in B cats;[6] that's *why* they've gone back there. So they didn't put me off. You find that most of the people who are negative about Grendon either have never been here or got kicked out!
>
> (Michael, Grendon)

> Grendon gets loads of slagging off but, at the end of the day, I came here for myself and what anyone else says about it, don't bother me, 'cos in five years time, I'll have changed and got out but they'll still be making the same mistakes, going nowhere.
>
> (Patrick, Grendon)

Type two: followers

> [The ex-Grendonite] told me about the TC vibe, what happens in therapy … And he said, 'Forget what all the fucking idiots here say, if you want to look for something, that's the place to go.'
>
> (Chris, Grendon)

Almost one-fifth of interviewees, all male, were *followers*. This second category of applicant met many of the same criteria as enthusiasts: they enjoyed problem recognition and were expectant of positive treatment outcomes. Their decision to apply, however, was extrinsically motivated, originating from the recommendation of either a former resident – TC followers – or a criminal justice system (CJS) professional – CJS followers – to which they were receptive. In marked contrast to the disparagement of TCs as refuges for 'wrong 'uns' described above, *TC followers*, all Grendonites, were encouraged to apply by men who had not completed their therapy but who nevertheless stressed that their 'failure' should not deter others: '[The ex-resident] said it was too much for him at the time, but he'd still got tons out of it – was more tolerant, less violent … [and] he would recommend it for *real* rehabilitation' (Andrew, Grendon). Moreover, the opportunity to learn from the first-hand experiences of these Grendon evangelizers enabled TC followers to make a uniquely well-informed choice about what the regime involved and would demand from its residents. Consequently, they were far better prepared than other applicants for, as I discuss shortly, the 'culture shock' the TC delivers.

CJS followers accepted the recommendation, usually from an influential pre-sentence report writer such as a probation officer or forensic psychiatrist or psychologist, that TC treatment 'would be beneficial, to address my issues' (Ben, GTC). Notably, three of the seven GTC participants in this research fell into this category; men who were genuinely eager to act upon advice they respected and believed would help them to explore their offending and 'deal with emotional problems … grief and guilt' (Raymond, GTC), whilst still in the early stages of an indeterminate sentence. Although there are clearly instrumental incentives for savvy prisoners, desirous of efficient sentence progression, to engage with recommended risk-reducing interventions sooner rather than later, these men appeared to be motivated more by their need for palliative self-awareness than calculated self-advancement. Moreover, CJS followers had sometimes been astonished and, invariably, ashamed by their capacity to commit the crime(s) of which they had been convicted, and TC treatment appeared to offer them a singular opportunity 'to find some answers to my questions about myself' (Johnny, Grendon).

Type three: desperados

> It was either this, or a lifetime inside.
>
> (Winston, Grendon)

The most criminologically interesting of the typologies, and accounting for nearly a third of the sample, *desperados*, as their name suggests, were plainly distinguishable by their affective state and limited expectations, of themselves and the TC, at the time of application. These residents were most likely to voice disquiet about TCs' 'nonces and grasses' reputation, but reasoned that 'beggars can't be choosers' (Charles, Grendon), since they had either 'tried everything else', or else reached out to the TC from a position of personal crisis. The former subcategory, *last resort desperados,* appeared particularly troubled by their recidivism which – amongst all those in this category at Grendon – had resulted in them spending most of their adult life in prison. These applicants had, over time, come to the conclusion that if they did not prioritize doing 'something' to change, they would spend their 'lifetime' in prison, either on their present indeterminate sentence or through the life sentence by instalments that a succession of lengthy determinate sentences can represent. The increasing demoralization and bewilderment they experienced because of their seeming inability to 'go straight' and, for many, their dissatisfaction with themselves and their hedonistic, 'futile' lives, had therefore led them 'to at least *try* something different' in the 'last chance saloon' (Brian, Grendon) of the TC. The 'leap of faith' this required was often remarkable, and poignant, given that these desperados had – in their self-assessment – 'fucked up' all previous attempts at rehabilitation, were unaware or unconvinced of the potential merits of TC treatment, and had minimal confidence in themselves to change:

> I done loads of courses; psychology love me! Makes no difference, though. Last time, I went out fully intending to go straight – hand on heart, Alisa, I did, but – it's circumstances, ain't it? [laughs]
>
> *Is it? That sounds like it had nothing to do with you …*
>
> Yeah, minimization! But in a way, it weren't really. I mean, I got out, my mates come round with some puff,[7] I started selling drugs again, got a new motor, some guns, started running around again like a fucking idiot, and boom! Nicked!
>
> *So is this time likely to be any different, if you complete your therapy?*
>
> I don't know. I'd like to think so. Worth a try, ain't it?
>
> (Nick, Grendon)

> Half of me wanted to change but half of me was quite comfortable where I was. It gets a bit monotonous, going in and out of prison, but I didn't mind it, really … But I suppose deep down, I knew it wasn't right … [and] I thought if I come here, maybe I'd find the motivation to change my ways.
>
> *Why did you think you might find that motivation here, when you hadn't found it elsewhere?*
>
> Because it's so different here. I didn't know much about it – but I knew it was different! Put it this way, nothing had worked up to

> then, so perhaps I needed to try something completely different. And if it didn't work, I was nothing lost, was I? It was that kind of attitude.
>
> (Nate, Grendon)

> This is my longest sentence. I didn't have no expectations of it but on my other sentences, I haven't done nothing constructive and I thought, if I don't do something now, to address my issues, I don't think I ever would. I'd get out of jail, go back to drug use, back into crime, and back into jail. And I didn't want that. So I thought, fuck it! What's the worse that can happen, you know? [laughs]
>
> *Sure. But it sounds like you didn't really know what you were getting yourself into?*
>
> No, no, not at all! [laughing] I thought this would be a piss in the park, to be honest with you!
>
> (Adele, Send)

Other last resort desperados perceived themselves to have become 'stuck' at the level of a category B prisoner and/or second stage lifer; a distressing failure to advance through their sentence and the system which they hoped the TC's more pluralistic mode of treatment and assessment might remedy. This motivation particularly applied to lifers who were returning to the TC after an earlier, prematurely curtailed residency. They attributed their non-progression in part to psychologists' use of algorithmic risk assessment instruments, in which actuarial relationships between specified variables (static risk factors, drawn from large datasets of offenders' characteristics) and outcomes are used to quantify levels of risk and estimate the probability of reconviction. They opposed, in other words, the 'unjust' application of *aggregate* statistical data, with the homogenising tendencies and mathematical certainties this seductively seems to suggest, to *individuals*; and the 'unforgiving' reference back to one's unalterable past to forecast, with alleged reliability, one's future. All efforts at risk prediction produce, sometimes substantial, margins of error (Hood *et al.* 2002; Hart *et al.* 2007), the consequences of which for indeterminate sentenced prisoners may be unnecessarily prolonged incarceration in secure conditions. These desperados anticipated, however, that the TC's routine integration of actuarial assessments with clinical judgements (Shuker and Jones 2007) might eventually (if they completed their therapy) permit their more individualized, favourable assessment:

> There's more opportunity for the *real me* to be seen here – not the person in the file, but the one I am now. The problem in the system is being bunched up like a statistic, with a lot of other people, and your individuality goes.
>
> (Muktar, Grendon)

For the smaller subset of *tormented desperados,* the decision to apply was precipitated by a traumatic event or profound sense of personal crisis.

Desistance scholars will be unsurprised to learn that neither this catalyst nor the intense psychic and emotional anguish it produced was associated with the act or experience of imprisonment – it had not occasioned any dramatic Damascene conversion – but rather from a reflective resident's self-diagnosis of an alarming, internally attributed, 'problem' which could no longer be ignored. For Bill (Grendon), for example, this was his potentially fatal misreading of another prisoner's demeanour:

> I think the final straw was I thought there was someone who was looking at me as if I wasn't there, and I thought, you cheeky fucker, I'll plunge him up a few times and that will teach him to mug *me* off.[8] So one day I saw him go in to the kitchens by himself and I got me tool[9] and went to do him, and he turned round and asked me if I wanted a sandwich, real friendly like, and I realized then, it was me, it wasn't him. That was the point I thought to myself, I need to change; I can't live my life like this no more. I nearly stabbed someone up because of *my* paranoia. I felt like I was starting to lose my mind and needed to do something about myself before I got into some serious bother.
>
> *And that was on this sentence, for murder?*
>
> Yes. This was about five years in, at [a high security prison].
>
> *So didn't this sentence already count as 'serious bother'?*
>
> No, not really, because the way I was thinking then, [the victim] fucking deserved it and getting life, well, I know it sounds mad but I know how to do prison, you know what I mean? So even then, I didn't really think I had any problems. It was only because of this geezer that I thought, I *need* to get a grip.

In contrast to the intrinsic, self-propelling motivation of the enthusiasts, and notwithstanding the abrupt 'defining moment … when I thought, hold on, what's happening here?' (Neil, Grendon), tormented desperados, like followers, tended to require external encouragement before applying. Unlike followers, however, this support – or forceful ultimatum – was typically provided by family members, as Keith (Grendon) recalled with dry understatement:

> I was getting into too much trouble. I was not happy … [and] was heavily involved in drugs at my last nick – supply, distribution – and people were getting stabbed up; it was a bit chaotic. I [was] down the block[10] and my family was beginning to ask some serious questions about me.
>
> *So did you come here mainly for you, or for them?*
>
> For them; they badgered me into it. I thought it sounded a bit crap, but they wanted me to try it and I thought, it's the least I can do.

Desperados, then, sometimes understood little about the TC regime upon which they pinned what remained of their hope, and had none of the self-belief of enthusiasts or faith in 'expert' advice of followers. They had, however, reached a symbolically significant turning point, which encapsulated all of their frustrations with themselves and their imprisonment and demanded from them, even if reluctantly or regretfully acknowledged, some affirmative response.

Type four: escapees

> I thought that you all cuddle and things like that! That you sat around all day chatting and didn't have to do any work! Course, I soon found out it weren't like that at all! [laughs]
>
> (Caroline, Send)

Just two Send residents comprised the last category, self-confessed *escapees* from the system. Clearly, this number is too small to allow one to generalize, yet these residents demand their own category as their motivation was quite distinct. These women, who had both previously served a number of short custodial sentences, candidly admitted that they were motivated solely by a desire to enliven the spectacular banality of prison life and evade the 'hassle' of the mainstream. Although neither had been 'picked on' or had otherwise struggled to adapt to and survive in prison, they disliked or were 'bored by' the prison in which they were living at the time of their application and imagined that a therapeutic prison 'sounded like it would be nicer; an easier time' (Josephine, Send). The irony of the 'harder time' that awaited them within the 'emotionally exhausting' TC was therefore not lost upon them. Whilst men, then, might be thought to have greater reason to wish to flee the casual violence and hypermasculine aggression endemic to their penal environment, none of the male interviewees alluded to an attraction to the TC because of the potential escape route it offers; nor implied that they had been enticed to the TC solely in anticipation that it might offer a more relaxed and less physically threatening environment. Residents of both sexes, however, frequently attributed these motivations to peers whose commitment to therapy they found lacking. Perhaps, then, a larger (random) sample of TC residents would have uncovered more men and women for whom escaping from the mainstream for a seemingly 'cushier' prison experience was, at least initially, the primary reason for their application.

'Voluntary' participation and the TC alternative

The decision to apply to the TC was taken in the context of applicants' near universal dissatisfaction with, and often scathing derision of, cognitive-behavioural OBPs, *combined with* their stoical acceptance of the non-negotiable necessity of completing 'courses'. It is, of course, desirable that offenders undertake some kind of rehabilitative intervention to reduce their likelihood of re-offending. In post-modern neo-liberal societies, however, 'dangerous' people are no longer perceived as candidates for welfarist therapeutic treatment focused upon *their* psychological and social needs; but rather as 'actuarial subjects' and quantifiable sources of risk *to others*, requiring ever more sophisticated layers of assessment, containment, and precautionary management (Feeley and Simon 1992, 1994; Rose 1998; Hannah-Moffatt 2005; Hebenton and Seddon 2009). This institutionalization of 'risk thinking' as a new mode and technique of control has regrettably transformed forensic psychologists, in the eyes of most prisoners, from people vocationally drawn to 'a helping profession', to assessors of existing and potential harm in the cause of public protection, with almost absolute power to direct the terms and duration of serious offenders' sentences (Crewe 2009). It has also forced such offenders, however, to become more aware of their own 'risk profile' and the paramount importance of being able to evidence reduced risk of dangerousness and re-offending, if they are to persuade prison governors, and ultimately the Parole Board, of their suitability for recategorization and (early) release. Since OBPs are now the preferred mechanism by which offenders are expected to 'address their offending behaviour' and so demonstrate their rehabilitation, 'prudent', 'responsibilized' (O'Malley 1992; Garland 1996) offenders accordingly understand that they *must* do courses to secure sentence progression. They must, in other words, visibly submit to and reproduce the Foucauldian 'regime of truth' these programmes prescribe (Fox 1999; Lacombe 2008) in order to provide the required tangible, recordable evidence of their rehabilitation. Even enthusiasts and CJS followers accordingly acknowledged more strategic and self-serving – though entirely sensible – supplementary factors which had motivated their application to the TC:

> From a personal perspective, it was about wanting to know myself a lot better and understand my reasons for committing crime. And then, from a prisoner perspective, every lifer has to do one big course and it was here or the CSCP[11] … [which] seemed a very rigid course, very plotted, and I don't really get on too well with that kind of thing … [so] I preferred here.
>
> (Ross, GTC)

> Probation kept recommending it in my reports, it was on my sentence plan – I mean, if it's going to keep coming up, you kind of have to say yes at some point. Well, you can say no – but you stand *no* chance of getting parole. And if you're a lifer – forget it! You have *got* to show that you are addressing your offending behaviour.
>
> *So do you consider you made a totally voluntary decision to come here?*
>
> [long pause] Not really, no. I mean, I did *choose* to come here but I sort of volunteered with my arm twisted up my back.
>
> (Nigel, Grendon)

The discourse of 'voluntary participation' in OBPs therefore obscures the direct or implicit pressure or coercion, the stick rather than the carrot, pervasive throughout the contemporary risk-focused criminal justice system. Claims that prisoners in general and that TC residents specifically make an 'entirely voluntary' choice, implying 'considerable continuing motivation … [and] consent informed by experience' (Morris 2005:361, 364), need to be qualified by the recognition that the 'choice' to participate in an OBP is informed by prisoners' knowledge of the likely adverse consequences of refusal, which, for some, can feel awfully much like arm twisting. Voluntariness, in the inherently coercive penal environment, is a relative concept. Applying to a TC, however, afforded prisoners the opportunity to make, if not a wholly voluntary and autonomous decision, at least a positive choice from their limited options.

That choice, then, was to reject what they perceived as the tightly focused, time-limited, manual-compliant, 'tick box' approach of cognitive-behavioural programmes, in preference for a more holistic, ambitious alternative. Interviewees' criticisms of 'standard' OBPs ranged from humorous incredulity at the scale of financial and ideological investment in programmes which, they argued, were erroneously founded upon 'simplistic' assumptions about offenders' alleged thinking errors and anti-social attitudes; to bald repudiations of the worth of programmes in which, by apparently offering the obviously correct, socially acceptable responses to questions and scenarios, one was deemed to have 'addressed' problematic behaviours; to concerned complaints that OBPs offered no meaningful insight into crime and criminality; or were simply irrelevant to, and unrealistic about, prisoners' quotidian battle to endure their criminogenic environment:

> I do not know how [NOMS] can believe that them things do any good, that it's worth the money they put into it. They must be trippin'! [laughs] … They think like, we don't know right from wrong, or don't think, can't think, right! It's a waste.
>
> (Francis, GTC)

> Those courses have absolutely no credibility with inmates. People just do them because they have to … and all you have to do is sit there and tell [staff] what they want to hear.
>
> (Steve, GTC)

> You can do them courses a hundred times over but you'll not get to the root of your problems … Anger management, to be truthful, left me more angrier. I thought a lot of it was like, talking down to you; it just wound me up! [laughs] They don't sit and *explain* things to you in-depth, *why* you get angry, like the therapist does … Psychologists think them courses are great and I really wonder why!
>
> (Louise, Send)

> ETS – totally unrealistic. Nice idea and everything but as soon as you walk out the classroom, you're back into a very hostile environment. Like you're supposed to use 'I' statements: 'This is how I feel when you do this.' You try saying that to someone in the system and they'll tell you to fuck off! Probably stick one on you![12]
>
> (Clive, Grendon)

Tellingly, it was those offenders who evidently *were* labouring under cognitive distortions – about men's sexual entitlement, children as sexual beings, victim precipitation and culpability, and the minimal harm caused by sexual abuse (inter alia, Burt 1980; Ward and Keenan 1999; Blumenthal *et al.* 1999) – who most frequently offered some qualified praise for the 'right thinking' focus of OBPs. For these men, the range of sex offender treatment programmes (SOTPs) were thought to be 'useful first steps' (Eddie, Grendon) in restructuring their erroneous schemas; appreciating the sequence of decisions and emotions that had effectively enabled their (repeat) offending; and in equipping them with the skill development, coping behaviours, and effective strategies to avoid and prevent 'relapses' (inter alia, Pithers 1990; Eccles and Marshall 1999; Laws *et al.* 2000). These programmes were still criticized, however, as ultimately 'surface' interventions, whose 'here-and-now' focus excluded consequential consideration of one's past (and hence, often a history of victimization), 'brought up lots more questions than answers' (Tim, Grendon), and so, unlike 'the real deal' of multi-factorial TC treatment and 'the *real* work' done at TCs (Colin, Grendon), failed to excavate the 'deeper' causes and cues of their offending:

> ESOTP[13] was as much as I could do in the system. I needed to talk about my childhood, delve into hidden feelings and motivations ... [But the facilitators] only wanted to talk about specific things that's in their book,[14] and if you tried to go beyond that, they couldn't help you.
>
> (Leslie, Grendon)

> ESOTP was good because I went right into my distorted attitudes towards women, how I interact, why I see them the way I do ... [But] I still needed to go into more depth, to really understand where it started, why, and how I came to this.
>
> (Eddie, Grendon)

The residents interviewed for this study, then, had not been, as is often assumed of TC applicants, uniformly highly motivated, self-selecting individuals who make the TC's distinctive regime 'work' for them because they always believed it does 'work'. Whilst some were very enthusiastic about or demonstrated well-informed confidence in the TC, others were unconvinced of its likely merits, knew little about what TC residency entailed, and displayed questionable treatment readiness. Enthusiasts, followers, and desperados were united, however, by their decision to marry their desire for change to the atypical TC method. As architects of their own rehabilitation and personal development, and prompted by their generally poor opinion of 'standard' interventions, they rejected NOMS's reliance upon cognitive-behavioural OBPs as, to borrow from Mathiesen (2006:142–43), the 'action function' by which the government appears to be 'doing something' to reform offenders. Instead, aspiring TC residents agentically determined to seek out an alternative penal environment and rehabilitative method which they hoped, though in some cases could scarcely believe, might help them to change, would be superior to their mainstream options, and would allow them to contribute more proactively to the reiterative appraisal of their 'risk'. It is the reality of the TC way that awaits new arrivals to which I now turn.

First impressions

In Goffman's (1961) famous study of asylums, he explored how admission into any total institution involves 'a leaving off and a taking on', in which one's past identity and role is compulsorily discarded through a series of humiliating entry rituals and subjection to 'civil death'. In prisons, this relinquishment of one's 'free world', autonomous self is strategically and systematically engineered through the 'status degradation ceremony' (Garfinkel 1956) of reception, in which new arrivals are transformed into (or for transferees, reconfirmed as) prisoners. This mortification of the self begins with the quite literal shedding of one's former status through the removal of one's clothes, in the mandatory strip search, and their possible replacement with uniform garb; the forfeiture of prohibited personal possessions; and the assignment or checking of the individual's identifying prison number. In such ways, the prison communicates to the prisoner the absolute necessity of submitting to the institution's will and the inferior, circumscribed social roles it envisages for its captives. The manner in which these, arguably indispensable, identity reconfiguring tasks are accomplished, however, signals the particular establishment's approach to its custodial function in general, and the occupational culture within which its officers perform their duties specifically (Coyle 2002a).

It is thus significant that reception into Grendon was, almost without exception, generously praised by interviewees as a welcoming, relaxed, and reassuring experience, which favourably contrasted with the dehumanizing processing of the system they had previously known:

> As soon as I got off the bus[15] it was first name basis, shaking my hand – that put me so much at ease right off and it shocked me as well; I've never had that from staff before … [Elsewhere, it's] 'You, stand there, do this, do that, get your gear off', really snappy, unpleasant …
>
> (Clive, Grendon)

> The moment I came through to reception, and saw the way the staff were with me, I knew I was in a different environment. The relief was straightaway for me.
>
> (Wesley, Grendon)

Over a typically two- to three-month induction period, new arrivals are introduced to the process of therapy and the rules and wider regime of prison-based therapeutic communities. They are encouraged to start talking about their thoughts and feelings about what they have experienced that day, and are schooled in the TC way, both formally, through the mandatory induction presentation and distribution of the written constitution to which residents must adhere and, more importantly, through informal 'anticipatory socialization' (Merton 1957). Through their observations and interactions with other residents, newcomers begin to conceive of the norms of behaviour, attitudes, and obligations expected of an established community member, and can consider whether this is a role they truly wish to assume. This process of appraisal is mutual: the multidisciplinary clinical and disciplinary staff measure (through a raft of psychological tests), observe, and evaluate the resident's motivation, treatment readiness, and ability to engage with the TC dynamic. Swift withdrawals – being 'returned to unit' (RTUd) and transferred back to the prisoner's sending establishment – are commonplace at this time, due to staff's determinations of 'unsuitability for therapy', or the resident's inability to adjust to, or dislike of or disappointment in, the new normative environment.

Only a minority of participants, then, described their negotiation of this initial assessment stage as 'very good … I liked the idea of living as a community and took to it straight off, really' (Shelley, Send), or 'fairly easy, no big problems' (Joe, Grendon). For these fortunate few, the peculiarities of the TC way provoked only amused astonishment:

> My first community meeting, I was like, what the fuck's going on here? Cons slagging off officers, officers apologizing; two cons had had a ruck[16] and were having to explain it … I couldn't believe that they were sticking it on each other and it weren't going off in the recess later![17] But then, they were walking around the yard, talking! It was proper mad!
>
> (Sandeep, Grendon)

> It was *so* weird! Especially community meetings, I couldn't get my head round them at all. I thought, I'm in a nuthouse here, everybody talking about their feelings all the time! What the hell have I done? [laughs]
>
> (Raymond, GTC)

For most participants, though, 'learning the ropes … deciding whether it's right for you' (Lee, GTC) was experienced as a testing 'sink or swim period'

(Muktar, Grendon). In particular, the expectation that 'cons' should almost immediately interact with other prisoners with whom they were barely acquainted, and with officers, was considered 'bizarre' and 'unrealistic'; whilst the discovery that one could argue with other prisoners without fear of physical reprisals, or 'challenge [staff] and they can't give you an IEP[18] for it!' (Josephine, Send), was 'unsettling' and 'strange'. Such adaptational difficulties were most evident at Grendon which, given its dedicated purpose, is able to quarantine all new arrivals in an induction and assessment unit, F-wing, situated at the end of a long corridor away from the other communities. At one F-wing community meeting I observed, for example, it was revealed that one-fifth of its residents had recently tested positive for illegal drugs. The subsequent discussion exemplified the sometimes arduous transition new arrivals must make from the system's contempt for 'grassing', towards the TC conception of 'therapeutic feedback'. The majority of the non-using residents repeatedly called upon the users to name the supplier, with an animated outrage which suggested they had already internalized some of the TC's values and informal social controls. These men spoke of how 'let down' they felt by the 'disrespect' shown to the community, some of whose members had long struggled to become drug-free and now felt 'unsafe' due to the ache of temptation. By contrast, none of the (soon to be RTU'd) users would 'name names'; one explaining that having only been at Grendon a few weeks, he 'wasn't into all that – it's too much to ask, too soon' (fieldnotes). These men, then, implicitly rejected the TC by explicitly rejecting its prohibition against drug misuse; a reluctance to commit to the regime which could be interpreted psychodynamically as indicative of a fear of attachment, failure, and indeed, the panic-inducing possibility of hope and change (Mackenzie 2007).

Typically, then, the simultaneous combination of acclimatization to something 'a million miles away from the system' (Andrew, Grendon) and assessment 'when you have to *prove* you're worthy' (Colin, Grendon) made for an anxiety-inducing induction:

> F-wing was fucking hard for me and I think it is for a lot of people, because in the system, you just get in your cell, shut yourself away, put your telly on, and crack on. But there, everyone was on you, you didn't have no time to yourself. The officers like you to be in the wing office, mingling, talking to them and the others; it was weird … A worrying time because I thought, I'm having such a shit time up here and if I get to a wing and it's all like this – fuck!
>
> (Patrick, Grendon)

> Straightaway they expect you to do certain things that you're not used to doing. Just simple things: the way you talk to other inmates, the way you get to know someone. In the system, you may not talk to your next door neighbour for a year. Here, you're expected to integrate straightaway, to

> come forward with information if there's any drugs or if anyone's been threatened ... I found that difficult to get my head round.
>
> (Wesley, Grendon)

> I *hated* F-wing. I just desperately wanted to get a wing. I felt like one of them performing dolphins or whatever, jumping through hoops.
>
> (Don, Grendon)

First names

Newcomers were immediately confronted with one cultural indicator that, unfailingly, pleasantly surprised them: the reciprocal use of first names. The TC expectation is that all residents will be addressed by their first name, and they in turn will address all members of staff, regardless of role or rank, by theirs. Whilst mode of address may seem a trivial matter, denotative perhaps of political correctness, this mutually agreed usage of first names enjoyed real symbolic power, both as a declaration of individuality and as an indicator of the respectful, 'decent', and less hierarchical staff–prisoner relationships they could expect to enjoy. Proper names, after all, are pivotal to one's integrated and unified sense of self, and guarantee 'the visible affirmation of the identity of its bearer across time and social space' (Bourdieu 2000:300). They are chosen with great care by parents who, if only instinctively, understand the ways in which a name can evoke a stereotyped image or familial referent; practised as one of the first words a child learns; and sometimes shortened or adapted as one grows up to reflect better the 'real me' of its bearer. Yet, only in the women's estate, the contracted-out estate, and at particular institutions like Gartree, whose distinguished history of and expertise in working exclusively with lifers encourages the formation of long-term relationships, is the use by officers of prisoners' first names commonplace. In men's public sector prisons, repeated attempts (for example, Pilling 1992; HM Inspectorate of Prisons 1999; HM Chief Inspector of Prisons 2007) to encourage officers to address prisoners by their first name or other preferred title (including the endorsement of the Prisons and Probation Ombudsman[19]) – rather than an unadorned surname – have met with implacable resistance, as these participants explained:

> It felt strange at first, being called by my first name – and calling [officers] by theirs. In the system, you could find yourself on a charge for that! I've done many a sentence and never had it before.
>
> *How would officers normally address you?*
>
> Surname. They *refuse* to call you Mr.
>
> *Why's that?*
>
> They'd say, 'Who the hell do you think you are?' They think if they say Mr, it means you're as good as they are – you know, a human being! When obviously, we're just cons! [laughs]
>
> (Wesley, Grendon)

> I'd forgotten I *had* a first name. It's sad really, what you get used to – your surname shouted down the Tannoy. But *you* have to call [officers] 'gov' or Mr so-and-so … But there's none of that here – it's all first names, even governors and psychologists.
>
> *Why do you think some officers won't call you Mr or by your first name?*
>
> Because system screws[20] think that would put them on a level with us, like it's demeaning to them. I think that's bollocks; they're still the ones with the keys. Them being polite ain't going to change that.
>
> (Winston, Grendon)

The antipathy of public sector staff towards prisoners' use of officers' first names, meanwhile, needs to be situated within the context of the instruction from the officers' trade union (the Prison Officers' Association) not to wear name badges, as proposed in 1993, on the grounds that identifying officers by name may make them vulnerable to assault or intimidation. Instead, officers are required to wear a prison-specific numbered epaulette; a regrettable and supremely ironic 'retrogressive step' (Coyle 2002b:80) which further embeds the reductionist and identity-stripping institutional preference for numbers over names.

From a psychoanalytic perspective, however, such unilateral formality may speak to the instinctively defensive tendency of (in particular) people working with those who have committed the most serious and repellent crimes to differentiate themselves from such 'deviants', and to deny that the capacity for 'deviancy' is ubiquitous, when in reality 'everyone functions to some degree psychopathically' (Morris 2004b:50). Given the working-class background, cultural affinities and, especially in local prisons, regional ties officers and prisoners frequently share (Crawley 2004), and the close working proximity and easy rapport they may establish, officers may find themselves wrestling with a powerful counter-transference[21] dynamic which demands reassurance that, despite their superficial similarities, they are not 'like that' and could never become so. To reduce symbolically the power and status differentials between officers and prisoners by using terms of address which place these two groups 'on a level' may therefore reactivate officers' apprehensions about commonality and undermine their confidence in the continuity and integrity of their personal identity. Language that depersonalizes prisoners, whilst reprehensible, can then be understood as an organizational defence against anxiety (Brown and Walker 2010), as this contributor explained:

> If you are working all day with people who have committed utterly horrendous crimes, it does get inside you, and one of the ways you manage that is to say, 'I'm not like that'. And the moment inmates start to have the same rights as you, then, you *might* be like that and you can't do it; you can't keep coming to work … So it's about survival.
>
> (Jane, therapist)

For TC staff who could 'survive' this threat to their identity, however, the agreed and reciprocated use of first names positively impacted upon the perceived identities of *both* officers and residents. Using officers' first names made it easier for residents to begin to reconstruct the occupational identity of their custodians, not as indistinguishable disciplinarians, but as individuals who were equally committed to rehabilitation within a partnership-oriented, trusting, enquiring culture:

> If you're working with someone, like colleagues – even though we are residents, prisoners, we are working *with* an officer – we'd be calling each other by first names, wouldn't we? … I found it odd at first but now I do think it's about being treated as an individual, and from our side as well.
>
> (Nate, Grendon)

Equally, the use by staff of residents' first names privileged the singularity of the individual over the stigmatized homogeneity of 'the offender', and so powerfully conveyed to residents that they too were unique 'human beings' and not 'just cons':

> Just being called by your first name, having staff accept that you can call them by theirs, that does feel special. In all my other prisons, I've just been a number; they didn't even want to know your name. And you become that number for a while, just a nothing; it's a strange feeling. It's like if you went out every day and had to give your national insurance number and not your name, it would start to depersonalize you, wouldn't it? … It's like you've lost your identity because of your offence; that's *all* you are. But using your first name gives you that bit of respect back. I think it's really important.
>
> (Danny, Grendon)

Moreover, this mutual recourse to first names fostered mutual respect or, more specifically, as distinguished by Butler and Drake (2007) after Liebling, assisted by Arnold (2004), respect-as-consideration. This requires the expressive performance of respect, 'finding the words and gestures which make it felt and convincing' (Sennett 2003:207). Mainstream officers who seemingly believe that affording a prisoner a title or first name would be akin to 'bowing down to us, when we don't deserve that because of what we've done' (Ravi, Grendon) are confusing respect-as-consideration with respect-as-esteem, which does need to be earned through one's status within the social hierarchy, personal conduct, or achievement. To show respect-as-consideration, however, is to recognize the inherent rights and needs of others and the intrinsic value of, and respect due to, any human being (Sennett 2003:53–45); an admission that self-evidently benefits prison staff as much as inmates.

Combined with the preferred language of 'residents' not prisoners, and of 'communities' not wings, the use of polite and courteous discourse therefore helped to communicate to TC neophytes that they were now in an environment quite unlike a 'normal' prison, in which essentialist differentiations and the social distance between staff and residents would be diminished, and in which they could expect to be treated as, and hence could hope to become, someone 'different' to their former offender/prisoner self. It was this acknowledgement of *everyone's* intrinsic dignity and individuality, fundamental and equivalent humanity, and entitlement to respect-as-consideration that accounted for the extraordinary symbolic potency of, and substantial 'meaning' ascribed by participants to, such an otherwise seemingly unremarkable civility.

Remaining in therapy: adaptation and ambivalence

> I can't *stand* Grendon! But I think it's working, so I'm staying.
>
> (Ravi, Grendon)

For the resident who had passed the preliminary tests of suitability and adjustment, and, at Grendon, transferred to one of the five main communities, 'full' membership status now beckoned, and with it, the need for full adaptation to the TC way. Although scholars differ as to how adaptation by newcomers to the prison is achieved, it is always a process that requires some conscious, and sometimes considerable, effort. The indigenous (deprivation or functional) model of adaptation, for example, argued that 'prisonization' – the assumption and assimilation of 'the folkways, mores, customs, and general culture of the penitentiary' (Clemmer 1958:299) – emerged as a collective, proactive, problem-solving response to and accommodation of the structural deficits, 'pains of imprisonment' (Sykes 1958), and psychological assaults upon one's self-esteem that incarceration entails. Subsequently, the importation model (Irwin and Cressey 1962; Irwin 1970; Carroll 1974; Jacobs 1977) positioned adaptation as differentially experienced according to one's pre- or extra-prison, extrinsically derived social variables, cultural capital, and criminal career. The reproduction of the subcultural norms prisoners brought with them to the prison resulted in the development of more fluid, pluralistic, and conflict-laden subcultures, as they continued to gravitate towards and found support and solace in the codes of behaviour that best perpetuated their 'outside' self, whilst rejecting those cultures that for them held no resonance. Most scholars of the prison would now argue that adaptation involves the integration of elements from both paradigms (for example, Thomas 1977; Wright 1991; Dhami *et al.* 2007). The point is, though, that penologists recognize that people have to find a way to adapt to imprisonment generally and to the culture of the prison in which they are held specifically; a culture that, in large part, is determined by the prison's security classification, leadership, and institutional memory.

For new arrivals to the TC, the challenge is therefore twofold: they not only have to adjust to the peculiarities of the TC and the demands of psychotherapy, but as a penal counter-culture, that adjustment requires them to discard all that they have learned previously about how to adapt to and cope with long-term high- and medium-security imprisonment. Accounts by participants of a seamless and entirely enjoyable transition were accordingly distinctly in the minority. For most, adaptation to 'full-on' therapy and TC life was experienced as a demanding, dynamic process of acculturation, or what, after Clemmer, one might term therapeutization. Outwardly, this required new residents to establish their sincere motivation to join (psychologically and socially) their small group through beginning the work of in-depth psychotherapy; and to pledge their engagement to their community through performing beneficial, if relatively menial, service to others: an aptly named 'commitment job', such as cleaning or working in the kitchen, or an often similarly low status rep job.

Inwardly, the commencement of 'therapy proper' required new members to begin to review their life story, disclose highly personal and sensitive 'secrets' from their past, 'unpick' problems, and 'access' and 'get in touch' with often long-repressed, 'split-off' or dissociated, emotions and anxieties, which for many was immensely challenging: 'My issues are deeper than I thought and there's more of them … I can talk about the things I've done, but not how I feel about them' (Roger, Grendon). Participants recalled, in particular, finding themselves repeatedly questioning the wisdom of 'opening up a can of worms' about their past, and of being 'just not really sure any more' whether they wished to expose themselves to the intense scrutiny of and the internal torment resulting from therapy and 'bringing your insides out … feeling that you're being mentally raped' (Chris, Grendon). Reports of insomnia, tension headaches, and psychosomatic stomach pains, and of feeling 'very low' and being 'exhausted' by this 'head work' were commonplace. Some interviewees also described how they had for a while relied upon stress-related and stress-relieving behaviours, such as smoking (nicotine or illegal drugs) or eating more (or occasionally, less) than usual, or spending long solitary hours playing computer games or watching television, to try to distract themselves from the assaults upon their psyche that commencing therapy inflicted.

For others, and evidently notwithstanding their successful induction, it was 'the general vibe' of TC imprisonment and the need to 'do *everything* differently' that could induce deeply disconcerting 'culture shock' (Ross, GTC). Whilst TC followers were the mentally most prepared for the challenges of the TC's counter-culture, even enthusiasts who had so wholeheartedly desired a 'different' rehabilitative and penal experience could find themselves 'sometimes uncomfortable' with the scale of the TC 'difference'. For although the largely unambiguous, socially unified, and interdependent 'prison community', as depicted by Clemmer (1958[1940]), Sykes (1956, 1958) and Sykes and Messinger (1960), no longer exists, adherence to the unwritten codes of mainstream prison culture still remains a key element of the 'system head' way of thinking and continues to exert considerable influence over everyday social relations within the prison. This normative 'inmate code' traditionally – even if only as 'an ideal rather than a description' of actual behaviour (Sykes 1995:362) – has approved, amongst other things, self-sufficiency, stoicism, and prisoner loyalty and solidarity which must at a minimum oppose the authority of, and fraternization with, staff ('them and us'); resisted institutionally instigated attempts at rehabilitation; and respected the hierarchy of offending: the penal caste system by which all offences are ranked and classified, by inmates and some staff, for acceptability and excusableness (Einat and Einat 2000; Winfree *et al.* 2002; Crewe 2005a, 2009). Particularly for those experienced 'cons' who had over many years become adept at 'doing prison', then, the unceasing demand now placed upon them to display emotional honesty; to monitor and, if necessary, offer critical public 'feedback' on their peers; to cooperate and socialize with officers within the shared resource of the wing office; to engage in 'change talk'; and to live peacefully alongside 'nonces', left them conversely longing for the simplicity and predictability of the system and the clarity of a historically defined, non-negotiable, 'comforting con way of looking at the world' (Ross, GTC). Even the less overt emphasis in TC prisons upon security and situational control, which one might expect to be welcomed, and the expectation of shared decision making and more egalitarian relationships, as required by a resident rather than prisoner role, could induce unease at first because of their unfamiliarity and create uncertainty as to how one should now behave: 'It's shit at times because I want to go back to what I know. It's easier, ain't it?' (Nick, Grendon).

For GTC and Send residents, therapeutization could be further complicated by the necessity to attend, for example, workshops, gym, education, or healthcare in the mainstream establishment; thereby having to retain, in effect, a foot in both penal camps. A few GTC residents avoided leaving the unit whenever possible, with one newcomer explaining that he 'needed to get a proper handle' on the TC before he would once again feel able to 'deal with the aggro of normal location' (fieldnotes). Counter-intuitively, however, most interviewees from these units said they valued their access to a range of mainstream activities. They felt they benefited by preserving some connection to the 'reality' of mainstream imprisonment to which they would return post-therapy; and from the relief gained by briefly absconding from the TC, particularly during times of interpersonal tension when such small communities could otherwise provoke feelings of claustrophobia. Provided residents were sufficiently immune to the stigmatized misconceptions surrounding TCs, and were able to manage 'the distractions of normal prisoners and the normal routine while doing therapy' (Sarah, Send), these episodes of readjustment to system culture could cumulatively reinforce their sense of differentiation and group identification in their treatment choice and social environment, and offer valuable opportunities for reality testing of their therapeutic progress. As one GTC member who had previously resided at the much larger, more self-contained Dovegate TC explained:

> I prefer it this way. It's good to have two hours in the afternoon when you can have a normal conversation, *not* about therapy or people's problems. And sometimes it's encouraging for me because I can look at the way some of the guys carry on over there, and think, yeah, I *used* to be like that …

For some people, however, therapeutization was unachievable. These residents would take themselves 'out of therapy' – no longer participating in small groups and sometimes, community meetings – whilst they awaited transfer to another prison. During a series of lengthy and painfully honest conversations with one such man, it became apparent that his specific prison history and self-perception as an 'old-style con' rendered aspects of the TC regime – especially, again, the expected 'friendly' relations with officers, the use of officers as therapy facilitators, and 'grassing' upon one's peers – 'totally repugnant'. Although he had sought 'something different', the regime he encountered was '*too* different, there's too much love going on here; it's not what I'm used to'. His attempts to adjust had so consumed his mental and emotional energies that he had been unable to 'open up' about his 'issues', the hoped-for resolution of which had initially brought him to the TC. He therefore felt that the 'lack of commitment' for which he had been criticized by staff was 'very unfair', and this could perhaps more accurately have been interpreted as a lack of therapeutization which may have been resolved with more time and greater patience. For this soon-to-be ex-Grendonite, TC culture had become an obstacle, rather than the intended gateway, to change. Rather than setting out on a path towards reinvention, his 'failed' residency had only communicated to him a sense of hopelessness about his problems – because 'if Grendon can't help me, where else am I going to get any help?' – and potentially, had therefore only confirmed him in the appropriateness of his prisoner/offender identity (fieldnotes).

Joining a TC is therefore a gamble – and, as with all gambles, both the rewards and losses can be high. For those who reject, or are rejected by, the TC, either during induction or later into their residency, the institutional and their individual perception of progress towards rehabilitation may be harmed, and their self-esteem dented. Drop-out rates, especially in the first year, are substantial: at Grendon, 39 per cent of all new arrivals between 1995 and 2010 left, either by choice or compunction, within 12 months;[22] and, similarly, 34 per cent of residents departed during the first year of Dovegate TC's operation (Miller *et al.* 2004). (Both these figures include those who did not progress from the respective assessment unit to a main therapy wing.) By comparison, Cann *et al.* (2003) reported that adult prisoners' non-completion of the cognitive-behavioural ETS and Reasoning and Rehabilitation OBPs was 9 and 12 per cent respectively. Such high levels of attrition underline the peculiarity and minority interest of the TC offering, but also the heavy responsibility placed upon assessment staff to select new recruits wisely. Particularly at Grendon, it was a common complaint from residents and prison officers that reduced demand for TCs from prisoners, combined with 'unhelpful' pressure to 'fill beds' (that is, to meet NOMS's key performance target for the number of prisoners held), meant that more fundamentally unsuitable or unmotivated applicants were accepted for assessment, only to be subsequently (and often, swiftly) RTU'd. Whatever the factual veracity of this widespread perception that it was now 'too easy' to come to a TC,[23] it was certainly not easy to stay.

'A love–hate relationship'

Beneath the surface of the many accounts of adaptive struggle ebbed an undercurrent of ambivalence and indecision about the merits of TC residency in general and forensic psychotherapy in particular. Residents – of all original motivational types – could find themselves conflicted by their mutually exclusive desire to dissect their lives and take responsibility for their offending, and to protect themselves from the anguish and discomfort that 'digging and delving' into one's past guaranteed. Inevitably, therapy as a task and a process only became more difficult and more distressing the deeper one mined the recesses of childhood memories and exposed the emotional chaos and emotion-driven thinking in adulthood which had prepared their path towards crime. In trying to 'make links' between the humiliations and hurts inflicted upon the offender and upon the offended against, residents often had to find an accommodation between the insight they gained into their dysfunctional upbringing and familial dynamics and an acceptance and, perhaps, continued love for that family; and between a past that could not be changed but had to be revisited, and habitually defended against emotions which had to be re-experienced, if the re-manifestation of that past in, and the 'acting out' of those emotions through, crime were to be avoided in the future. A life story that had appeared, at least to the newly arrived TC resident, to consist of a series of disjointed and unrelated events and experiences now began to reveal the coexistence of emotional connectivity and psychic compartmentalization flowing through their self-narrative, which illuminated 'the horrible feelings I couldn't deal with … [and] what was *really* going for me' (Belinda, Send), at the time of their index offence. These insights were not always welcome or easy to assimilate. As new residents battled to reconcile their competing desires to stay and to leave; to explore and to retreat; to internalize TC values whilst still, for many, tempted by the comforting familiarity of the system; so their faith in, and commitment to, therapy and community living could fluctuate dramatically:

> [Therapy] hurts, it's painful; sometimes you don't even want to go there because you know when you go to the dark places of your life, your

sadness, your upset, you're going to feel that pain, but I do feel it's the best place for me … [My therapist], sometimes I cussed her so bad; we have such bust ups and I take my frustrations out on her! Always asking me questions, questions, pushing me to say more. There's loads of times I'm thinking I'm going to quit and I'm not coming out of my room!

(Josephine, Send)

There was an issue I had to bring up about my mum and that was hard. I broke down, it ripped me apart because I felt like I was grassing on my family … I struggled with myself after I said it in group for ages. I still feel that way, even talking about it now to you is making me croaky … I feel proper disappointed in myself that I done that to them.

(Adele, Send)

You're talking about yourself day in, day out, really personal stuff and even though I know the end result is absolutely joy, at the present time, it's hard and I feel like I'm being punished every day. I don't sleep. I'm talking about things that I never thought I'd talk about and it's daunting; it really is. How horrible it is when you're lying in your pad[24] knowing you've got to come down here next day and talk some more. Sometimes I just hate it and want to leave, but I know I'll benefit in the end and so will everyone else, because I won't be running around causing mayhem.

(Don, Grendon)

I've thought about putting my 48[25] in loads of times. I don't like talking about my stuff … When you use your group in the morning, you've got all day to think about it and then you're banged up. It hits home what you spoke about or where you are and you can't go and have a walk; you're stuck in that little cell. It gets you depressed. If I was on a normal wing, I wouldn't have to think as much.

(Richie, GTC)

Such ambivalence also characterizes the 'zigzag path … from noncrime to crime and to noncrime again' (Glaser 1969:57–58), as Burnett's (1992, 2000, 2004) longitudinal research with 130 formerly imprisoned property offenders cogently demonstrated. (Re-) offending mostly reflected, not neutral and non-committal 'drift' (Matza 1964) but rather, the confusion that results from metaphorically riding 'a pendulum of ambivalence … swayed by the weight of alternative desires and rationalizations' (Burnett 2004:168). Just as Burnett's cohort could vacillate between the contrasting attractions of desistance and persistence, so TC residents' commitment to remain, and hence to try to change, could be equally unstable; contingent upon what they uncovered about themselves in the TC and which they accepted would have to change, if they were realistically to believe in the possibility of post-release desistance from crime.

At Grendon, it was apparent that residents' doubts about their progress and 'love–hate relationship with the place … very up and down' (Dominic, Grendon) were often embedded within vehement complaints about their physical environment; (at that time) deleterious changes to the core day, instituted by 'Top Corridor' (senior management) partly in the Sisyphean pursuit of 'efficiency savings';[26] and NOMS's general attitude to TCs. Men who had been accustomed to more recently constructed, 'all mod cons' prisons could find Grendon's ageing fabric, absence of in-cell sanitation,[27] and low wages, a genuinely powerful disincentive to remain. Others worried that the regime was steadily being eroded by a persistent lack of ideological and financial investment in TCs because '[NOMS] views us as a money pit; we're a cancer on their side … they care more about money than rehabilitation' (Bill, Grendon). Many residents, then, recognized that they had made a conscious cost-benefit calculation to stay at Grendon and a reasoned decision 'not to go down that negative road' (Peter, Grendon) of allowing themselves to become fixated upon their complaints as a way of avoiding or displacing more troublesome emotions and thoughts. This is not to suggest that these criticisms were unfounded, but for someone who is ambivalent or anxious about the process and consequences of rehabilitation and is weighing up the 'pros' and 'cons' of remaining in treatment, it may seem preferable to accentuate Grendon's structural or regime deficits and under-resourcing on the drop-out decisional balance sheet, rather than one's unwillingness or inability to confront one's problems and live within a therapeutic community:

> When you're having a bad day, you can feed into that – the crap wages, 'nightsan', the regime changes which are all wrong for this place … [but] the work that goes on here is absolutely *phenomenal*, it's powerful. So then you have to challenge yourself: am I here for a nice time or am I here to change? You kind of have to weigh it up: what's more important?
>
> (Eddie, Grendon)

TC 'persisters' were therefore people who could first survive, and then embrace, the transition to a markedly 'different' penal culture, code, and treatment modality, and who could tolerate any subsequent disappointments or intermittent disorienting ambivalence they felt about the reality of the TC way. They began to redefine the nature and scale of their 'issues' and to search for the complicated latent causes of their offending, rather than merely describing its symptomatic features, and they learned to accept the often perpetual discomfort and enervating anxiety that accompanied their therapeutic explorations. They swiftly disengaged with the generic identity of the offender or prisoner to adopt instead their agentically chosen role of a TC resident who, to varying degrees, 'bought in' to the idea of therapy and the ideals of the therapeutic community. They belonged now to a 'different' penal club, the criterion for membership of which was to regard the pursuit of rehabilitation as laudable and achievable. This new identity then became the prop by which their, at times, fluctuating motivation to complete their therapy, and to progress towards desistance, could be supported.

By applying to, entering into, and persevering with the TC, residents could therefore find the kind of hook for change or turning point upon which the precarious pathway towards desistance often depends. Joining a prison-based TC provided them with the opportunity to create a credible plot development in their life story; one which might eventually permit a happier (non-offending, non-imprisoned) ending than that seemingly already scripted by the offender's 'backstory' and narrative trajectory. Whether applicants actively wanted to change, or reluctantly recognized the need to change, their encounters with the institutionalized use of first names, the starkly 'different vibe', the abandonment of the usual inmate code and culture, and the commitment to a therapeutic retelling of one's 'true' life story and (re)discovery of one's 'real' self, all indicated to neophytes that this was a place where they could be something more than 'just cons', and could create precisely the sort of 'other self' and 'other life' that studies of desistance through identity reconstruction have identified.

As a final illustration of how the all-important hook for change can result from exposure to the TC way, I conclude this chapter with the heartfelt testimony of James, whose faltering first steps towards rehabilitation began by 'coming clean' in the TC about his offence. Although upon admittance to Grendon, James's intention had been 'to start over and fess up',[28] his concern for his 'image' initially proved more compelling. Within weeks of his graduation to a main therapy wing, however, his 'bullshit lies' were exposed by a member of his small group who realized that James's account of his crime 'had more holes in it than a colander':

> And I thought to myself, you know what, I have come here to change, I've come here to do what's right, I've come here to challenge myself in every area possible, and I said to myself, you need to start being honest … And I proceeded to tell [my group] the truth about what had actually happened the night I committed the murder. And that was the first time I had revealed to *anyone* – probation, my solicitor, my missus – the whole truth. … Afterwards, at first I felt really shitty, I felt exposed, vulnerable; I had a whole lot of horrible feelings going on, Alisa, right, but after a couple of days, I felt my shoulders straightening out, I felt myself like, kind of, physically growing taller because I was actually being truthful. And I thought to myself then, I don't have to be that person no more; I *can* change. And it felt really good. It was a powerful moment for me.

4 Care, trust, and support

> To see that there are people who value you and care for you is really important. It helps residents to build an inner core that says, I'm an okay person and I deserve good things. Feeling cared for can change the way they feel about themselves and the way they think about their future.
>
> (Elizabeth, therapist)

In therapeutic communities, the relationships between community members, and the experiences of care that should result, are understood through the framework provided by attachment theory. This theory, derived from the eclectic theoretical, clinical, and empirical work of the psychiatrist and psychoanalyst John Bowlby (1969, 1973, 1979, 1980, 1988) and developmental psychologist Mary Ainsworth (1967), presumes that, from the umbilical attachment of the baby in the womb to the adult's search for romantic and sexual love, human beings possess a biological propensity to forge intimate attachments (emotional bonds) with others. The ability to meet this innate basic need initially depends upon the quality, accessibility, and consistency of care experienced by the infant child, and provided by his or her principal 'attachment-figure' (usually, but not of necessity, the mother). In response to these earliest experiences of caregiver responsiveness, the child develops a 'pattern of attachment' – secure, ambivalent, avoidant (Ainsworth *et al.* 1978), or disorganized (an incoherent mixture of ambivalent and avoidant styles) (Main and Solomon 1986) – and creates 'internal working models' or cognitive maps, which persistently define how the individual sees him or herself, relates to others socially and psychologically, and anticipates others will behave towards him or her. Attachment theory accordingly postulates that, 'Human infants … are preprogrammed to develop in a socially co-operative way; whether they do so or not turns in high degree on how they are treated' (Bowlby 1988:9).

Extensive longitudinal research into the developmental consequences of early attachment (for example, Sroufe 1983; Hazan and Shaver 1994; Bartholomew 1990; Grossman and Grossman 1991) has since confirmed that a child who is 'treated' to an insecure, traumatic, chaotic, or abusive attachment – whether through death, divorce, abandonment, rejection, or neglect – will tend in adolescence and adulthood intuitively to seek out and reproduce equally deficient and pathological attachments and inflexible relating styles. A person's mental representations and experiences of ambivalent or avoidant attachments may lead him or her, for example, to create intense, all-consuming, but volatile attachments with people whom he or she jealously and obsessively seeks to control, or to deny and denigrate any need for intimacy and so prospectively relate to others in a defensive, dismissive, and manipulative manner. A primary corrective focus of (psychoanalytic) psychotherapy is therefore to provide a 'corrective emotional experience' (Alexander, cited in Yalom 1995:24) through the reappraisal and modification of self-perpetuating and unproductive cognitive and affective schemas and, through the therapist–patient dyad, the modelling of attachment as reliable, trustworthy, responsive, and attentive (Bowlby 1988). Moreover, the TC has, from Main and Jones onwards, laid particular claim to providing attachment disordered individuals with the hitherto denied comforting and reassuring 'safe haven' and trust- and confidence-enabling 'secure base' (Bowlby 1988) from which to re-experience earlier dysfunctional experiences of care, explore new internal working models, and create prototypical empathetic and supportive patterns of relating to others.

Attachment theory is similarly valued by clinicians and practitioners working in forensic settings for the contribution it can make to assessing and explicating the offender's 'backstory' and attachment schemas, their affect upon the therapeutic alliance[1] and transference relationship, and the correlations between early attachment trauma and later psychosocial and emotional impairment, including personality disorder (de Zulueta 1993; Fonagy *et al.* 1996; Pfäfflin and Adshead 2004; Ansbro 2008). Such work assumes special relevance when one considers the potential influence of attachment style, intimacy deficits, and emotional loneliness upon the aetiology and maintenance of sexual offending (Marshall 1993; Ward *et al.* 1995; Bumby and Hansen 1997; Cortoni and Marshall 2001; Rich 2006); and that (especially female) victims of violent and sexually violent crime are typically drawn from the (male) offender's attachment network (Myhill and Allen 2002; Finney 2006). Adshead (2004:149, emphasis added) notes that it is 'highly unusual for offender patients … to have had early childhood experience which *would* promote attachment security'; a statement quantified by Shine and Newton's (2000) findings that 69 per cent of Grendonites had experienced loss or separation from either their natural or surrogate parents for at least one year before the age of 16, whilst 63 per cent reported being the victim of physical, and 40 per cent sexual, abuse during childhood. It is part of the work of prison-based TCs to attempt to assuage pathogenic parenting, and to demonstrate that the dysfunctional relationships residents have previously known, and inflicted upon others, are not inevitable; but can be replaced with reparative, secure, and coherent attachments to staff members and their peers, who are able to give care *to* them and, perhaps even more alarmingly to some offenders, successfully elicit care *from* them. As Bowlby (1988:136) comfortingly reassures us, '… at no time in life is a person impermeable to favourable influence. It is this persisting potential for change that gives opportunity for effective therapy.'

To understand the transformative potential of therapeutic community treatment, then, one has to appreciate the importance of care to people who, on average, have received little care in their life and have been little inclined to show care to others or, indeed, themselves. The two are not unrelated, as attachment theory demonstrates. The purpose of this chapter is therefore to detail residents' experiences of learning to accept care from, and in time to return it to, staff and other residents. Care from officers was predominately communicated through the performance of their custodial duties in a considerate and conscientious manner, congruent with a criminal justice credo based upon liberal and humanitarian values (Rutherford 1993) which consistently and implicitly acknowledged, and hence respected, the symbolic meaning and practical importance of these tasks to the prisoner and his or her quality of life. Care from residents was predominately experienced through the provision of emotional support within the small therapy groups. Both contributed to residents' improving sense of self as an empathetic and emotionally responsive individual, capable of change and of assisting and supporting others to change. The chapter concludes by considering the distinctive institutional factors which further ensure that an ethic of care is embedded into the TC way.

Experiences of care: attachment to officers

Relationships between officers and inmates have always been recognized as central to the prison experience. The affective quality of individual relationships between 'screws' and 'cons' can determine the influence, for good or ill, the former can have upon the latter, and to what extent, or even whether, the pains of imprisonment are mitigated and the regime is perceived as fair and constructive (Sykes 1958; Home Office 1984; Woolf 1991; Gilbert 1997).

When the resident participants in this research were asked to describe TC officers and their relationships with them, the most frequently attributed, spontaneously chosen adjective was 'caring': 'They're very caring and compassionate; they've always got time for you' (Mark, Grendon); 'I'd describe them as caring; I get a strong sense that they really do care here' (Muktar, Grendon); 'They're so caring. The officers make it like a family up here' (Richie, GTC). Although 'the word "care" causes considerable controversy in prisons, with some staff finding it unutterable' (Liebling, assisted by Arnold 2004:15), and has historically been found to induce role conflict between those officers who seek to find an appropriate accommodation between the otherwise seemingly oppositional demands of care and control (Liebling *et al.* 2011), the importance of care, as a legitimate and critically important facet of the prison officer's role, has of late gained wider recognition (Tait 2008, 2011; House of Commons Justice Committee 2009).

To theorize the contribution of 'care' is therefore to focus theoretical attention upon the normative relationships between, and social responsibilities of, people. Caring relationships become possible when the inherent connection and commonality between morally interdependent but fundamentally similar people results in a recognition and acceptance of responsibility for each other, and of the perceived imperative to react to the expressed or implicit needs of others (Gilligan 1982; Noddings 1984; Tronto 1993; Held 2006). In describing TC officers as 'caring', residents were responding to officers' multiple, small – though evidently, symbolically large – acts of civility, kindness, and individual attention, which consistently conveyed to them that they possessed the ability to comprehend, respect, and respond sensitively and empathetically to residents' perspectives and concerns, as if they were their own. The provision *and* acceptance of care developed from practical to emotional issues; or as Harvey (2007:82) found in his research with young offenders 'the response of staff to practical concerns served as a testing ground for trust to be established or distrust to be confirmed'. For example, residents complained about the institutionalized (and institutionalizing) requirement that prisoners routinely submit written applications to acquire information or lodge a grievance, and the apparent tendency of such forms to disappear into some curious administrative vortex. 'Caring' officers, by contrast, were more willing to use their own initiative to problem solve informally and to respond creatively to residents' requests for practical help:

> In the system, it's apps[2] for *everything*, isn't it? ... There are some things, small things, and you could just ask the prison officer. You can see they're just sitting in the office; they're not doing anything and it wouldn't kill them to pick up the phone and resolve [your question] in a matter of minutes. But no, they just go, 'Put an app in', and you put it in, and they lose it [laughs], and it takes weeks and weeks to get a simple answer.
>
> *How does that make you feel?*
>
> [pause] Frustrated, like a child. It's absolutely tedious and unnecessary, I think. You feel like you're shunted to one side, like an inconvenience. And with some people, they feed into that and then really start to dislike staff because they don't see them doing anything for their benefit ... But one thing I have noticed here is, most of the officers, if they can find out for you there and then, they will. They're much more proactive and helpful, I find. You feel like they understand that it matters *to you.*
>
> (Leslie, Grendon)

> My personal officer[3] was willing to go out of his way to go over to Spring Hill[4] stores and collect my property which I badly needed. And it wasn't

> nothing to do with him; it was for the staff over there who weren't doing their job. So that shows me that he's a caring bloke who thinks about me.
>
> (Callum, Grendon)

> [The officers here are] like friends – really helpful, supportive, approachable; very different to normal officers! [laughs]
>
> *So it sounds like you're saying you don't generally find mainstream officers to be helpful or supportive?*
>
> No. Some are but generally, I think, to most prison officers, it's just a job and they can't wait to bang us up. That's my opinion. But here, they are more willing to help and I think they take their job, well, more seriously really; they care about *you* and where you're at. Like, say you need to speak to an officer but they can't stop and talk to you right there and then, they'll say, 'Give me ten minutes and I'll be back.' And they do come back! Normally if you hear that, it's like, yeah, right, I'll see you next week sometime. But here, if they say they'll do it, they do it. They don't mug you off. You can trust them.
>
> (Shelley, Send)

Simply, then, by understanding that the enquiry is important to the enquirer, responding in a timely manner, and keeping their word, officers could come to be considered as caring and trustworthy. Their behaviour indicated to residents that residents' needs were understood and respected, and implied an understanding and respect for the individual prisoner. The officers having 'proven' themselves in the execution of standard custodial duties, residents then became more willing to seek care and support from these same officers for emotional and personal matters, and felt more able to talk openly and candidly to them about their past and ongoing 'issues'. Officers' responses to – and, importantly, sometimes initiation of – sensitive discussions determined whether they would enhance their reputation as 'really caring ... they understand a lot more than your average officer ... rehabilitation is what they're about; they're as committed to change as much as some of us are, which is important' (Lee, GTC). Indeed, amongst the many polarized comparisons between TC officers as 'a different breed' (Francis, GTC) and 'system screws'[5] that TC residents tended to make, this perception that TC officers genuinely believed in the ability of people to change *and* wanted to contribute actively to that process of change, as evidenced in part by their volunteering to work in, and continue to work in, a TC,[6] was critical in its contribution to the transformation of uniformed, discipline officers into partners in rehabilitation:

> Certain officers will say things to me that I spoke about on my group like weeks later, and that shows that they really listen and they're thinking of me, doesn't it? ... [Names of two officers], they're honest with me and talk

> to me on the level. We have some deep conversations. They're very into therapy and change, and they give me good feedback and things to think about.
>
> (Nick, Grendon)

> [Name of officer] I admire him, I respect him, I look up to him. He's a role model for me, he is. I would like to have a father like that, to be honest … He believes in this place and gives me guidance to do the right thing. He's really helped me with what I need to do here.
>
> (Wesley, Grendon)

> The majority, their desire to help people just sort of oozes out of them. For starters, they've chosen to come here, so that tells you something. Why work here, on the same pay, when they could go and work at [another category B prison] and just open doors and drink coffee all day? Do you know what I mean? So most of them, they believe in change, otherwise they wouldn't be working here.
>
> (Brian, Grendon)

Of course, as with all human relationships, the quality of individual attachments between residents and officers varied considerably. It was noticeable, however, how, in each community, certain highly supportive and individually attentive 'role-model' officers, who were 'interested in you as a person and really try to understand what you're about' (James, Grendon), were consistently singled out by different resident interviewees for praise. Conversely, a handful of officers were repeatedly accused of being 'system-like', with all the disdain that implies in a TC. The recently arrived (and evidently untherapeutized) officer who, for example, whistled down the Tannoy and barked out a surname as a way of summoning a resident to the wing office, was speedily 'picked up' on his 'disrespectful' error by another resident in the next community meeting; as was the officer who was unequivocally reminded that his preferred reliance on the completion of formal applications was '*not* the way we do things *here*' (fieldnotes). Whilst interviewees attributed such 'system thinking' to mainstream occupational culture and the realities of mass imprisonment, no such mitigation was made for officers whose choice to work in a TC, as Brian argued, implied a commitment to its 'special' purpose. Residents accordingly reserved their strongest opprobrium and 'censoriousness'[7] (Mathiesen 1965) for the small minority of officers whom they judged to be uninterested in prisoners as individuals, unsympathetic towards any personal difficulties they were facing, and cynical about their potential for rehabilitation, and condemned them as 'indistinguishable from system screws … they're lazy, they've just come here for an easy ride … no therapeutic value to them whatsoever' (Peter, Grendon). Such officers appeared to have never truly joined, or had allowed to lapse their membership of, the TC club.

Overwhelmingly, however, residents were unstinting in their praise of TC officers. For these therapeutic 'champions' (Wilson and McCabe 2002:285), their emotional support – being 'like friends' engaged in the human service of custodial *care* – and demonstrative correctional orientation towards rehabilitation in general, and psychotherapy in particular, ensured they could approximate the influential attachment-figures Bowlby described. This enlargement of role and espousal of purpose is not something many prison officers would want or even consider appropriate (Crawley 2004). TC officers, however, were contentedly aware of their stigmatized reputation amongst their peers and managed their 'dirty work' with this particular 'out-group' (Hughes 1962:8) through taking satisfaction from, and enjoying confidence in, the merit and appositeness of their work: 'We're "care bears", all pink and fluffy! … [But] I absolutely love working here and this to me is what the job should be about. I'm making a *real* difference and I certainly wasn't at [my previous establishment]' (Kevin, officer).

That '*real* difference' for residents included experiences of care which were not exceptional, but routine; they were 'lived' in omnipresent and normalized episodes of diligent responsiveness, genuine concern, and humanizing social relations. Care came not from the minority of staff one finds in any prison who are, in Tait's (2008, 2011) typology of officers' caring styles, 'true carers' (or even 'limited carers'), but from nearly all the members of staff with whom residents had daily interaction. Care, as 'the most powerful treatment tool available to staff' (Wood 2007:156), incrementally enabled residents to see themselves as 'normal' people, greater than the sum total of their offending, *worthy* of care and capable of change. This improved self-concept was further encouraged by the care shown by, and to, their fellow residents.

Experiences of care: attachment amongst residents

Whilst the sociology of imprisonment has had much to say about relationships (or otherwise) between officers and prisoners, attachment amongst prisoners is less well understood, often framed within discussions about the inmate code and 'the dilemma'[8] of friendship, its gradations, and limitations (Cohen and Taylor 1972; Jewkes 2005a; Crewe 2009). When interviewees were asked, however, for a recent example of 'something that's happened … that you thought was really good about this place', two-thirds volunteered an incident that evidenced care shown by their fellow residents. This suggests that such care, whether in its frequency or quality, impressed and influenced my participants more than the still evidently appreciated care from staff.[9] Prisoners may expect prison officers to care, to some degree, as part of their occupational role and for which they are remunerated, but care from other prisoners, and particularly care from men to other men (discussed further in Chapter 6), was evidently something of a novelty.

Care from residents was conveyed by concern, in the trusting disclosures of personal experience, and the provision of emotional support. Care was often first and most regularly encountered when residents received 'incredible, very humbling' (Dave, Grendon) encouragement and guidance from their small group members, as they periodically struggled with therapy, the TC way, and their efforts to change. Such care emanated from the camaraderie of shared purpose – 'we're not here to fuck about and fight; we're here to do therapy and help each other' (Luke, Grendon) – and the shared experience of enduring 'excruciating embarrassment and shame' (Raymond, GTC) and 'terrible turmoil and pain' (Jenny, Send) as residents gradually unfurled the story of their life, including their entire history of offending and the smallest details of their index offence(s), to their small group. As more recently arrived residents listened to the wisdom and insight of senior residents and sensed that their peers wanted to help them accept and work through their 'issues', as once they had been helped, so they began to accept this care as genuine. Stewart (Grendon), for example, explained how he had become 'panicked' by the revelations he had made in therapy and the consequent crumbling of his 'mask' of confidence and bravado. He announced to his small group his intention to leave but was dissuaded from doing so by his fellow Grendonites:

> What was amazing was the number of people who came up to me and sat me down and said, 'I think you're doing the wrong thing.' They told me – inmates, not psychologists or officers – [they] were saying that this place was the best for me and they were speaking like they know me, because they've been listening to me for months and they had my best interests at heart; that I should stay and deal with my issues … So I didn't even put my papers in.[10] It was just the care and concern from them, it touched me, that they actually give a toss about me, and I've never felt that before from no one.

For residents to accept the wisdom of such advice *from* their community and to respond to their overtures of care, however, required a willingness and ability to trust *in* their community. Trust, like care, was a word used by participants with all the reverence its infrequency and desirability demands. Sociologically, trust in others acts as a form of social lubricant, promoting confidence, collaboration, communication, and cohesiveness. Psychologically, one's ontological security – an elemental sense of confidence in the reliability and continuity of one's personal identity and social and material world – is founded upon the formation of trust relationships; relationships that ideally begin, of course, with secure childhood attachments (Giddens 1990; Misztal 1996). Axiomatically, then, trust is also integral to the creation of a therapeutic alliance, but – and therefore a complicating factor for prison-based TCs – the achievement of such a relationship is made more difficult by the intrinsically power-imbalanced, *low*-trust custodial environment.

Trainee officers, for example, are specifically taught to develop a suspicious, hypervigilant 'mindset' and 'never to trust the bastards!' (prison officer quoted in Crawley 2004:69). Although, of course, some degree of trust 'is essential to social co-operation *even in the prison*' (Liebling, assisted by Arnold 2004:241, emphasis added) and thus does exist, albeit 'unevenly' and at times, tenuously, a fundamental principle of 'jailcraft' is that officers should be continually alert to the potential for conflict, misbehaviour, compromise, or conditioning, and should not divulge personal information about themselves to prisoners, in order to maintain appropriate boundaries (Arnold 2005). The primary purpose of the prison officer's job is, after all, to ensure that prisoners remain in custody and either obey, or are detected as disobeying, the prison rules, and this necessary preoccupation with security and discipline cannot but position the keeper in opposition to, and at some social distance from, the kept.

Offenders, meanwhile, do not easily trust officers' discretionary, and hence unpredictable, use of authority and tactics of persuasion or 'soft power' (Crewe 2009); nor the objectivity and expertise of those staff tasked with monitoring, assessing, and reporting upon offenders' behaviour. In particular, residents frequently asserted that report writers nowadays possess almost unquestioned and unquestionable power to 'screw you over' and 'knife you off'[11] by committing to paper their assessments of prisoners which could have, in residents' opinions, 'malicious' and disproportionately severe, long-term consequences for their sentence progression. (This pervasive fear of perceived or actual self-incrimination made it more difficult, some residents said, at least in the earlier stages of therapy, to 'open up' fully about their 'issues', lest such honesty exacerbated, or invited previously unappreciated, concerns about an individual's 'areas of concern'.) Finally, prisoners trust their peers only minimally and conditionally, recognizing in each other the proven potential for deception, violence, and all manner of 'trouble'; yet accepting of the need for some wary collaboration, if only to pursue activities of interest to 'us' in defiance of 'them'. As classic ethnographic research with both men and women contends, 'The worst thing about prison is you have to live with other prisoners' (prisoner quoted in Sykes 1958:77 and similarly, Giallombardo 1966:99).

Whilst residents therefore acknowledged that trust was essential – 'You *have* to trust people here to be able to do the work. It's hard, it don't come easy to many of us, but you've got to do it, otherwise you might as well go' (Ravi, Grendon) – some participants were, or initially had been, simply unable to trust anyone. To articulate one's innermost feelings and thoughts and to 'let people in … [to] tell them my guilty secrets, hidden things, nasty things about me, that I'm ashamed of, that I've never told no one' (Alan, Grendon) is to cede knowledge about oneself and, thereby, some degree of control over and regulation of the presentation of that self. Yet, in a deliberately disempowering environment, impression management is one of the few activities that prisoners *can* seek to regulate, even if it tends to result in the assumption of psychological masks which are every bit as imprisoning as physical structures. Allowing others to glimpse the 'real' individual was therefore instinctively resisted by some residents, not least when the agony of 'letting people in' was compounded by the imprint of earlier attachment experiences and thus the fear that to trust is to make oneself vulnerable to betrayal, deceit, and others' questionable ulterior motives:

> No, I don't trust anyone, end of … I've learned the hard way: people always shaft you in the end.
>
> (Richard, Grendon)

> I always thought that anyone who was being nice to you, it's to get something from you. I got really paranoid with the officers thinking, why are they being nice to me? What's their game?
>
> (Louise, Send)

For these residents, and in language reminiscent of the last resort desperados, summoning up the necessary trust was therefore akin to an act of will and a gamble, in which the risk of treachery was balanced against the hope of benefit:

> When I first come here, all my barriers were up; I didn't trust anyone … I thought the girls would spread lies and nasty rumours about me around the prison … [but] nothing bad seemed to happen to the girls who did speak about their stuff, so I thought, well, maybe I can trust them.
>
> (Theresa, Send)

> I don't trust people because I've been badly let down, too many times. But I'm having to do it on my small group.
>
> *And how is that working out for you?*
>
> [sigh] I struggle with it every day but [pause], some of the things my group tell me, I can see that they are saying it out of caring; that it's well intentioned. So I'm beginning now *sometimes* to trust what they say. They haven't lied to me or let me down yet. And there's something about [my facilitator] that I do trust. I respect her because she's an intelligent woman and she talks a lot of sense. But if that trust goes, I'm gone.
>
> (Keith, Grendon)

For all residents, though, being required to re-experience in therapy traumatic experiences and reclaim the associated 'split-off' 'unacceptable' emotions of anger, shame, despair, jealously, and sorrow against which they have been psychically defended for so long, was periodically 'very, very difficult and *really* painful' (Sarah, Send). The support and encouragement of other community members was therefore pivotal in determining for individuals whether the possibility of change was worth the difficulty and pain of its pursuit through psychotherapy. One of the cited advantages of group, as opposed to individual, psychotherapy is its 'strength in numbers' (Manor 1994:251). It is easier to summon up the courage to continue with one's therapy when one realizes that one's apparently unique problems are, in fact, familiar to and well understood by others. In the TC, deeply personal disclosures – experiences of, for example, as children and/or adults, being physically and sexually abused, or degraded by drug or alcohol addiction, or victimized through prostitution and violent and sexually exploitative relationships – were routinely met with the empathetic understanding of people who have also endured such traumas, and similarly struggled to contain the resulting disassociation and disempowerment: 'We all have the same sort of issues, so the shame is taken away' (Belinda, Send). Shame inhibits openness to therapy and prevents the growth of trust (Yalom 1995), and thus it was significant that residents found, sometimes to their immense surprise, that their peers, as responsible and responsive auxiliary therapists, neither judged nor rejected them, nor abused the trust placed in them: 'You don't have to fear here that any openness will be used against you, i.e. that whatever you've revealed will be thrown back at you and seen as a weakness' (Michael, Grendon). The respect and sensitivity shown to those who shared their stories confirmed to other residents that it was psychologically safe to 'open up' emotionally; and the resonance of experience and resulting realization of commonality that so often followed, powerfully lessened residents' embarrassment, social isolation, and existential loneliness, and increased their understanding and acceptance of themselves:

> When you divulge intimate things about yourself, you learn that you are never alone; there is always somebody else who has suffered a similar thing and they can share that pain with you. So in a way, that's quite comforting, quite refreshing, relieving. It's nice to know that you are not alone.
>
> (Mark, Grendon)

> Getting this crap out does seem to lighten you … It's fucking horrible but really, it's weird as well, because it gives you a lot more confidence. The first time I broke down in front of my group, I cried, and [a group member] put his arm around me – and I thought, how powerful is this place to give me the confidence to talk about this and to take that comfort from him.
>
> (Patrick, Grendon)

> I hadn't felt no feelings about things that had happened to me before but here, hearing other people's stories, just to know you're not the only one that's gone there or done that, it does help … Just hearing the other girls talk about things what they've been through, and their feelings about it, makes it easier for me to feel my feelings and get support with them feelings.
>
> *Why does it take a TC to get that kind of support?*

> Because in the mainstream, everyone just gets on with their own sentence; they've got their own problems, you know what I mean? And you have to put on a front to keep yourself safe because otherwise some girls see you as vulnerable and then they take advantage ... If you got close with a few girls, well, you might hear their stories and that, but it's like you don't *feel* them. It's just a story, that's all it is ... Here, because we do go deep with each other, it makes for a different relationship. There's a lot more support and care for everyone and you know they ain't going to go around and chat your business, so you can trust them.
>
> (Caroline, Send)

This experience of receiving care from one's peers translated in time into a willingness to bestow care. Simply stated, receiving care from others made it easier for residents to accept that they were worthy of care, and thus to reconfirm the importance of caring for others *even in* an environment more usually associated with cultural assertions of the need to 'do your own time' (Sykes and Messinger 1960) and be self-sufficient. As they gained in therapeutic insight, residents wanted to impart the understanding and experiential knowledge they had acquired to those, generally less experienced, residents who were struggling with aspects of their therapy. They also found, however, that supporting others was emotionally satisfying, enhanced their self-confidence and self-esteem, and provided reassuring and tangible evidence of their personal development:

> The level of care for people that are struggling is just amazing. I've been there myself; I've struggled and the guys have given me the inspiration to keep plodding on with it.
>
> *And how does that make you feel?*
>
> It makes me feel good, that I'm worthwhile. Some guys build you up and say, 'You *are* doing well, and half the reasons *why* you probably are feeling so bad is that you're going through the motions of change ...' It's like gaining things as well because I can talk about those feelings now when they're going through a hard time.
>
> *So they gain because you can support them, because you understand their feelings, and you gain because you can talk about your feelings now?*
>
> Yeah. It feels like I'm giving something back to the community and I feel good about myself now ... When I first came up here, I couldn't talk about my own feelings, let alone want to hear about another man's feelings! But now I do, and I can give some good advice. So you find out here different sides of yourself; you find you can do things, good things, worthwhile things, that you never thought you could do.
>
> (Ben, GTC)

> I've given advice to other people and they took it, and that makes me feel worthwhile. People never listened to me before, but they do now.

> *But is that more about other people not listening before?*
>
> No, it comes back to the vocal thing – I can explain things better. I wouldn't have been able to do this [interview] a year ago. I first tried it out on here with [name of resident]. He was asking me about something and I went on this massive speech, and he came back 15 minutes later and said, 'You know what, that's the best advice I've ever got off anyone.' I heard him talking about it the next day and I felt really proud of myself. And that's a big achievement for me.
>
> (Richie, GTC)

As substance abuse self-help organizations such as Alcoholics Anonymous have found, and research in the fields of mental health and social care suggests (for example, Davidson *et al.* 1999; Solomon 2004; Loat 2006), 'giving something back to the community', being both recipients and donors of care and support, 'helpees' and helpers (Riessman 1965, 1990), and, in time, role models and mentors, can bolster one's own emerging sense of competency and intrinsic worth. Peer support provides a sense of purpose beyond one's own 'recovery', reinforces for the helper the magnitude, and continuing importance, of their ongoing rehabilitation, and can create a sense of generativity or 'concern for and commitment to promoting the next generation' (McAdams and de St Aubin 1998:xx, cited in Maruna 2001:99). In the TC, then, successive generations of residents consolidate their own progress by contributing to the progression of others. Wisdom, as well as care, is shared, and understanding and tolerance, of oneself and others, deepened.

Residents' attachment to the community as a whole was therefore strengthened by what Yalom (1995:5–7), in his consideration of primary therapeutic factors, terms the 'universality' or commonality of experience they found within the community. Residents found it easier to return care to other residents because, given the entirely prudent, ethical, personal, and professional boundaries that govern the officer–resident and therapeutic relationship, fewer opportunities exist to reciprocate the sharing of personal information and confidences with staff, who simply cannot 'open up' to the extent that residents, if their therapy is to succeed, must. Furthermore, uniformed and clinical prison staff, it is safe to assume, do not have first-hand knowledge of many of the types of 'issues' that afflict TC residents. They probably have not been subjected to, or subjected themselves to, the abyss of misery these – and indeed, many – prisoners have, and the fundamentally flawed sense of self-worth that results; and they certainly have not committed the usually violent, sometimes fatal, criminal offences that bring prisoners to TCs. It was therefore residents, who truly *know* what it is to live through and with diverse but similar experiences and how it is that one's internal victim can become projected into the vicitimization of others, who represented a particularly potent source of support to other residents.

Changing conceptions of friendship

As Caroline (Send) explained, developing trust, sharing experiences, and learning from each other, 'makes for a different relationship'. In the mainstream, the majority of 'relationships' were described as merely utilitarian, situated quid pro quo alliances of convenience, in which it was neither prudent nor feasible to elicit sustained emotional support from others when 'they've got their own problems'. Such '*prison* friendships' ranged from the most superficial of acquaintances alongside whom one could peacefully coexist; to 'lads you're reasonably friendly with, you'll watch each other's backs … but I wouldn't call them friends as such' (Alan, Grendon) but with whom some material resources might be shared and to whom physical assistance, when faced with 'aggro', might be offered; to 'business associates', meticulously calibrated according to their contribution to the informal economy and 'what each of us can bring to the table' (Tony, Grendon). As a result, 'unless you've got a *really* good friend that you can *really* trust, you are basically on your own' (Natalie, Send).

TC friendships, by contrast, were understood to be 'based on different values: openness, honesty, trying to do the right thing. There's a different dynamic to friendships here because we haven't got all the trappings of the system – drugs, booze, mobile phones' (Bill, Grendon). With the trade in these valuable commodities largely removed in accordance with the TC's rules, the instrumental, strategic, and defensive partnerships they necessitate in mainstream prisons were rendered redundant (Crewe 2005b). Instead, 'more genuine, more mature friendships … [of] true emotion and affection' (Raymond, GTC) could emerge from the reciprocal sharing of intimate details of one's life and internal world, and the admission of thoughts, feelings, emotions, memories, fears, and secrets which would be unthinkable in other prisons:

> I've got a mate I've met here; he's a proper, like, friend.[12] I can say he's a friend because he knows everything about me, and I know everything about him, so our friendship is more than just taking drugs and having the screws over,[13] you know what I mean? He knows my problems, my issues, and I know his. So you can get close to people here.
>
> *Could you have that sort of friendship in the system?*
>
> No way. You just don't talk about personal things with your mates in the system; the things that happened in your childhood and all that. It just don't happen. You'd get the right piss taken out of you.
>
> (Don, Grendon)

This is not to suggest that TCs magically conjure up some fairy tale setting in which everyone harmoniously co-habits, happily ever after. The sustainment of a community requires sustained effort: residents may share 'issues' but this does not automatically translate into a propensity to coexist harmoniously. Relationships with residents who had to be 'tolerated' but with whom one need only politely but perfunctorily acknowledge, in passing, still existed; and combustible personality clashes were commonplace and sometimes ignited into verbal (and infrequently, physical) confrontations, the 'meanings' of which would then be subjected to the therapeutic examination of the whole community (as discussed in the next chapter). A small minority of men (and only men) also stated that they *never* made friends – either at all or only when in prison, with the socially restricted circles of potential companions it offers – but appeared neither perturbed nor disappointed by their continued rejection of friendships in the TC.

The intensity of a small community was more frequently credited, however, with enabling the formation of a 'different' – superior – type of friendship, and friendships with a 'different sort' of person – including men who had raped or who had murdered their partner – than those possible in other prisons, for reasons of cultural prohibition or institutionally enforced segregation (see Chapter 6). Residents' shared participation in the community, and the requirement for full and credible disclosure of their personal and criminal histories, ensured that, over time, 'a *knowing* bond' (Brian, Grendon) could develop, based on more profound and authentic judgements of personal character than that available from the more immediate markers of, for example, race and ethnicity, home area, or offence affinity. Since TC friendships could be 'different', they *produced* differences within residents, in what they valued in and wanted from their attachments. Instead of conversations limited to one's former lifestyle, present commercial interests, and the objectively petty but subjectively portentous preoccupations of daily prison life – or 'how many sugars are in the tea pack' (Robbie, Grendon) – the openness, sincerity, trust, and excoriating honesty that therapy required prompted changes to the content and calibre of everyday discussions, and hence to the quality of the attachment that could ensue:

> Me and [name of resident] are close and the conversations we have is like with brothers. But in a normal jail, if I spoke to him like that, he'd probably chin me because I'm speaking to him on a deep level. I'm asking him about his mum and dad, and in a normal prison, why would I want to know that? There are barriers, ain't there? Everyone's got an image and there ain't no deep conversations in normal jails. It's just about who made the most money, who's the hardest, who's going to sell drugs when they get out, what drugs they done, how many girls they've had, how fit their girlfriend is, and all this macho bullshit talk; that's all it is, *bullshit*. Here, we are dealing with stuff that's relevant. I'm getting to know [him] and who he really is. If he's got problems, I sit there and listen to him, to his intimate problems, and he does the same for me.
>
> (Stewart, Grendon)

Residents' (re)considerations about the true meaning and possibilities of friendship sometimes explicitly related to their individual criminogenic needs.

Leslie (Grendon), for example, described how he now understood that his sexual offending against children had been facilitated by his secretive compartmentalizing of his life:

> I had my friends, who knew nothing about my offending, and I had my offending. Here, for the first time in my life, I'm talking to people who *are* friends *about* my offending behaviour. They're mixing, my two lives. For me, that's helped a lot … It's made me realize, I need to be more open with people around me so that they can accept my attraction to children and help me with it … It's a much stronger friendship when you're not hiding, not dodging, this whole other part of you.

More frequently, though, participants acknowledged that sometimes they had committed offences because they had surrounded themselves, out of an overwhelming need for friendship and a desire to belong, with a network of people whose anomic delinquency (often accompanied by chronic substance abuse) was, at best, hardly conducive to 'staying out of trouble' and, at worst, actively supportive of and pivotally integral to the commission of crime. Others, from erroneous beliefs about the legitimate demands of friendship and loyalty, had felt unable to refuse 'a mate' who requested help in avenging a slight, or committing or concealing crime(s). Indeed, delinquent peers are implicated, with varying degrees of causality and agency, in the onset and maintenance of anti-social and criminal behaviour in a dizzying array of theories of crime. Conversely, and as Laub and Sampson (2003:32) succinctly explain, 'the account of desistance is the account of initiation in reverse'. Thus, to renounce offending, one needs to disassociate from such peers and forge instead attachments with people whose fundamental antipathy to deviance not only models and reinforces the attractions of 'going straight', but effectively reduces, if not actually eliminates, the former offender's exposure to criminogenic subcultures, temptations, and situations (Elliott and Menard 1996; Warr 1998, 2002; Giordano *et al.* 2003; Byrne and Trew 2008). To be able to criticize friends, to countenance discord or disapproval, or even to recognize and renounce a fundamentally unhealthy friendship, was accordingly understood by participants as a personal change which could reduce their susceptibility to malign peer influence in the future:

> Now I can be honest and open with people and say things, even at the detriment of them not liking what I say. That isn't going to take away from the fact that we're still friends. If I say something to someone and they don't necessarily agree with me, I'm not going to get the hump … And that works both ways: I appreciate them more for being honest with me and telling me some things which maybe I don't like to hear, but that are good for me, 'cos actually, a *true* friend does try to help you, don't they, rather than turn a blind eye?
>
> (James, Grendon)

> I knew [name of resident] from previous gaffs[14] … I do like [him] but I no longer feel the need to placate him or have him agree with me … I feel a bit of an outsider now, but maybe that's not such a bad thing because I've always needed to be in the mix of it, you know, the life and soul of the party … It's a shame because at one time, we were great mates, but I think I've kind of learned here to be more of my own man, you know, and that's a positive for me because in the past, I've done some really mad things to back up a mate.
>
> (Dominic, Grendon)

Participants were therefore clearly able to identify the ways in which establishing new conceptions of friendship were positively impacting upon their existing self-concept, changing the type of behavioural concordance with others they now sought, and informing the desistance-friendly 'new me' they hoped to become. In Sutherland's (1939) terms, the TC provided residents with a penal culture in which they could differentially associate with 'like-minded people who aren't going to wind you up and aren't going to take the piss, that you're actually *able* to have sensible conversations with about changing' (Callum, Grendon), and with whom they could therefore receive and reciprocate differential reinforcement of definitions and an emerging self-narrative which was less compatible with crime and criminal values.

The experience of *bidirectional* care amongst residents could therefore be of vital importance to offenders seeking to redefine their understanding of who they were and how they related to others. Residents' gradual acquisition of trust enabled them to share their experiences, receive – and, in time, to reciprocate – care, support, and assistance to others; and to change their conceptions of the nature and possibilities of genuine and pro-social friendship. In accordance with attachment theory, the safe frame provided by the therapeutic milieu could provide receptive residents with the opportunity to enjoy perhaps the first trusting, reliable, secure attachments of their adulthood. The 'toxic shame'[15] (Bradshaw 1988) engendered by their past was then reduced; a sense of self-acceptance and belonging, commonality and connection with others (re-)established; and feelings of self-efficacy, understanding of oneself, and empathy for others consequently enhanced.

Experiences of care: institutional factors

Opportunities for attachment formation and the demonstration of care were also institutionally advanced, through a number of uniquely TC situational and cultural factors. As the previous chapter detailed, the reciprocal use of first names bridged some of traditional 'them and us' divisions between prisoners and staff because 'first names, they put you on a level, don't they? As people, not just screws and cons' (Steve, GTC). Grendon – uniquely amongst similarly secure prisons – has no segregation unit: the traditional place of exile for prisoners who might most kindly be described, after Gelsthorpe and

Loucks (1997), as troubled *and* troublesome. Amongst Grendonites whose sentences had been punctuated with lengthy periods spent 'down the block', its absence therefore compounded residents' sense that their relationships with prison officers could be reassuringly 'different': 'They can't just twist you up[16] and dump you down the block, so you feel a lot safer with these screws. You know everything's above board here' (Richard, Grendon); and that prison officers expected different behaviours from residents: 'It just shows how much trust the staff have in us all to behave' (Dominic, Grendon). This mutual modification of conventional roles and assumptions was furthered by the easy sociability and inescapable 'intimacy' engendered by the limited size of the communities, the stability of a long-staying population, and the provision of communal spaces, which collectively ensured that all residents could become known to and regularly seen by all wing staff, and all wing staff could become known to and regularly seen by all residents. Self-evidently, one cannot become securely attached to people whom one rarely sees or with whom opportunities for meaningful interaction are highly curtailed.

Whilst residents frequently asserted, then, that 'in the system, I don't think most screws know you from Adam, and don't particularly want to' (Nigel, Grendon), they also conceded that in 'normal' long-term prisons, informal and supportive interactions between prisoners and officers were often difficult to achieve for various reasons, not least the large number of prisoners held on an average wing, shorter association periods, and normative prison culture which discourages socializing between officers and prisoners: 'In the system, if an officer talks to an inmate, he's bent. If an inmate talks to an officer, he's grassing. That's what it is' (Nate, Grendon).

In TCs, however, such distinctions and the constrained time frame for social communication is diminished. For example, mainstream prisoners cannot enter without invitation the wing office – officers' designated work space – and indeed to do so might incur the suspicion of other prisoners as to what was being discussed. At Grendon and GTC, however, the 'open-door' policy allowed residents to 'pop in' to the wing office throughout the day for a relaxing chat or to read newspapers *whilst* officers answered the telephone, made announcements on the Tannoy, and dealt with routine paperwork.[17] This afforded residents constant, 'legitimate', informal access to officers and normalized good-natured conversations and humorous banter between both parties, '[which is] important for someone like me because I struggle badly with authority, so I really need to sit in there, talking to officers' (Shane, Grendon). This in turn ensured that officers were approvingly perceived as permitting themselves to be known 'as people, as human beings; you can actually see who they are' (Chris, Grendon), behind the uniformed façade and authoritarian stereotype, and thus as individuals about whom residents could form and re-form their own 'evidence-based' assessments of trustworthiness and character. This ability 'to really suss out what sort of people they are, whether you can trust them' (Steve, GTC) was furthered on some communities, particularly during evening association, when residents and officers played board or card games together, or competed, individually or in mixed teams, in occasional 'quiz nights' or daytime sports.

Perhaps most significantly, though, a core TC service standard is that members are able to eat together in a communal room (Keenan and Paget 2008). Food has always been acknowledged by prison staff as 'one of the four things[18] you must get right if you like having a roof on your prison' (governor, cited in National Audit Office 2006:1). Meals punctuate the day and, if appetizing, can offer instant pleasure and consolation. Less obviously, as recent penological enquiries have uncovered, food can also represent a powerful source of rebellion and autonomy, individualism and agency. Such meanings may be gendered: whilst Valentine and Longstaff (1998) and Godderis (2006) emphasized the role of food in the complex contestation and negotiation of power relations amongst male prisoners and between prisoners and staff; Smith's (2002) research evidenced how women's dietary choices – whether of self-starvation, disciplined rejection, or conversely the 'comfort eating', of unhealthy foods – helped them to regulate their emotional response to, and resistance and survival of, imprisonment.

Considerably less attention has been given, however, to the significance of *where* one eats in prisons. To 'dine in association' with 'a decent tone of conversation' was introduced as a privilege from the 1920s (Prison Commissioners 1927:20, cited in Pratt 1998:494), and remains normal practice in the female estate. Send TC residents therefore ate in the prison's pleasant dining room (organized into three sittings, the order of which rotated), which notably allowed them, if they so chose, to socialize with mainstream women.

By contrast, from the 1980s onwards, dining rooms were largely removed from men's prisons in order to maximize 'occupational capacity' and so prioritize the provision of cellular accommodation over communal space, and because of their recognized 'flashpoint' potential.[19] The collection and consumption of institutional food, with its variable quality, limited variety, and controlled portion size, can become a metaphor for all of the diffuse frustrations, indignities, and dependencies occasioned by imprisonment, which sometimes translate into dissent, aggression, and violence among prisoners or against staff. The majority of male residents had therefore never eaten, in prison, in a dedicated dining room. They were accustomed instead to collecting their meals from wing serveries to consume on trays in their cells – 'feeding time, as the officers called it at [my last prison], like we're animals in a zoo' (Mark, Grendon) – or, if unlocked, as Robbie (Grendon) joked ironically, to eat 'standing up at the railings, talking to someone: classy, like Starbucks without the stool!'.

The expectation and enablement that residents of each community will eat together therefore represented a rare and 'very welcome change' (Roger, Grendon), which nearly all participants in this study thoroughly welcomed. Indeed, some male residents reported that they had no prior experience of commensality *at all*. The depth of familial neglect and childhood deprivation revealed by some responses to my innocuous question about the dining room was affecting, but, as this excerpt from my interview with a GTC resident shows, hinted at the remedial power of the TC's approximation of 'family meals':

> The first time [in the dining room], I was very uncomfortable. I didn't realize they done it here; no one told me until I got here.
>
> *What was it that made it so uncomfortable for you?*
>
> Because I've always ate on my own, always, through my life.
>
> *Even as a child?*
>
> Yeah. My mum was a drinker, do you know what I mean?
>
> *Right, so she couldn't really look after you …*
>
> No. She weren't interested. I mean, she gave me money for the chippie or whatever, go to the shops, you know, so it's not like I starved or nothing, but I always ate on my own.
>
> *So how do you feel about eating with other people now?*
>
> Oh, now it's great, 'cos it's like we're one big family. I'll eat with anyone now, now I done it. Yeah, I really like it now. I think they should do it in other prisons and all, 'cos I'm not the only one who's never had, like, family meals.

Moreover, the opportunity it affords to eat from plates 'at proper tables, like you're in a café or restaurant' (Raymond, GTC) contributed to residents' collective sense that they were living in a (relatively) normalizing, sociable environment where they were trusted and could trust their peers to behave appropriately. As a practical embodiment of the principle of communalism, dining together provided residents with thrice daily 'living-learning' opportunities for gaining social confidence and for expressing responsibility and care, for oneself and others, by maintaining a hygienic eating environment, sharing foodstuffs, and by acknowledging special occasions:

> I really do like the whole dining room thing. You get all the lads together, it's very sociable, a bit of banter, a bit of chat, and it really helps you to build strong relationships. I was kind of shocked to discover that I liked eating together but actually, it's very important; surprisingly powerful.
>
> (Ross, GTC)

> Some people are quite shy and do struggle with talking in front of people and being assertive, asking for things, and I think, just little things like the dining room, to have people around them, gives them some support and strength that they can build on. You know, maybe they've been bullied when queuing up in other nicks, so normally they'd alienate themselves, and I think to be able to eat with others here without any of that happening, and have meal times become an *enjoyable* event, can be a big step and a positive challenge for them.
>
> (Dave, Grendon)

> I'm a big fan of the dining room. You come here to join a community and eating together is part of it ... We all take turns cleaning the table, filling the salt, pepper, vinegar, whatever needs doing ... Our table, we've got all the sauces because we all take turns to buy something, so we have a really good selection! ... Normally in nick, it's every man for himself.
>
> (Dominic, Grendon)

> The leaving dinners[20] and Christmas, New Year, I like those. Obviously it's not like having a proper family Christmas dinner, but it makes it a bit more special, a bit more of an event, being able to sit down with people I get on with it and have a laugh. It lifts everyone's spirits because Christmas, you know, it's depressing for a lot of people.
>
> (Luke, Grendon)

The privilege of social dining also represented to residents further confirmation of the greater decency and respect accorded to them in a prison-based TC. Although food, in the form of a meagre and monotonous diet, may no longer contribute to the punishment of 'less eligible' prisoners, the 'very degrading' typical mainstream practice of 'eating in a toilet' (Bob, Grendon) continued to serve as a similarly acute signifier of residents' punitive exile from civilized standards, as these sentiments – made repeatedly by my participants – convey:

> You shouldn't have to eat where you shit. Sorry to be so blunt, but that's what they make you do on normal location. It's not right, it's not humane, is it?
>
> (Steve, GTC)

> Prison can really mess up your head, 'cos you don't do nothing normal. When I'm out, I don't get my dinner and take it to the bathroom to eat it, do I?
>
> (Stewart, Grendon)

> In your cell, it's where you live: you have to do everything in there, sleep and wash and use the toilet. So to have some elsewhere to go to eat, that's proper, well, it's not a lot to ask, is it?
>
> (Don, Grendon)

For most (male and female) residents, then, commensality was appreciated for its sociability and normality; for further forging a sense of shared experience of, and connectedness to, the TC way, outside of the structures of group therapy; and for the expression of care and decency it represents from penal institutions that do not require prisoners to eat adjacent to a lavatory, whilst enabling them to care for themselves and each other. The symbolic 'meaning' and importance of communal dining is therefore much greater than might at first appear to those 'on the out', or only accustomed to system incarceration, but as Andrew (Grendon) remarked about the dining room, 'Little things make a big difference, don't they?'

An ethic of care was therefore embedded into the very core of the TC's culture, expectations, and institutional practice (Stevens 2011). The TC enabled the social production of care through its creation of an alternative penal milieu in which both prisoners and prison officers were allowed and encouraged to behave differently to their conventional roles and ways of relating, working, and living within prison. The range of both structured and naturally, spontaneously occurring opportunities for sociability encouraged attachment formation between residents, and between residents and officers, and affirmed the greater equality residents enjoyed with prison staff in this, by penal standards, relaxed and informal environment. Moreover, residents' bidirectional experiences of care and emotional support, the reciprocal relationships of trust this promoted, and the depth of therapeutic discovery this allowed, contributed to an improving sense of self as a more empathetic and emotionally responsive individual, who was entirely capable of change and of assisting and supporting others to change.

5 Responsibility, accountability, and safety

> You have to be *very* responsible here: for yourself, for your behaviour and therapy, and also for other people and what's best for the community.
>
> (Raymond, GTC)

The neo-liberal discourse of personal responsibility pervades contemporary penal governance. The Prison Rules for England and Wales stress the rehabilitative imperative of treating prisoners so as 'to encourage their self-respect and a sense of personal responsibility' (Prison Rules 1999:5, para. 6 [3]); while early contributors to what became 'the decency agenda' espoused the importance of giving prisoners greater responsibility for their lives in prison and the life of the prison (Woolf 1991; Pilling 1992). In some establishments, prisoners may be able to participate in prisoner representative associations and (variously called and differently utilized) inter-wing meetings, joint consultative committees, prison councils, and lifestyle committees (Solomon and Edgar 2004; User Voice 2010), and restorative justice schemes (Edgar and Newell 2006); whilst peer support schemes, notably the adult literacy course, Toe-by-Toe, and the Samaritans-trained Listener scheme, which provides confidential emotional support to distressed and suicidal prisoners, are well established.[1]

Precisely what responsibility does – and ever can – mean in an environment more frequently associated with the painful and coerced deprivation of autonomy and the intrinsic denial of meaningful choices is considerably less clear, however, than these commendable pronouncements and initiatives suggest. For some observers, penal rhetoric about responsibility is obviated by the infantilizing reality of incarceration in secure conditions. Long-term prisoners are *expected* to comply dutifully with a micro-managed, largely non-negotiable, extensively regulated, repetitive, and restricted regime, and thus to become regressively and pervasively dependent upon the decisions, instructions, and discretionary powers of prison staff (Goffman 1961; Irwin and Owen 2005). The prison's understandable preoccupation with, if sometimes 'excess of caution' about, security, control, and order, has the regrettable tendency to produce a 'fearful loss of self-determination' amongst its captives

(Sykes 1958:133), so that prisoners' very capacity for mature agency, so necessary upon release, is eroded (Goffman 1961; Irwin and Owen 2005); and to breed institutionalized practices which unnecessarily remove responsibility from – and hence, effectively deny responsibility to – prisoners (Pryor 2001, 2004). As one of my interviewees cheerfully confirmed: 'In the system, you're not even thought *capable* of being responsible, so you don't have to be, which of course suits a lot of cons perfectly' (Ross, GTC).

Other scholars have documented how the concept of personal responsibility *for* offenders has become confused with and contaminated by the less noble aims of 'responsibilization' *of* offenders. This ensures that while the state 'retains all its traditional functions ... and, in addition, takes on a new set of co-ordinating and activating roles' (Garland 1996:454), it discursively transfers its responsibility for rehabilitation and risk management to the individual offender. Through, for example, the 'nudge' provided by admission and orientation literature (Bosworth 2007); Offender Assessment System (OASys) and sentence plans which identify risk factors and recommend, as discussed earlier, that prisoners 'volunteer' for OBPs; the provision of education and skills training; the inducements of the IEP scheme, security recategorization, and temporary and early release, including parole; and regular reporting upon prisoners' perceived attitudes as well as observable behaviour, the prison communicates to its captives the desirability of becoming a 'responsible' – meaning here, a self-reforming, self-regulating, utility-maximizing, regime-compliant – prisoner. Simultaneously, however, the prison employs ever more detailed and prescriptive, at-a-distance and automated arrangements of surveillance and monitoring – closed-circuit television, random mandatory drug tests (MDT), cell searches, mobile phone detection, and so on – lest prisoners should persist in being 'irresponsible'. The institution thus demands self-governance and autonomy from the individual whilst augmenting its mechanisms of control and disciplinary governance over the individual (Hannah-Moffat 2001, 2005; Garland 1996, 1997).

To some then, the notion of a truly 'responsible prisoner' (Pryor 2001) remains an oxymoron. This chapter, however, shows how the prison's incoherent inclination to reduce prisoners 'to the weak, helpless, dependent status of childhood' (Sykes 1958:75) while simultaneously demanding their responsibilization, is negated in the TC through its promotion of '*real* responsibility'. The chapter begins by analysing how residents were encouraged to claim ownership of their community, before detailing how their responsibilities extended beyond accountability for their own conduct to include the monitoring, policing, and challenging of others.

Experiences of responsibility: consultation and contribution

To reiterate momentarily, then, Pryor's (2001, 2004) argument (amongst others) that prisoners are often institutionally impeded from being responsible, it was significant that in discussing responsibility, interviewees invariably stressed the myriad ways in which, by comparison with the mainstream, they felt they were required in the TC to be more responsible for their day-to-day conduct:

> My last nick, absolutely everything was done for me … When I first come away, I had a seriously nice watch and after a few months I handed it out to my people, 'cos I didn't need it. The screws told you what to do, when. Here, I've got to keep track of time and what I'm doing all the time.
>
> (Sandeep, Grendon)

> You have to get up and get to groups on time; you're not called. You're not called to dinner; it's your responsibility to turn up. If you're ready for a ROTL, the staff won't come up to you and say, 'You should go for this'; it's your responsibility to get the forms and get backing for it.
>
> *How is that different to the system? You have to get up and go to work there …*
>
> But there are no *major* consequences of not getting up, not going to work – you'll get a nicking,[2] loss of privileges, something like that – but here, you're answerable to everyone. And I don't know anyone who wouldn't rather take the nicking than explain themselves to their group! It's about learning the consequences of what we do, and owning that responsibility, and having respect for others.
>
> (Tim, Grendon)

Besides this promotion of self-reliance, punctuality, and being 'answerable to everyone', discussed in the second half of this chapter, residents were enabled to contribute responsibly for their living environment through their participation in community meetings and their performance of 'rep[resentative] jobs': two different tasks which produced very similar beneficial results.

It will be remembered, then, that the bi-weekly community meeting, chaired by an elected resident, provides the forum in which the whole community can deliberate and decide upon, with votes cast by a show of hands, 'everything that affects our community, because it is *our* community' (Belinda, Send). This 'everything' literally can include consideration of administrative issues – decisions about, for example, proposed changes to the community's constitution or the redecoration of the community and members' preferred choice of colour scheme – and a 'deeper' search for the 'meaning' behind residents' requests for 'backings' for particular employment opportunities, education, recategorization, or ROTLs,[3] or the reasons for the problematic behaviours of, and difficulties between, individual members. The meeting's dual executive and psychotherapeutic function therefore pits the structure, efficiency, and reasoned calm of agenda-led 'business' against the unstructured, chaotic, raw exposure of group dynamics and individual psychopathology; producing a creative tension that can be as instructively uncomfortable for the residents as it is clinically informative for the staff. Indeed, the very unpredictability, in both content and experiential quality, of community meetings – the routine coexistence of scripted order, soporific mundaneness, respectful negotiation, liberating enfranchisement, and considered debate *and* nerve-shredding confrontation, regressive defensiveness, internal politics, collective bargaining, and individual evisceration – explains why participants' evaluations of the 'average' meeting were so equally diverse:

> I love them! The place wouldn't work without them; it's like the glue that holds everything together. And you never know what's going to happen. If you miss one 'cos you're ill or something, it's like missing your favourite soap: you haven't a clue what's happening!
>
> (Alan, Grendon)

> I *hate* them! Tell me to run round the prison a hundred laps for that time and I'll do it rather than them meetings! Who puts prisoners in charge? I don't like the voting thing! I don't like prisoners making rules! I don't like the responsibility! [laughing]
>
> (Louise, Send)

> Fascinating and very beneficial.
>
> (Raymond, GTC)

> Dull and monotonous; tedious beyond belief.
>
> (Keith, Grendon)

> They're very important, but not enough good work gets done on them. Often, that time is wasted in talking about trivial things … On occasion, it'll be mind-blowing, when it's like an extension of the small group but involving the whole community in someone's therapy. Then, you can learn something … So I'd say some are good, a few are *great*, and some are just laborious.
>
> (Brian, Grendon)

The TC's enthusiasm for resident-led consultation and non-hierarchical social relations, however, does not confound the Orwellian maxim that whilst all members are equal, some are more equal than others. The staff group retains the ultimate power to veto or remit for further debate residents' expressed wishes, and to exclude them from certain managerial discussions and decisions. Residents' involvement in the community's governance therefore constitutes democratization (Rapoport 1960), not democracy; or as one therapist succinctly noted: 'It's democratic to the point of us saying no!' (Anne). This limitation was accepted by participants, however, as entirely realistic – 'the bottom line is that this *is* a prison!' (Roger, Grendon) – and sensible: 'I have faith that the staff are functional people who have got my best interests at heart and know more than me and see the bigger picture' (Brian, Grendon). In other words, residents were 'very happy' to 'have *a* say' and were little troubled by the fact it was not and could not be '*the* final say' (Lee, GTC).

Moreover, residents emphatically distinguished consultation, the TC way, from the various consultative committees available in a minority of mainstream prisons. Here, prisoner representatives from each wing convey the views of their peers to, and are consulted by, governors upon regime-related topics. Interviewees who had experienced these councils, however, whilst enthusiastic about their underlying principles, were critical of the councils' very limited and narrowly defined remit in practice; disappointed by their seeming ineffectiveness; opposed to any employment of 'rent-a-cons' (Andrew, Grendon), that is, reps selected by prison officers rather than elected by their peers; and amusingly sceptical about governors' motives for supporting prisoner engagement:

> We had a lifestyle committee at [a high-security prison] but it was just to do with canteen problems, facilities list, and the like. It wasn't about inmates' behaviour or offending, like here. Nothing ever came of it. Everything we suggested was given the elbow. To be honest with you, I think it was just a paper exercise, so the governor could say, 'Look, we're talking to 'em, aren't we good?' You know, to look good for the Inspectors! [laughs]
>
> (Eddie, Grendon)

Community meetings were accordingly perceived by participants as an exercise in empowerment, self-governance, and democratization without parallel in the penal estate: 'You feel part of how things are run … valued as a person [and] trusted to be able to think for himself and to have, you know, *sensible* opinions' (Leslie, Grendon). The greater depth and breadth of their terms of reference, the onus placed on residents to 'make things happen' and to make sure that 'things happened' as agreed – including, when necessary, chivvying along residents *and staff* to follow up enquiries or complete their allocated tasks – and the staff's relinquishment or sharing of at least some power to residents, was widely welcomed.

This trusting delegation of power was evident in the chairing of the meeting by a resident, not a member of staff: 'Can you imagine that in the system? I mean, really, isn't that *amazing*? They let one of us be in charge!' (Joe, Grendon). The chair's responsibilities extended beyond presiding over the meeting to encompass deciding which agenda items were discussed, in what order, for how long, and whether it was necessary or desirable to hold a commitment (or at GTC, reflection[4]) vote, and to act at all times as the chief conduit for bidirectional liaison between staff and residents. The chair was assisted by a deputy who took the minutes, and who in some communities had to first serve in (and so train for) this position before being promoted to the 'top job'.

The complexities of the chair's position are best illustrated by the following entirely unexceptional example of a fractious (GTC) community meeting. The chairman repeatedly encouraged – or from an alternative perspective, pressurized – one curtly communicative and darkly brooding resident to explain why he had walked out of his small group when asked to discuss his alleged involvement in a recent controversy, but without success. The chairman then had to decide whether this resident might 'open up' if the meeting were extended beyond its scheduled finish time; a suggestion residents debated at length, rather irritably, and in an atmosphere of rapidly escalating tension. No member of staff offered any opinion on how to proceed. Another resident then began denigrating – in imaginatively scatological and anatomically specific language – the chairman's abilities and character, and stormed out of the meeting; immediately followed by the tight-lipped resident – who noisily displaced his frustrations onto items of furniture en route to his cell – and one other who said he was 'fed up' and couldn't 'be arsed a moment longer' with the 'pointless and stupid' proceedings. The meeting then concluded at its normal time without any resolution of the original issue, and with these new misdemeanours now automatically added to next week's agenda (fieldnotes).

In their subsequent debrief, staff members opined that this chairman – a 'people pleaser' – had yet to learn how to take difficult and sometimes inevitably unpopular decisions, and to remain in control without being overly controlling. When I interviewed the chairman, however, he described how he had felt 'badly let down' and unsupported by the community and, in particular, by staff, that day – 'I felt alone in my courage … no one shared in my experience and that was frustrating' – because he considered himself to have been in 'a no-win situation': criticized by some residents for not showing 'strong leadership' because he declined to decide unilaterally to close or extend the meeting; whilst others – including the 'fed up' community member, also an interviewee – berated him for 'having a go' at the silent resident because '[the chairman]'s an inmate who thinks he's an officer!'

As other present and former chairpersons recounted, then, the successful performance of this role required a taxing blend of leadership qualities and diplomatic sensibilities, and an appreciation of the intricate dilemmas that power and boundary setting can entail. One must try to make impartial but decisive judgements in volatile situations, to which there may be no 'correct' or universally palatable solution, to assert one's authority without being aggressively autocratic, and to tolerate the discomfort of being both a personally responsible prisoner and a community member 'in charge' of one's peers:

> You sort of have to see all sides, what everyone needs, but you can't have no favourites. You have to give everyone their go, no matter what you

> think of them or what bullshit they're spouting off about. That's hard to do. I get on with most people, right, but being chairman, it kind of learns you that if you have some power, not everyone is going to like you no more when you don't do what they want or call it the way they see it, and you have to suffer that.
>
> (Lenny, Grendon)

'Community service', the TC way

Whereas only a few residents become chair, all residents were expected to undertake a succession of diverse rep jobs, 'doing things not just for you but for other people, and if you don't, things are messed up for everyone, so that teaches you something about responsibility you won't get elsewhere' (Muktar, Grendon). Examples of the more demanding rep jobs (particularly in evidence at Grendon), obtainable after the initial commitment period, included responsibility for the community's entertainment and for health and hygiene compliance; contributing to the prison's drug strategy and violence reduction meetings; and all aspects of planning and orchestrating social events for one's visiting family and friends or for invited members of the public.[5] As with the chairpersonship, residents had to apply for and be elected to rep jobs on the basis of their demonstrable developmental need. Thus, rather than work being assigned to them by prison officers or selected upon the basis of availability, residents had to make a consciously reasoned and defendable choice:

> It's very worthwhile to be challenged about what rep job you want. When I first heard about it, I thought, you can't be serious! But actually, when you think about it, we've all made wrong decisions otherwise we wouldn't be here, and it gives you a chance to hear other people's comments on your decision making. It's hard to take sometimes but it's good because it makes you think again; to take a step back and look at your reasons. Whereas in the system, you would just do it without thinking.
>
> (Leslie, Grendon)

Whenever residents were in competition for the same position, it was not necessarily awarded to 'the best person for the job', but rather to the resident who would 'get the most out of it, therapeutically; it'll bring up issues for them' (Peter, Grendon). This could require residents to elevate the therapeutic needs of others over the interests of their friends, and thereby to learn the potentially desistance-supportive lesson that there could be 'other norms, held to be more pressing or involving a higher loyalty' (Sykes and Matza 1957:669), than fulfilling the perceived demands of friendships:

> Obviously, you would think criminals would be staunch for each other and would abide by their mates. [On a recent rep job vote], I felt like

> I was going against my mate, against all my criminal values. But the other fella's reasons were very strong, so I voted for him. He needed it more.
>
> *How did your friend feel about that?*
>
> He was all right about it; he knows it's a Grendon thing. You've got to learn to do the right thing here, the responsible thing, and not just follow the criminal values you've lived by all your life.
>
> (Paul, Grendon)

Sometimes the 'issues' raised by rep jobs related to the individual's risk factors and therapeutic targets: one Grendonite who had 'liquidized his hamster' as a child, for example, accepted responsibility for cleaning the community's fish tank.[6] More typically, though, this principle meant that, for example, former drug users joined the drugs strategy; those who lacked organizational or social skills took on roles requiring a high degree of organization or sociability; and those who had experienced difficulties with budgeting or gambling 'on the out' became the finance rep, responsible for accounting for residents' weekly contributions to, and the collective expenditure from, the community's social fund. To some degree, then, all rep jobs were expected to test and hence, through practice, to develop, residents' interpersonal, communication, decision-making, and problem-solving skills:

> Even the simplest job has certain challenges. It may even be that it's boring and simple and how do you tolerate that? If someone is going to leave prison and get a job, he may have to stack shelves in Tesco and how does he feel about that? How does he manage being bored rather than saying, 'Sod this, I'm going down the pub!' So there is a therapeutic challenge in everything: not to take decisions impulsively, to be responsible, to get on with people, to focus on doing the job well.
>
> (George, therapist)

What community meetings and rep jobs shared was that they were perceived by interviewees as self-esteem enhancing and dependency-reducing. TCs, with their psychiatric origins in rebuilding men traumatized by war, understand that one way to make a damaged person less damaging to others is to improve self-esteem: people who feel good about themselves do not generally feel compelled to make other people feel bad. Specifically, self-determination theory (Deci and Ryan 1985, 2000; Ryan and Deci 2000) (a macro theory of human motivation and personality) postulates that human beings are predisposed to seek autonomy, relatedness, and competence – 'a propensity to have an effect on the environment as well as to attain valued outcomes within it' (Deci and Ryan 2000: 231) – and that these fundamental needs (or 'innate psychological nutriments') are essential for ongoing psychological health and development, motivation, and the achievement of effectiveness, connectedness, and coherence. When these needs are thwarted, individuals will inevitably suffer psychological distress and, Deci and Ryan contend, develop dysfunctional compensatory strategies and 'substitute fulfilments', as seen most acutely in the emergence of psychopathy. Supportive social contexts or environments, however, which satisfy these three core needs, can provide an important emotional corrective and act as a powerful influence upon the maintenance or enhancement of the motivation necessary to contemplate and realize change (Stevens 2012). Through choosing and successfully undertaking work, then, which residents perceived to be intrinsically worthwhile and which resulted in some mutually beneficial consequences ('valued outcomes') for their community – whether that be a 'voice' heard and responded to in a managerial meeting, an enjoyable and efficiently organized social event, or a sparklingly cleaned fish tank – the resulting sense of achievement and competency, validated by others, further improved residents' self-esteem, self-respect, and sense of self-efficacy and prompted them to re-examine any disempowering beliefs they held about who they 'naturally' were and of what they were capable:

> I never really believed I could be anything better; it's very hard to think highly of yourself when you're a drug addict and committing crimes, you know? … [My rep job] showed me that I've got a good head on my shoulders and it can be put to good use; I am capable of *more*; I can be someone totally different, basically – that's what this place gives you … Having that say [in community meetings] – although obviously there are limits – it doesn't make us feel as if we are convicts. It makes us feel as if we're humans, adults; we're part of the process of what goes on here and not just here to do therapy. What we say actually counts for something. It's our community and we have a big say in the running of it. Where else would you get that?
>
> (Nate, Grendon)

> I never had a high opinion of myself at all. I just generally hated myself and never thought I would amount to anything … But it's started to change for me, from actually achieving things … I always hated speaking up before and now I go into meetings with governors and what have you and say my piece, and the lads look to me to get things done. That's a big responsibility and, you know what, I'm bloody good at it! [laughs]
>
> (Callum, Grendon)

> [Being family day rep] allows you to better yourself and prove yourself to the lads and to know that you've done something worthwhile for the community and it's been massively appreciated. I never really thought of myself as an organized person before or a generous person but I am, that's what people have told me, because of the way I did that job. Yeah,

> I put a lot of energy into that, I got real satisfaction out of it, and I felt proud of myself – which ain't normal for me!
>
> (Alan, Grendon)

Two other themes can be gleaned from the above quotes. To assume a role successfully is to commit to the normative behaviours and attitudes associated with those roles (Ebaugh 1988). In successfully enacting a positive social role in the community – as an organizer, a committee member, a responsible and autonomous individual upon whom others rely – the resident began to perceive that he or she was responsible, autonomous, and reliable. This subjective sense of accomplishment was objectively confirmed by the community's affirmation. Since one's identity consists of both one's private self-image and one's social identity, perceived, bestowed, and sustained by others, the latter influences the former, ensuring that the 'looking-glass' self always responds to interactions with, and the evaluations of, others (Cooley 1902; Goffman 1959; Tajfel 1982; Jenkins 2004). Accordingly then, whenever residents received the recognition, praise, and gratitude of their peers for their well-performed and effective 'community service', and had their responsible behaviours and pro-social inclinations validated, this positively reflected upon and powerfully reinforced their improving self-concept because, to pursue the 'looking-glass' metaphor, they could 'see' themselves as others told them they 'saw' them. Put simply, people who want to desist from crime are more likely to do so when significant others – here, community members – believe in the offender's ability to change *and* communicate that belief (Maruna *et al.* 2004, 2009).

Second, and similarly, although labelling theory has tended to emphasize the dire consequences of stigma and spoiled identity (Goffman 1963), and the 'Golem effect' of low expectations leading to poor outcomes, the converse can occur: a 'Pygmalion effect' when high expectations of 'better things' propel a would-be desister to greater self-belief and behaviours that concord with the attainment of 'better things' (Maruna *et al.* 2009). In overcoming the challenges presented by the demands of 'speaking up' and of rep jobs, residents were enabled to focus not upon their cognitive-behavioural deficits, failings, and risk factors, but rather upon their skills, abilities, and potential. This capability-building emphasis, as advocates of a good lives model of offender rehabilitation (Ward and Brown 2004; Ward and Maruna 2007), strengths-based resettlement (Maruna and LeBel 2002; Uggen *et al.* 2004; Burnett and Maruna 2006), 'altruistic activity' (Toch 2000), and active citizenship and volunteering (Farrant and Levenson 2002; Edgar *et al.* 2011) by prisoners have identified, bestows self-worth and the agentic determination to reorder the direction of one's life in pursuit of these strengths. The acquisition of new skill sets and discursive resources which are not only consistent with rehabilitation, but positively exclude the behaviours, cognitions, and self-concepts favourable towards offending, therefore further contributed to the process of differentiation from the 'old' identity and the certification of a 'new', 'better' 'possible self' (Oyserman and Markus 1990) committed to change. In short, and in addition to the self-esteem enhancing experience of providing peer support discussed in the previous chapter, the forms of community service available to TC residents transformed them into a 'giver rather than a consumer of help' (Maruna and LeBel 2002:169). The opportunities they enjoyed to 'try on' and rehearse new pro-social roles encouraged them over time to conceive of themselves as someone worthy of esteem and respect, and 'capable of more', mastery, and generative contribution (Stevens 2012).

The experience, then, of 'some *real* responsibility, which, let's be honest, is a novelty for most of us!' (Steve, GTC); of taking decisions and exercising choice; of completing tasks – or, to revive an unloved term, performing community service – of benefit both practically to others and developmentally to the individual; and of developing – or for some people, pro-socially redeveloping – their repertoire of transferable and marketable skills, was unequivocally welcomed by participants and recognized as an important facilitator of change:

> [Being chair has] heaped responsibility on me and as a con, it's taught me something about power and the responsibility that comes with that … We've got some characters in the community that just like to create[7] and I find that really quite tiresome now. It's made me realize that anger is still there for me, and will probably always be there, but it's also made me aware that I deal with it differently now. I can feel aggrieved, and feel under attack, and sit back and approach it in a different way, instead of just firing off … I've always been quite organized in my criminal activities, but what I've done here is, I've used those skills for the benefit of our community – which is better, obviously!
>
> (Bill, Grendon)

> I'm drugs strat[egy] … It does feel surreal sometimes, like, I'm sitting here with governors and officers, *what* am I doing? I'm talking with them about inmates with positives[8] and how drugs get into prison – it's mad! … I suppose it is a bit uncomfortable at times, ain't it, but it does make you think about the serious harm drugs do and the violence and corruption that goes with 'em, which I'd never really took on board before. So I'm doing something beneficial with this job and it shows me I'm changing.
>
> (Nick, Grendon)

Experiences of responsibility: accountability and challenge

Criminologists have long sought to establish whether 'environmental effects' of different prison regimes can influence prisoner behaviour for the better (or worse) and, if so, why and how this is achieved (for example, DiIulio 1987; Bottoms *et al.* 1990; Sparks *et al.* 1996; Camp and Gaes 2005). Quantitative research at Grendon has revealed that it has consistently enjoyed the lowest rate of adjudications (internal disciplinary hearings) of any category B prison, notwithstanding that it admits men with alarming adjudication histories at other establishments (Gray 1973a; Cullen 1994; Newton 2010). Prison-based TCs prefer to address relatively minor misbehaviour through therapeutic enquiry, rather than formal disciplinary powers, so this finding could appear self-explanatory. No such discretion applies, however, to serious offences against prison discipline, including a positive MDT, which must be referred for adjudication. Newton (2006, 2010) was therefore able to calculate that Grendon's 2002 adjudication rate, when proportionately (per 100 prisoners per establishment) compared to other category B training prisons, was an impressive five times lower for all offences, and seven times lower for violent offences. Individual residents' adjudication rates of violent assault against staff, against other prisoners, and for drug-related offences, were also respectively ten, twelve, and again twelve, times lower at Grendon for these offences than at their previous establishments. Reductions in adjudication rates were also sustained to a significant extent when ex-Grendonites returned to mainstream prisons. Grendonites' improved behaviour cannot therefore be entirely attributed to the TC's avoidance of adjudications, but suggests that some TC-specific regime effect occurs (see similarly Cooke 1991; Dietz *et al.* 2003).

The greatly reduced levels of violence and general misbehaviour in TCs fostered a pervasive sense of safety: 'you're completely safe, you don't have to watch your back here at all' (Dave, Grendon); 'you feel very safe here, physically and emotionally' (Jenny, Send). This was maintained by the TC's reliance upon residents to monitor and challenge as necessary their peers' behaviour, and from the reiterative reassertion of its values and required behaviours.

The TC way of dealing with relatively minor infractions, then, is to hold residents accountable to their community, rather than an adjudicating governor. This was because, as will be elucidated further below, collective examination of the misdemeanour in community meetings invites therapeutically informative understanding of the 'meaning' and implications of that misbehaviour, of benefit to the whole community. TCs expect their residents 'to push boundaries' and indeed need them to do so because otherwise residents cannot learn where the boundaries lie; or, as Shane (Grendon) put it, 'making mistakes isn't seen as a bad thing here. They want you to fuck up really, because it will make you look at yourself and talk about your issues'. Moreover, by being able (mostly) to contain and tolerate within the community highly volatile emotions and 'unacceptable' aspects of personality and behaviour, the TC communicates to its resident that it is possible in time for them similarly to learn to contain their emotions and tolerate the less desirable aspects of themselves (Downie 2004).

Residents therefore had to accept that their private 'mistakes' would be subjected to public interrogation, in which they would be challenged – and in the process, receive candid corrective information or 'therapeutic feedback' – on any and all aspects of their conduct *which their peers thought* was unacceptable and detrimental to a safe, respectful and, hence, therapy-conducive environment. Such public examination of individual problems possessed a wider educational purpose, in which both the resident and his or her community were encouraged to look for indicators of mental and emotional rehearsal of the 'issue' and thus of how thoughts and emotions had propelled actions. To borrow from the language of cognitive-behavioural offending programmes, the value of challenges therefore lay not just in understanding what had happened and why, but how the cycle of offending could be broken, risk awareness and relapse prevention prospectively promoted, and alternative coping strategies prepared.

These challenges occurred mostly within the individual's small group – the experience of being 'grouped' – but, for more serious matters or problems concerning members of other therapy groups, were continued in community meetings – being 'winged' – and could culminate in a commitment vote to ascertain residents' views on whether the offender's commitment to the TC was so irrevocably weakened that his or her membership should be revoked. Since I could not attend small group therapy sessions, all my observations of, and most discussions about, challenges occurred when residents were winged for a variety of prison offences: the supply and consumption of illicit drugs and alcohol, for example, or assault and intimidation, theft, the possession of 'unauthorized articles', and other sundry forms of 'skulduggery and mischief; you can still get up to all sorts in prison if you put your mind to it!' (Paul, Grendon). Accordingly, my data do not fairly represent the much wider and more minor – some residents suggested, 'trivial' – assortment of challenges that related to (person-limited) 'failings' and (interpersonal but, as yet, inconsequential) conflicts that could remain within the jurisdiction of the resident's group, and may therefore give the wholly inaccurate impression that 'naughty stuff' (Bill, Grendon) was an extensive problem. On the contrary, the difficulties discussed below must be understood within the context of their *relative* infrequency compared to mainstream prisons, where, in particular, drug misuse and violence are prevalent, if woefully undetected and under-reported.[9] However, the pronounced thematic similarities between factually disparate incidents in the TC explored below illuminates how prison-based TCs seek to attain penal order, control, and safety through the inculcation of personal and collective responsibility and the pre-eminence of social incentives over situational deterrents.

Residents could be challenged on their attitudes or behaviours either by confessing to and seeking advice and support on some 'issue' that troubled them, or, more frequently, following an allegation of wrongdoing made against them by another resident (known as putting someone 'in the book' or 'on the agenda'). The responsibility therefore lay with residents themselves to identify 'issues', a fortuitous bi-product of which was that it rendered the subsequent challenges both more credible and less threatening than if they emanated from prison staff. Fellow 'cons' were already acutely attuned to prisoners' propensity for self-pitying 'sad tales' (Goffman 1961) and were very familiar with every possible permutation of justificatory and comforting tactics for denying, minimizing, or rationalizing one's less admirable characteristics or objectionable behaviours (Sykes and Matza 1957). Any attempt by the person 'in the hot seat' to gloss over the negative consequences of what he or she had done was therefore easily defeated, and could not be as lightly dismissed as the predictable disapproval of an adjudicating governor. After all, 'you can't con a con'. Given the culture of challenge and feedback, it was also harder for residents merely to 'talk the talk' in the public 'frontstage' arena of small groups and community meetings, whilst maintaining the same anti-social attitudes and behaviours in the private 'backstage' world of the residential landings (Goffman 1959):

> If I'm going to sit in my group and spout shit, I can't then go on the landings and say the exact opposite, 'I'm blagging them', because the next day, it will be put on me. So if you're going to hold up a false front and blag, then you've got to blag every day for three years, so you've got to be really good at it and have a really good memory!
>
> (Stewart, Grendon)

Many disclosures therefore related to residents' observations of transgressions of which staff were, and would otherwise have remained, unaware[10] – and hence, in prison parlance, required residents to 'grass up' a fellow 'con'. As noted earlier, given that, to most prisoners, informing on one's peers is still only 'understandable' or excusable in certain exigent circumstances (Crewe 2005a), this was an instinctively difficult aspect of therapeutization for many new recruits. Some residents reported, however, that they continued to feel that they could not, or could not *always*, proffer information or therapeutic feedback on their peers. This was conspicuously the case when the 'naughty stuff' in question involved drugs, and its usual companions, an incessant layer of subterfuge and the lingering stain of compromise. For these participants, the stigma of 'grassing', the fear of reprisals upon return to the mainstream, and/or, more murkily, their complicity, effectively ensured their silence. Intermittent incidents of the failure of therapeutic feedback and the abdication of responsibility that this entailed were therefore pragmatically – though certainly regretfully – accepted by staff as 'an inevitable fact of prison life' (Gareth, officer). Several Send and GTC participants also argued that, in this regard, their location within a mainstream prison – to which they returned daily – detracted from their ability to give feedback:

> Grendon is its own prison, so you wouldn't have to worry about the normal prison rules so much but here, you really do. You put it on someone and they will go back on the mains and tell everyone you're a grass, and that can have some *serious* consequences and follow you

> around for a long time, specially for a lifer … So for staff to expect us to, basically, grass someone up is not very realistic.
>
> (Francis, GTC)

For others, their willingness to feedback was contingent upon their judgement of the severity of the offence, and concerns about the disproportional or 'unfair' penalty that might arise should that offence become known. These residents differentiated between drugs, for example, notwithstanding the TC's clear prohibition against consumption of all illicit substances. They argued that the occasional and 'harmless' use of cannabis did not need to be disclosed and so risk exposing the user to a commitment vote and the possibility of expulsion. It might, however, warrant 'a quiet word' between residents; in effect, a private challenge:

> I will say anything to anyone if I think it will help them, but there are things I *won't* say in the small group or the community meeting. [Cannabis], for example. There is not a chance in hell I would mention that in front of staff but I would go to the person's cell and ask him what he thought he was playing at … There are some things I will not do and grassing is one of them – and it is a very fine line between grassing and therapeutic feedback, *very fine.*
>
> (Ross, GTC)

'Hard stuff' such as heroin, conversely, was thought to pose a much greater risk to the individual's health and the psychological and physical safety of the community and thus should 'probably always' be challenged publicly:

> That's different; that can fuck things up for everyone else. It's not just about you then. He'd just have to take his chances in a vote. But I'm not putting someone in the book for a harmless bit of puff. No way.
>
> (Nigel, Grendon)

The majority of interviewees, however, did not feel the need to question or redefine which TC 'offences' were 'really' serious or to second guess whether any resulting penalty would be 'fair'. They reinterpreted 'grassing' as constructive criticism, intended to help the recipient, and more consistently felt able to feedback whenever the TC's rules were broken or its values undermined:

> I used to be staunch about no grassing; it's just a major rule of prison life. But I have no qualms about it here because it's not grassing: it's feedback to help someone with his behaviours and to keep the community safe.
>
> (Steve, GTC)

> In this environment, we are the best police. We know what's going on. The staff don't know what goes on upstairs. It's us that brings it into the room and says, 'You threatened him' ... If I see someone doing drugs or smuggling drugs in, I'll stick it on[11] them. I'd tell one of the staff, I'd do it blatantly because I don't want that for this place ... We've got very little naughty stuff going on here and that's down to us, you know, because *we* decide it's going to be a safe environment.
>
> (Bill, Grendon)

> If there are any fights or arguments, we're the ones that stop it. I was nearly scalded with a boiling kettle on the threes[12] and it was other guys who stopped it. They got in the way, took the kettle off the guy, took me to my cell, then went and got staff. They didn't know nothing about it – they were in the office. It could easily have got brushed under the carpet.
>
> *And perhaps would have been elsewhere?*
>
> Oh for sure, because if you went to staff, you're a grass, aren't you? ... Sometimes people will say, 'Why weren't staff around when it kicked off? Why was it left to us?' But on the other hand, it's good that the responsibility is put on us because if staff are doing everything, then it's the same as a system prison, isn't it? We've been irresponsible all our lives, most of us, and it's good that a lot of responsibility is put on our shoulders to deal with the issues in our community.
>
> (Danny, Grendon)

Resident responsibility 'to keep the community safe' and 'to deal with the issues in our community' was at its most visible when members met to deliberate and vote upon whether the residency of one of their number should continue. The community's discussion on these occasions revolved around three principal but closely interrelated concerns: namely, the need for absolute honesty; the importance of an appreciation of the consequences, for oneself and others; and the reassertion of the desirability of TC norms.

At minimum, then, residents needed – even if only after initial denial – to be honest about their behaviour: 'People will work with you, *if* you're honest' (Bob, Grendon). A refusal to acknowledge one's culpability, however, indicated to the community that the resident was unwilling and/or unable to engage in therapy and the pursuit of rehabilitation with the requisite sincerity:

> I've made mistakes and admitted them and been allowed to work through them ... So I do believe in giving people a chance but if someone totally denies it, well, then I think, what can we do to help you if you won't help yourself? So like [name of recently expelled resident], I said to him when he failed his MDT, 'You're talking bollocks, mate, and you just need to own up to it, and then we can talk about it and move on.' But because he wouldn't admit it, I was thinking, as much as I want to help

> you, you've got to go, because for therapy to work, you have got to be honest.
>
> *So you voted him out?*
>
> Yeah, I did. If he'd just been honest, but when he couldn't even do that … Sometimes you feel like *you* want someone to change more than he does, which obviously, is no good. So then, unfortunately, he has to go.
>
> (Neil, Grendon)

The significance of honesty extended beyond factual veracity to an implied understanding that deceit and wrongdoing not only harmed the individual but also the community, and thus could impact upon a wider network of people, in less obvious ways, than the 'offender' and any primary 'victim'. A resident who abdicated his responsibilities to himself, in effect, could be 'worked with', but not necessarily one who demonstrated – or more likely, *continued* to demonstrate – an irresponsible attitude towards the physical, emotional, and psychological safety of the community. A failure to comprehend that one's own substance abuse, for example, elevated the risk of relapse amongst other community members, and 'linked into' residents' wider anxieties about attachment and trust, could therefore quickly exhaust the limits of the community's patience. As with rep job selection, residents might then prefer their higher loyalty and obligations to the community over the undoubted rehabilitative needs of any one individual.

The commitment vote of a Grendonite who had failed a MDT for the second time within six months illustrates this observation clearly. The perpetrator seemed contrite, cited in mitigation recent distressing events in his personal life, and pleaded for 'one more chance'. Residents who had advocated his continuing membership after the first occasion of drug misuse, however, were now amongst the most vociferous in demanding his expulsion because of the 'devastation' his abuse of trust and friendship had created: 'You've badly let me down, I feel mugged off by your lies'; 'I can't understand how a mate could do that to another mate'. Other members were irate that he had neither spoken to his group about the 'emotional turmoil' that apparently precipitated his self-medicating recourse to the anaesthetizing oblivion of opiates, nor to the drugs strategy rep about the presence of drugs on the community, nor volunteered his 'lapse' until confronted with a positive test result. He had therefore repeatedly failed to be honest, to access the peer support available to him, to protect 'clean' members who might similarly be 'tempted', and to 'face up to' the consequences of his '*choice* to use'. Accordingly, the consensus was that 'enough is enough: you had your chance last time and you threw it back at us', and he was voted out; a decision subsequently ratified by staff (fieldnotes).

Conversely, for a first-time offender, the community's exploration of the damage caused by deceit could assist that resident in understanding the consequences for others of seemingly unilateral actions, as Theresa's (Send) account of her commitment vote, for brewing 'hooch' (illicitly distilled alcohol), indicates:

> I got really challenged because at first I lied about it and said I didn't do it but then I owned up.
>
> *So did you get more challenged about making the hooch, or lying?*
>
> Lying. The biggest issue is always about lying. I blatantly lied to everyone and a lot of the girls on here, they have been lied to a lot, their whole lives have been about deceit, and when you come on here, you are supposed to be honest. So when you come up with a load of bullshit about how you haven't done it, then it puts a load of barriers up because it is all about trust. It takes forever for people to build trust and if you lie, that trust is gone and you have start all over again.
>
> … *How did it feel to be the subject of a commitment vote?*
>
> Oh god! It was the worst time of my life; really, it was much worse than the trial! … Although the community was supportive, some girls were *very* angry with me because it made them feel unsafe, because some girls have alcohol issues, so it brings up cravings, and because it linked into the trust thing. And people had to say how they felt and that makes you think, oh my god, what I do actually affects other people and it's not just me.

Consequential thinking, social perspective-taking, and empathy acquisition: these are, of course, standard objectives for offending behaviour courses. The 'added value' provided by the TC approach, however, was the opportunity for interpersonal learning it provides in real life situations, rather than the artificial and sequestered environment of an OBP classroom. Residents learned about their maladaptive social behaviours and how they are perceived by others from community members' therapeutic feedback, and the sanctions they received emanated from their social peers, not disciplinary custodians. They could therefore literally see and hear from the expressions of disappointment and anger from their community the adverse effects their behaviour had on people about whom they cared and/or whose good opinion they desired; and indeed the possibly severe repercussions for themselves, if they were to persist with, or revert to, their problematic behaviour:

> [Being] up for my commitment was *horrendous* … I grabbed hold of someone. I still say to this day, as far as I'm concerned it was banter, two blokes messing around. But to the community, it was an act of violence … [and] actually if I was to do that on the out and then someone else took it wrong, I could be coming back to prison for a long time 'cos I'm a lifer. So I could see the benefits of what happened there as well. I learned from it: I'll never fucking touch anyone again. It was a good lesson, without a doubt.
>
> (Patrick, Grendon)

> [The commitment vote] was just awful. The guilt was so bad, seeing what I done to other people on the TC, and the upset and the mistrust that I caused, and having to build that all back again. It *devastated* me. But it taught me a lesson, it really did. If I hadn't had the community around me and seen what I done to them, I don't know that I would have realized fully what a big mistake it was ... I think it has made me stronger and my barriers against drugs are straight back up. I thought I'd cracked it and I realized, from what other people said as well, that I'd not cracked it and I never will; it's something I've always got to be on my guard about.
>
> (Natalie, Send)

As these comments also indicate, being challenged by one's peers was a gruelling experience, and one can easily imagine how such robust inquisitions into one's mistakes, motives, and personal failings might be experienced as intimidating or humiliating. The term 'bullying' was not applied by participants[13] to these challenges, however, and therefore I hesitate to attribute it; indeed, many interviewees were adamant that 'there is no bullying here. The community wouldn't allow it' (Luke, Grendon) (and see similarly, Sullivan 2007). Some did allude, however, to the ways in which a resident's grouping or winging could provide an opportunity for a so inclined resident to 'have a go' 'forcefully' at a disliked peer. Under the guise of offering seemingly constructive feedback, such a resident could subvert the challenge into the discharge of personal animosity; and this might well be thought to be akin to the persecution of a, certainly at that moment, more vulnerable person, and thus to approximate the experience of being bullied. Conversely, a popular resident might escape detailed cross-examination:

> I think your popularity will depend on whether you're heavily challenged sometimes when you're winged. It does happen, unfortunately. If someone dislikes you, if they was really devious, they could use the therapeutic process to really hammer you. And it's not to help you, it's because that person's got issues with you ... Other people, because of their popularity, get off lightly.
>
> (Clive, Grendon)

Challenges, or the avoidance of challenges, for reasons other than the requirements of therapeutic feedback might therefore occur, thereby comprising the TC's commitment to a truly dispassionate, egalitarian culture, open to the questioning of all members by all members. Most interviewees, though, maintained that 'digging out' each other's imperfect rationalizations, undigested emotions, and psychic defences was integral to an honest examination of residents' problems, even if this might on occasion lead to certain individuals being 'picked upon' more than others. The key to a successful (therapeutically valuable) challenge was therefore to focus on the behaviours indicated by the 'issue', its emotional antecedents and less obvious but significant 'meanings' and, where relevant, how it mimicked or paralleled and 'linked into' characteristic ways of (dys)functioning and/or elements of the index offence; rather than the personal characteristics of the resident 'in the hot seat'. In focusing upon the act rather than the actor, constructive challenges approximated what Braithwaite (1989) terms 'reintegrative shaming', because the disapproval of the resident's behaviour was couched within an implicit respect for his or her ongoing therapeutic work and concern to retain the resident within the TC family. Uncomfortable and unvarnished words of advice were also more palatable if offered by residents who could relate how they had determined what the problem under examination 'meant' for them and how they had proceeded to 'deal with' it:

> In another jail, I'd say, 'Get the fuck out my way, you fucking screw.' Now I'd get adjudication for that but I wouldn't care, that's not being accountable; that's just getting a nicking. But here, you are accountable and your group goes into detail: 'Why are you always so aggressive? Why are you anti-authority? Have you got something against that officer? Was there some other way you could have said that?' You'd get none of that in another prison.
>
> *And have you found that sort of questioning helpful?*
>
> Oh yeah, I've not sworn at an officer now for, oh, a couple of weeks! [laughs] ... When I'm challenged, it's not nice to hear, but it makes me think about why I'm pissed off and how I make other people feel around me. It gets explored and the questions you're asked can lead anywhere; one minute you're talking about anger, and the next, your childhood. But that's how you make links, isn't it? You have to look for the *true meaning* behind your behaviour.
>
> (Charles, Grendon)

> I think what I got out of being winged most was to learn how differences can be sorted out the *correct* way, which I've never seen before. I've always seen differences sorted out violently; that's what I'm used to. So having to talk through my beef with [a resident], with all the other members chipping in and giving me their opinions, I did find helpful. Some of the things I didn't like to hear, but I got support with it too. It's like a whole new way of dealing with things.
>
> (James, Grendon)

> I went to the pod[14] and asked for a juice, and I took it bad when [the pod worker] said no ... I threatened him because I was pissed off ... So I got grouped and had to talk about why the juice was so important to me [laughs]. And then [name of resident] started asking me loads of questions and I ended up talking about my index offence.
>
> *How did you go from talking about juice to rape?*

> Er, he said my problem was entitlement; that I feel like I'm entitled to what I want and don't think about how my behaviours make other people feel.
>
> *Right. So that's how you make links between …*
>
> Between little things that you do that are a bit wrong and the big things you do that are very wrong. It's not easy but [name of resident], he's a sensible fella, he's got good insight into therapy, and him and me have similar issues, so I did take on board what he said.
>
> (Eddie, Grendon)

As explained earlier, in most instances, then, and certainly for transgressions that did not incur the potential penalty of expulsion, the threat that the conduct or rule-breaking posed to penal order was a secondary consideration to understanding why and how this problem had occurred and what it signified for that resident. Occasionally, however, a resident's behaviour so threatened the stability of the prison-based TC that the immediate demands of security had to override 'permissive' therapeutic goals. Given Grendon's lack of a segregation unit, in extremis, this TC can only keep the disreputable resident locked up whilst arranging a speedy transfer to another prison (an action known as being 'shipped out'). This happened once during my fieldwork, when a resident violently assaulted another. Even in these grave circumstances, however, it was instructive how the staff's response modelled the value of problem solving and de-escalation of volatile situations *through talk,* thereby helping to embed notions that there is a 'correct', or at least preferable, first resort way of surmounting conflicts. Moreover, the content and tone of the subsequent community meetings exemplified the way in which the TC collectively continued to enquire into 'true meanings', recognize and seek to learn from problems, and re-involve its members in the effective policing of their community.

The reassertion of social norms

The community's dialogue about the soon-to-be shipped out resident initially focused upon the psychoanalytic interpretation that this resident, serving life for rape, had (physically) 'acted out' after watching an 'extreme' pornographic DVD, reputedly featuring highly explicit images of rape of women and teenage girls. It quickly emerged, however, that a handful of other residents had watched, trafficked, and concealed on the community this and other 'hardcore' pornographic DVDs; revelations that were prompted by one or more residents informing staff anonymously, rather than by voicing any suspicions or challenging the other alleged culprits openly in a community meeting. The community, as a collective body, had therefore failed both to prevent recourse to and trade in prohibited material[15] *and* to hold each other accountable through challenge. The focus of the community meeting was therefore to discuss *why* residents in therapy should wish to reinforce their criminogenic sexual preoccupations, decline to seek help, fail to feedback therapeutically, and betray their peers in this way; rather than investigating the identity or identities of the supplier or suppliers and his or their methods of importation and concealment. The potential for pornography to serve to legitimate residents' coercive and abusive sexual fantasies and to affect adversely their relationships with, perceptions of, and respect for women was also explored (fieldnotes). In my interviews with residents of this community, it was striking that they stressed their '*huge* disappointment' in, and 'real anger' with, the violent and other viewers, the unknown supplier(s), and the covert informer(s) for the betrayal of TC norms, rather than concerns about the 'offending' per se:

> I am so pissed off with [the expelled viewer] … He could have brought it to his group, say he was struggling, say why he felt he needed porn, *this* type of porn, especially … That kind of secrecy and deviousness just makes a mockery of everything we're about. I feel *huge* disappointment in him and it really offends me personally that he did that.
>
> (Tim, Grendon)

> What [the original supplier] did was so damaging, not just for [the violent viewer] – who's had to be shipped out, obviously, and so has forfeited therapy he really needed – but because it's *such* a breach of trust. There's real anger about it amongst the community … Very irresponsible, very damaging, potentially.
>
> (Peter, Grendon)

> Notes in the box[16] are completely contrary to the ethos of this place …
>
> Whoever did that has a streak of yellow running through him. He should have taken responsibility for what he knew.
>
> (Eddie, Grendon)

Moreover, after this period of collective soul searching, exploration of 'causes' and peer-led condemnation, the debate progressed to consider how residents could be (more) involved in monitoring their peers' behaviour and assisting with relapse prevention. In choosing this approach to safety and security, then, the TC prison operates what one might call, after Liebling (2002:136), a 'social-plus' model of crime prevention, which marries fundamental, non-negotiable, situational measures to achieve 'good order and discipline' with, preferably and whenever possible, social, informal controls; and thus reverses mainstream prisons' reliance on 'a "situational-plus" model of social control, with a certain amount of self-governance added' (ibid.) Thus, a situational response to 'the porn problem' would have chiefly considered how importation and trafficking could be better 'designed out' by, for example, the extrinsic denial of opportunity to offend through more rigorous examination of 'sent in' items by reception staff, and more frequent or targeted cell searching. The TC's preference for social methods, however, can be discerned by its eagerness to include residents in both the prevention *and* cure of problematic behaviours, through seeking to understand and reduce the intrinsic inclination to 'offend' and thus, to transpose Wortley's (2002:4) maxim, to create safe individuals rather than (merely) safe situations. Leslie (Grendon) explained the difference in approach in these terms:

> In other jails, [the viewers] would have just gone in front of the governor, been told they're very bad boys, and given a nicking. No discussion, no understanding, no real attempt to put things in place so that they aren't tempted again … [But here] they know now how we think it's damaging; that their behaviour is not acceptable. So with a winging, you get the reasons *why* people think it's wrong; *why* it's not acceptable. It's much more in-depth and people can express how they feel about it and it's a chance for them to suggest how they've dealt with problems in the past and come up with other solutions.
>
> *So it sounds like the whole community becomes involved in 'relapse prevention', so to speak?*
>
> Yeah, absolutely, because we know now to keep an eye on them and to be aware that porn is an issue for them – and *they* know that we're on to them, so that's hopefully a bit of a deterrent as well.

As also indicated here, the reassertion of the TC's rules and normative expectations was further achieved by the engagement of residents in defining and reaffirming what constituted 'wrong' and 'damaging' behaviour. Sometimes this involved residents, in effect, in the judicial interpretation of the legislative intent of the (Prison Rules and) community's rules, and wherein lay the boundary of acceptable conduct. One community, for example, was required to deliberate upon the precise mental and behavioural elements of the offence of using threatening, abusive, or insulting words or behaviour; specifically, whether a statement of aggressive intent made to a staff member about a resident, but neither enacted nor made within hearing of that resident, amounted, in fact, to a threat and hence warranted a commitment vote. Besides these semantic considerations, members also reflected upon the feelings of staff members to whom the contentious statement was made, and of the intended target, once its utterance was made known to him. The community concurred that 'the preferred way' would have been for the agitated resident to challenge 'appropriately' – more delicately and evidently, effectively – the person whose behaviour had so displeased him (fieldnotes). From the perspective of Ravi, the Grendonite whose remarks initiated this discussion, however, the idea that his peers would 'side with' staff (and so choose 'them' over 'us') and endorse their understanding of the rules was difficult to accept, as he animatedly conveyed:

> I was *fucking raging*. *I* get put in the book 'cos I'm honest with staff about wanting to seriously hurt the fucker, 'cos they say that's a threat! But [names of residents] calmed me down and was taking the staff's side and saying, 'That *is* your behaviour.' They was saying, 'You're an angry guy who loves violence and you've come here to get that sort of character out in the open and look at it proper.' They pointed out to me, yeah, you wanted to hurt him because he was fucking out of order – he *fucking was*, Alisa, right – and it's good that you didn't, but staff were right to say it's a threat. Well, what the fuck's that about? My fellow cons siding with screws! Fucking mental this gaff, I tell you! [laughing]

If this were 'nihilation' of Ravi's views, the reinterpretation of and effort to redirect his perspectives came from other resident community members, not staff. If this were an iron fist of social control concealed in a velvet glove of 'care', that glove was worn by residents, and the control was exercised on behalf of all community members (cf. Sharp 1975). Ravi's problematic behaviours, generally and in this particular instance, were being explained to him by his peers and thus he could neither deny nor minimize the existence or effect on others of those behaviours. His depiction of rule affirmation, however, further attests that amongst highly committed, role model residents, there existed a fierce protectiveness of and expressed commitment to safeguarding *'our'* TC, including a readiness to expel 'fellow cons' who had 'broken and betrayed the way we do things here' (Michael, Grendon):

> The reason we have those rules is so that we can run a safe community and if people are willing to break those rules and risk a major breakdown in the community itself, then they should be gone, no question. Let them fuck off back to the system! They won't be missed!
>
> (Callum, Grendon)

> These are our rules: we police them, we enforce them, everyone who comes here agrees to abide by them, and if you don't like them, then you can leave; no one's stopping you. But don't think you can come here and try and change *our* rules that have been in place for years and years and make this into some sort of system nick with bells on, because you can't.
>
> (Winston, Grendon)

The responsibility and accountability most residents felt for their own and other's behaviour and relapse prevention, and for the safety of the community and the integrity of the therapeutic process, therefore equated to a social model of crime prevention. This finding also resonates, however, with Tyler's (1990) pertinent empirical investigations into 'why people obey the law', from which he concluded that a person's *normative* acceptance of, and personal commitment to, the law – or in this case, the rules and conventions of the TC way – coexists with, but is often more important than, an *instrumental* desire to conform.

As discussed, then, residents were keenly aware that their community's forbearance was finite and that egregious or repeated rule breaking would result in expulsion. Those who valued TC treatment were therefore inherently inclined to 'obey' because they did not want to risk ejection (and rejection) from the TC, and thus their compliance was born, to some degree, of calculated self-interest; just as rational choice and deterrence theory (amongst others) would suggest: 'I understand that if I want to stay, I have to refrain from violence and drugs, and I do want to stay, so that's what I do' (Tony, Grendon).

Most residents, most of the time, though, 'obeyed' because they not only wished to avoid jeopardizing their place, and to secure 'a safe environment' for themselves, each other, and the work of psychotherapy; but because of what Tyler (1990:3) terms normative compliance, in which people 'voluntarily assume the obligation to follow legal rules … [and] feel personally committed to obeying the law'. This involves the assumption of internalized (that is, identified and fully assimilated) obligations, deriving from a sense of legitimacy of those rules and/or through the desire to behave in a way that coheres with one's personal morality. By open communication in community meetings and by contributing to the enactment of justice and fairness in commitment votes, residents could therefore acquire a personal obligation to adhere to these democratically endorsed, communally 'owned' decisions and standards; an obligation which was more easily and more keenly felt than that demanded by any number of rules and regulations imposed by prison governors. Furthermore, the TC way could encourage, where needed, the *re*development of personal morality – that is, one's 'own set of normative values [and] sense of what is right or appropriate' (ibid.:24) – which would be more supportive of pro-social behaviour and, ultimately, desistance from offending. This is not to suggest that such morality did not exist pre-TC residency, for not everyone in prison is or was an inveterate rule breaker. Many participants freely conceded, however, that their personal morality had formerly been mired in criminal values and the inmate code, but from which they could now dissociate and replace with pro-social peer influence and TC culture, and hence be *positively* 'strongly affected by the normative climate created by others' (ibid.).

In other words, and as social control theorists and observers of the phenomena of group identification and socialization would more explicitly but equivalently explain, by developing a compelling social bond to their community, residents concomitantly increased, and through normative reiteration, strengthened, their interest or 'stake in conformity' (Hirschi 1969) and desire to do, as Raymond (GTC) put it, 'what's best for the community'. The internalization of the very specific Durkheimian 'collective conscience' that the TC engendered, and its very peculiar environmental effects, ensured that, over time, most residents genuinely *wanted* to 'obey' and comply with the social conventions, rules, expectations, obligations, and 'whole new way of dealing with things' they found within their community, to which and in which they had become (after Bowlby *and* Hirschi[17]) attached and involved. Residents who had never previously been overly concerned about breaking society's laws and prison rules could therefore find themselves, if often to their own surprise, developing a passionate enthusiasm for rule construction, interpretation, observance, defence, and enforcement; whilst behaviours that once they would have ignored or, indeed, facilitated, now offended their sense of what was morally 'right and appropriate' *for the TC* and for the people within it, to whom they felt personally obligated and responsible:

> On a normal wing, if my next door neighbour is bang at it,[18] it doesn't bother me at all. But when it's on *here,* and you've agreed to change, and they're just blatantly at it, it's like they're just playing a game, not just with the system but with me and other people who are trying to get the best out of it, you know? And that pisses me right off. And every time you're on a group or community and they say something, then you look at them and think, don't talk to me, you little shit. You want to talk about change and your eyes are pinned?[19] No, it ain't happening.
>
> (Francis, GTC)

> In other prisons, I sell drugs and smoke weed[20] and arrange parcels[21] and shit like that, ain't it, but here, I don't really want to be doing that because you build up relationships with people and you don't want to let them down … People are working through some serious shit, their heads are like, right mashed,[22] and you've got to, kind of, respect that.
>
> (Nick, Grendon)

As the nineteenth-century penal reformer Alexander Maconochie discovered, communal living and mutual responsibility 'created an atmosphere of "mutual watch, check, and self-command" that seemed to be valued by the inmates' (Clay 2001:175) – and contributed to their astonishingly successful rehabilitation. In the TC, its cherished principles and practice of peer accountability, therapeutic feedback, and challenge similarly facilitated and demanded '*real* responsibility'. Combined with exceptionally educational commitment votes, and the reinforcement and re-communication of the rules and social norms of their community that this entailed, these mechanisms ensured that, to an extraordinary extent, residents were self-policing and did actively cooperate with and contribute to the production and preservation of order and safety. The experience of social control was therefore not experienced as oppressive or 'top down', but as essential for the effective practice of group psychotherapy and, more tellingly, welcomed as a desirable and responsible (*not* responsibilized), 'bottom-up' response to the needs of the community. The TC functioned effectively because the residents themselves wanted to 'keep the community safe' and to protect and sustain '*our* rules', and were willing not only to do their 'own time' but to involve themselves in the monitoring of their peers' 'time' to ensure that this happened. Accordingly, these findings offer some persuasive qualitative elucidation of the paradox which Newton's (2006) quantitative research at Grendon identified; and moreover show how, within a supportive environment, the social role of convicted offenders could be transformed from rule breaker to rule enforcer, and their identity reconstructed from sometime irresponsible prisoner to that of routinely responsible resident.

6 Vulnerability, unmasking, and 'de-othering'

> It's okay to talk about your feelings here; in fact, you're *encouraged* to let out your emotions. And if that means crying, then cry. So a lot of those façades of being macho, they go out of the window. They're not sustainable here, and that's good, because it gets in the way of trying to change.
>
> (Muktar, Grendon)

In his consummate sociological study of a maximum security prison, Sykes (1958) described how the male prisoner's confidence in himself *as a man* is assailed by the enforced loss of normative indicators of masculinity. The deprivations of sexual relationships with women, security, autonomy, and consumerism ('goods and services'), all threaten to figuratively emasculate the male prisoner because of the ontological threat their absence poses to his self-concept as a heterosexual, inviolable, self-determining, individualist. The greater significance of Sykes's analysis, however, was his early problematization of performative masculinity, for these deprivations demand some compensatory, rectifying response – or a 'secondary proof of manhood' – which, amongst men keen to reassert their masculinity *to other men*, tends to ensure and perpetuate extreme displays of 'toughness', 'masculine mannerisms', and 'inward stamina' (ibid.:98).

In the half-century since Sykes's observations, scholarly interest in and understanding of gender have brought to the fore implicit themes in Sykes's depiction of prison masculinities: namely that gender is a social construction, an interactional and situational accomplishment, and a deeply internalized psychic structure, which has to be continuously and actively performed and affirmed as a constituted, negotiated, and authenticated aspect of one's personal and social identity. In other words, gender is a product of a number of historical, cultural, and structural contingencies and inequalities, which can be distinguished from one's innate and, without surgical intervention, unchangeable biological sex. The 'doing' of gender, however, varies according to, amongst other things, class, age, race, sexuality, educational and occupational attainment, and the specific circumstances in which the performance is required – alone or with others, and by reference to the expectations of one's environment (West and Zimmerman 1987). Accordingly, for men, there is no one-size-fits-all masculinity but rather a multiplicity of masculinities, defined and mediated by and manifested in differing interests in the 'hegemonic' or hypermasculine, 'subordinated', or 'marginalized' relationships[1] *between* men, and with women (Tolson 1977; Connell 1987, 1995; Morgan 1992; Messerschmidt 1993).

Within the specific social situation of the secure prison, then, when men 'do gender', they accordingly enact a particularly exaggerated notion of masculinity – hypermasculinity – which replicates understandings of what such masculinity should involve, if it is to be received receptively. Many aspects of this hypermasculinity are unsurprisingly mirrored by those 'free world' men whose testosterone-charged pursuits of both high-risk, high-reward offending and seemingly non-utilitarian delinquency populate the crime statistics (Messerschmidt 1993, 1997; Newburn and Stanko 1994; Collier 1998; Winlow 2001). Nevertheless, imported conceptualizations of what it is 'to be a man' are still accentuated within prison because of the greater deprivations indigenous to, and the heightened consequences of perceived weakness within, the penal environment. Consider, for example, this thoughtful description from Winston (Grendon) of what 'doing gender' entails for serious offenders in 'serious' prisons:

> In the system, you have to stand up for yourself, you have to look like you'll fight any fucker ... You can't trust no one; you can't talk to no one about your issues, personal stuff, or show any weakness at all. Specially in dispersals,[2] you need to be a man or else, seriously Alisa, you ain't going to survive them places. Not with your pride intact, any ways.
>
> *So when you say you've got to 'be a man', how do you show that?*
>
> [pause] It's a certain attitude. Aggressive, ready to fight, bit cocky, I suppose ... You've got to be, well, a *hard* man; harder than anyone else. You haven't got to be a bully – I despise bullies myself, I would never pick on the weak, but I wouldn't have them under my wing neither ... Don't show no emotion, unless it's anger. It's hard to explain to a nice woman like yourself; they're all soft,[3] posh blokes at [your] University, ain't they? [laughs] But basically, you've got to come across so that no one would even *think* of messing with you; if necessary, do the fuckers before they do you. You're constantly on your guard.
>
> *That sounds awfully tiring ...*
>
> It is. That's why I like the bang up; I think a lot of us do. 'Cos when you go behind your door, you can relax, yeah, just be yourself, know what I mean?

As Winston suggested, then, the enactment of hypermasculinity within prison serves both to provide a defensive mechanism or coping strategy for the pains of imprisonment, and to communicate, regulate, and reinforce the socially transmitted, gendered conduct of the prisoner and his peers. Most obviously, the use of aggression, physical force, and bravado – the convincing appearance of being 'ready to fight' – deters potential attackers and predators and directs them instead towards easier prey. The exceptional situational artificiality and pervasive 'toughness' of prison life demands the ability – or, at least, *appearance* of ability – to resort to (retaliatory) violence, as a primary, if primitive, survival skill, so that one will not be physically (or sexually[4]) assaulted or psychologically exploited: 'Everyone in prison has to create an image to some extent … I've never had a fight, but on normal location, I have to put on a bit of a hard front and *look* like I *might*, to keep people away' (Ben, GTC). If the male prisoner's ability to 'stand up' for himself is tested, however, he must respond aggressively, or accept an inevitable escalation in violence and victimization: 'You *have* to fight, otherwise you're fucked! There ain't no way back – short of going on the numbers.[5] It's the whole image thing, ain't it?' (Tony, Grendon). Even minor affronts that might be dismissed in the outside world cannot therefore be ignored within the social context of the long-term prison, where reputational challenges are widely known amongst the relatively static population and reappraisals of claims to 'manhood' are incessant (see further Butler 2008; Gambetta 2009):

> If someone calls you a dickhead in society, that can maybe be dealt with. But if it's said in front of other inmates, then you've got to have a fight because it's a threat to your image. If I let him call me a dickhead, then another fella might call me it, and before I know it, I'm seen as weak. So a lot of the time, you're having a little scrap now so you won't have to have a big fight later.
>
> (Robbie, Grendon)

Second, the standards of hypermasculinity caution against exposing (too much of) one's inner self. Emotions must be sublimated, distressing personal difficulties contained, and vulnerabilities denied, since to 'show any weakness at all' is fundamentally to weaken one's claim to 'be a man' amongst other hypermasculinity-endorsing men. Consequently, 'cons' are apt to develop an overtly Goffmanian dramaturgical conception of themselves and their role within the prison, in which they accept that a viable self-presentation depends upon their convincing, if often conflict-laden, public performance of hypermasculinity and an ability to maintain, at all costs, 'face' (Goffman 1959, 1967). To project a credible 'frontstage' mask, despite (not because of) the pains of imprisonment, however, can be psychologically burdensome in the demands it makes on the wearer to conceal his 'weaker' feelings. It is only when the prisoner is ensconced 'behind the door' of his private 'backstage' cell, that he cast aside the mask, drop his guard, and 'just be yourself'.

This chapter, then, explores how, in the less 'pumped-up' environment of the TC, the normative compulsions to conform to hypermasculine ideals could be jettisoned. Of interest here is not prisoners' performative hypermasculinity as such (for which see, for example, Newton 1994; Sim 1994;

Sabo *et al.* 2001; Jewkes 2002, 2005b; Hua 2005), but rather what happens when that hypermasculinity is rendered not only irrelevant by the TC but inimical to TC treatment. In revisiting the themes of care and safety discussed in the previous two chapters, the focus here is exclusively upon the experience of male residents, who are weighed down by gendered expectations to an extent unknown to women.[6] The chapter begins by detailing the incremental removal of 'hard man' masks, as vulnerabilities were uncovered and accepted. The Grendon experiences of one of the traditional targets of hypermasculine prisoners, men convicted of sexual offences, are then explored. Through the mostly successful, if incomplete, integration of these offenders, this chapter shows how 'regular cons' were able to form friendships and therapeutic alliances with 'nonces' and, as a result, re-examine the hierarchy of 'real man' offending, their position within it and, sometimes, the 'deeper meaning' of their own offending.

Experiences of vulnerability: hypermasculinity deconstructed

Winston's depiction of 'being a man' in the system centred upon two themes: aggression and emotional impermeableness. In the well-functioning TC, the former is unnecessary and the latter, untenable. As the previous chapter documented, TC residents assumed responsibility for the maintenance of a largely norm-abiding and self-policing community. The resulting pervasive and, amongst comparable prisoner populations, highly uncharacteristic sense of safety effectively eradicated the need for violence as a 'secondary proof' of one's manliness. Neither authentic 'macho men' nor those who had to fake 'a hard front' had to worry that they would be 'messed with'; nor confront the equally alarming prospect that they might fail to demonstrate the requisite 'transcendental courage' (Whitehead 2005:416) if they were. The significance of this decreased anxiety – about the potential for assault, upon one's body and one's ego – and increased protection from violence in the TC therefore fundamentally unsettled the foundations upon which much prison hypermasculinity rests: 'You *can't* fight, 'cos no one will fight you! It's against the rules. So you learn quite quickly, you don't need none of that front here' (James, Grendon).

Of equal importance to the TC's deconstructionist project, however, was residents' development of the ability to access and share 'unacceptable' emotions and to respond to and learn to tolerate the uncomfortable sensations of vulnerability this provoked. It is self-evidently impossible to engage in therapy in any meaningful sense without a willingness or, at least, a determination, to 'open up': to dismantle one's past and disclose one's entrenched pain, repressed fears, and shame-ridden secrets. Residents who cannot do so leave the TC, either by choice, in order to flee that encounter with one's true self, or following the community's judgement of a 'lack of commitment'. 'To learn that it's safe to trust people here and to let yourself be vulnerable around them' (Natalie, Send) was, of course, also problematic for women, but their experiences of vulnerability were clearly distinguishable from men's because their difficulties related solely to the necessarily prior acquisition of trust, rather than the demands of gender essentialism which so burden (hypermasculine) men.

Voyages into vulnerability were therefore more challenging for men because of the gendered meanings of those qualities whose polarity to 'weakness' helps define the male identity, both generally, in culturally conditioned expressions of masculinities, and specifically, in the excessively performative micro society of the prison. These include stoicism and psychological resilience; self-reliance: '[men] experience it as a sign of weakness to need the help of others' (Seidler 1992:1); circumspection about one's personal life; fearlessness (Goodey 1997); and a compunction to retain control, of one's self, others, and valued resources (Lipman-Blumen 1984). 'To get in touch with my feelings, and *allow* myself to be vulnerable and be sad' (Raymond, GTC) – in short, to admit to and show 'feminine' emotions *in front of other men* – was therefore invariably difficult:

> My main struggle is being vulnerable in front of men. I struggle with that, feeling vulnerable or showing emotion, sad emotions – I'm okay showing angry emotions … And I see that as being about what I've been used to for years in the system and outside, where you wear a mask and put up barriers and that. I know I've got to but I struggle with that, big time.
>
> (Wesley, Grendon)

> I've got to come and sit in [my group room] with eight people and question really manly things, you know what I'm saying? It's really tough with other men, other criminals, all in for violence, and I've got to sit here and talk about things that's confused me and hurt me …
>
> (Don, Grendon)

Moreover, men were anxious not only about their naked vulnerability in the TC, but that by permitting 'softer feelings to surface' (Seidler 1985:159), their capacity to re-exert emotional self-restraint would be permanently diminished. To relent their grip on their feelings might then, they feared, threaten their ability to function and survive upon their return to a more ruthless penal environment, with its expectations of *mental* and physical 'toughness':

> I'd never cried in all of my life before here but here, I've broken down, I've cried in front of 40 people plus. *You*'ve seen me cry, a man crying in front of a woman! … I feel weak when I cry, I feel embarrassed, and my image is gone and it's not nice. But it's better than holding it in and being angry all the time … I'm more in touch with my emotions now than what I ever was, which is a good thing, but …
>
> *But what?*

> Well, it's all right here, them feelings are understood. But back in the system, or outside, no one gives a fuck about my feelings. I'm on my Jack Jones[7] again. So you have to put the armour back on and all these emotions – it's like I've opened them up here and then I'm going to have squash them again.
>
> (Charles, Grendon)

Charles's concerns about the long-term viability of 'opening up' were understandable, although 'from a developmental perspective, strings are being added to [his] bow, rather than being removed' (Parker and Morris 2004:201). More brutally, some surrender of 'image' was inevitable and unavoidable, once residents' attachment needs, 'inadequacies', and 'weaknesses' had been ascertained *by other men*. The puncturing of hypermasculine pretensions could then not be repaired by patently false claims to invulnerability, as Don (Grendon) rather ruefully accepted:

> Here, you have to sit and be vulnerable and sort out the things that cause you problems. So how can you sit here and talk about your issues and then throw your weight about like some macho knobhead? People try it – of course they do – but they get laughed at. *I've* tried, puffing my chest up and that, but the other lads just deflate it. You can't get away with that here; people just won't have it.

This 'deflationary' culture benefited all male residents, however, in ways which relate back to and reinforce the themes explored in Chapter 4. Disclosing their 'issues' to empathetic group members led to the blossoming of mutual trust and caring bonds, and the realization that those 'issues' were shared with others. Since this continued gift of care and support was conditional only upon continued engagement with therapy and the community, and since sources of shame were understood and often familiar, men did not have to worry (so much) about how other men might perceive them as sometimes victim and always perpetrator of crime; nor be so constantly vigilant about their defence of a hypermasculine 'hard' image, or so dismissive of their 'softer' side. This sense of acceptance strengthened their secure attachments to other men, with whom their 'unmanly' emotions could be shared, and the integrity and validity of these emotions recognized, without fear of derision.

Moreover, the TC's ethic of care had reassured residents that men *can* care emotionally for other men, and enjoy, reciprocate, and benefit from that care, without any possible sexual imputation. Observers of men's same-sex relationships routinely depict 'intimate', emotionally supportive friendships in particular as bathed in unaddressed questions about homosexuality (Nardi 1992); anxiety about which results in pervasive homophobia, as defined by Kimmel (2001:277) as not just a fear of gay men but a fear of being exposed as less than a 'real man'. It is this paralysing fear that one's concern or interest may be misinterpreted as barely repressed homosexual desire, or certainly less than ideal 'manliness', that obstructs the development of genuine closeness between men and makes homophobia 'a central organizing principle of our cultural definition of manhood' (ibid.). From this perspective, much hypermasculinity, misogyny, and sexism dressed up as allegedly 'harmless' 'laddish' behaviour can be understood as part of the ceaseless quest and perceived necessity to prove to other men, and to reassure oneself, that one is *not* homosexual – a 'qualification' of particular importance, of course, in prisons inhabited solely by men. As Joe (Grendon) observed, 'You can't talk about your "relationships" with each other in normal prisons or show care for a man: people would say you're an iron!'[8]

With violence and homophobic fear of expressed emotion largely extinguished, so-inclined TC residents could therefore only establish and advertise their hypermasculine credentials through more subtle means. Teasing banter – or 'taking the piss out of each other' (Paul, Grendon) – about the relative merits of football teams or one's proficiency (or otherwise) with computer games, for example; a conspicuous fondness for designer labels which harked back to a pre-prison identity as a devotee of material markers of success (though 'earned' through crime); and wildly embellished, sexually explicit and objectifying storytelling (Thurston 1996), discursively overflowing with rampant heterosexuality – or 'talking bollocks about women and sex' (Lenny, Grendon)[9] – were frequently cited residuals of masculine self-expression. Such displays, however, were only tolerable in moderation, so that these culturally normative masculine pastimes did not morph into the dysfunctionally macho. Fitness activities in prison, for example, can offer important opportunities for self-care, achievement, and stress management, and team sports in particular provide a conduit by which men can 'do things' together, without the fear this enjoyment of close companionship and male bonding will be mistaken for intimacy (Messner 1992). Yet they also offer a particularly effective resource by which to signal one's allegiance to a conception of masculinity which is 'hard', powerful, and self-disciplined (Sabo 2001), and by which to create a muscular physique which quite literally embodies force, competency, and intimidation (Connell 1983). The 'meaning' of lengthy gym sessions and obsessive body building did not therefore escape the critical eye of the therapeutically insightful. Men whose dedication to the gym was judged to be excessive, resulting more from a narcissistic concern with their 'image' than any laudable regard for fitness, or from the erroneous equation of masculine power with corporeal dominance, accordingly attracted more criticism than admiration:

> The stereotypical macho guys here are the ones who go to the gym every day and they are not just going to exercise and maintain their fitness levels; they go to pump their muscles up and improve their own image of themselves which is based upon their physical presence. Wankers, basically!
>
> (Luke, Grendon)

> [Name of resident], on my group, he thinks he's a woman's dream because of his muscles and he lifts weights and I think no, you just look like a thug! He's one of those who goes to the gym every chance he gets, doing that 'dispersal walk';[10] what a dickhead! [laughs] So there is that culture amongst some individuals, but it's all about them. It's not needed here. And it certainly doesn't seem to give them confidence because they seem to be the most insecure people.
>
> (Peter, Grendon)

The openness to vulnerability, and greater scepticism about hypermasculinity, that men acquired in the TC, then, created a climate in which the yielding of image was not only permissible but logical: since weaknesses were now known, attempts to conceal them with a 'macho mask' were futile, and only likely to invite therapeutic scrutiny of why a hypermasculine performance might still be thought desirable when the requirements of one's audience had changed. The resulting 'loss of face' did not produce the sullied self-concept that such public exposure would usually incur (Goffman 1967), but rather enabled residents to restore their true 'face': 'to be who *you really are,* without any of that macho pretence' (Lee, GTC).

Yet, to be 'who *you really are*' was challenging for those men who no longer knew who they really were, since the mask they had so successfully worn in the system now fitted them so snugly that their true identity had long been erased. For these men, the challenge was far more fundamental than 'merely' relinquishing their prison mask – they had to resurrect their suspended, pre-prison identity in order to rediscover who they once were (Schmid and Jones 1991). This conundrum was explored most perceptively by Tony, an exceptionally imposing, self-identifying 'old firm' lifer who was struggling to adapt to Grendon after years detained in the *über*-hypermasculine culture of high-security prisons, within which he had felt psychically constrained yet also, given his entirely warranted 'hard man' renown, contentedly 'at home':

> You have to put a mask on in dispersal, be one of the lads, and obviously, I have a reputation so everyone expects you to be a certain way. Sometimes I felt like I wanted to change but I couldn't; I couldn't be no one different because they wouldn't let me … The problem is here, I'm finding it hard to tone myself down, know what I mean, 'cos I've been that way for so long, I can't even remember what I *should* be like. Like, one of my group, he said I have 'an intimidating walk'. Well, I can't start walking no different now, can I, darlin'? [laughs] So, you know, men don't call it on here,[11] so you don't need that macho mask, but at the same time, I ain't really comfortable without it yet. So I really want to change but I don't know to change to what, 'cos I don't even know what I'm fucking about now. I know I've got some good things about me, but I've put on so many masks in my life, to cover how I felt some times, so I forgot who

> I am. But, I believe Grendon can help me with that 'cos I can just be me here; I don't need no masks no more. It's fucking hard, though!

Reconfiguring one's self-identity was not the only incentive for unpeeling long-attached 'macho masks'. Residents came to appreciate that in the TC, one's reputation rests not on a talent to camouflage one's feelings in the pursuit of a suitably hypermasculine image but the converse: the willingness and ability to expose one's vulnerabilities and work through them in the pursuit of change. Again then, the TC inverted the mainstream prison's cultural norms and expectations. The 'tough guy' in the TC was the man who could decline to respond aggressively to behaviours that might otherwise be interpreted as a provocative status challenge, because his confidence in himself *as a man* no longer demanded such (self-)destructive affirmation: 'If you don't react when someone is angry, *here*, that's seen as sensible, and it's the other fella who looks fucking stupid and weak, 'cos he can't control himself' (Stewart, Grendon). From a psychotherapeutic perspective, the unconscious motivation behind hypermasculine violence is not just the self-affirming demonstration of power, but a desire to conceal and distract attention from one's intolerable suspicions of power*lessness*: it is ontologically less disturbing to induce fear in others than to confront one's own fears. Accordingly, it takes more 'manly' strength and courage to walk away from provocations, in the knowledge that in retreating, one apparently concedes one's hypermasculine deficiencies, than to defend through violence a false notion of honour. For those who were able to internalize this distinction, the transformation to one's self-concept and the implications for one's future conduct were revolutionary. One formerly 'exemplary' hypermasculine GTC resident, with numerous convictions for serious assaults on other men, explained his revised attitudes as follows:

> I had this image … I always wanted to be the toughest guy out there so I'd fight. It was just about putting other lads in their place … If they annoyed me, or done me wrong, to my image, then I would have to sort that, you know? Whereas now, up here, I can fall out with lads but I don't feel the need to do the violence.
>
> *So what has changed for you?*
>
> I think what it is now is that I'm more comfortable with myself and more confident about my manly – well, as a man, really … This place makes you look at yourself and question things that you've always thought were right but which really are crap, because they don't get you nowhere – but jail. Men fighting – it's just childish really, a lot of the time, isn't it? I think it's embarrassing now; I'd rather walk away than *need* to fight for my pride … So now, I don't feel that if someone comes bowling in here, giving it all that,[12] I don't feel the need to put them in their place. Whereas before, I would; I'd want them to know that I was the same as them, well, *better* than them! … That's a *massive* change for me; I'm really proud of that.

Respect in the TC was therefore accorded not to the 'toughest' fighter, nor to the strutting, posturing 'macho man' addicted to muscles, nor to the brooding, emotionally repressed 'hard man' who could recount the most horrific events without ever flinching or empathizing (with his victim or himself). It was the senior residents who had demonstrated and hence modelled the personal courage to excavate and 'work on' their criminogenic 'issues', underlying insecurities, and submerged emotions, to whom other residents now turned to for advice, and whose rehabilitative progress they coveted for themselves. A new notion of 'reputation' therefore emerged in the TC in which respected TC residents were those who had earned 'appraisal respect' for their personal qualities and commitment to change, rather than the 'prudential respect' commanded by those hypermasculine men who inspire fear amongst their peers in the system (Crewe 2009, informed by Darwall 1977). Emotional intelligence and interpersonal and communication skills were now the markers of truly masculine men: 'the "strong and brave" man here is the one who will talk and cry' (McLure 2004:82).

Through the almost complete removal of violence, the reduced value placed on embodied masculinity, and by learning 'to sit and be vulnerable', the reductionist values and dynamics of hypermasculinity were therefore deconstructed in the TC. 'Hard men' were enabled to 'soften' and to revise their internalized, essentialist, and often hugely unhelpful notions about 'being a man'. Men could then discover, and be encouraged by other men to discover, that 'sad emotions' are not 'unmanly'; that acquired wisdom attracts more admiration than instinctive aggression; and that the unmasking of vulnerability need not threaten the masculine identity, but can enrich and contribute to its positive and pro-social reconstruction.

Experiences of 'de-othering': sexual offenders at Grendon

Men convicted of sexual offences are typically perceived as modern-day monsters and folk devils (Sampson 1994; Simon 1998). They represent a highly emotive, non-rational, 'criminology of the other'; a wholly unacceptable, entirely 'alien', and essentially different criminal group whose 'dangerous members … bear little resemblance to "us"' (Garland 1996:461; Hudson 2005). Their crimes attract particularly hysterical and voyeuristically salacious media coverage (Soothill and Walby 1991; Benedict 1992; Howe 1998; Greer 2003); and the public's concern that such offenders can never be truly 'cured' of their sexually deviant predilections demands that their risk is managed and their activities monitored upon release with a rigour once reserved for lifers.

This exclusionary construction of 'othering' is one that extends to the mainstream prison, through the hierarchy of offending (discussed presently), the related imperatives of the inmate code, and operational practice; all of which endorse notions that sexual offenders should be distinguished and segregated from 'normal' criminals. Prison studies abound with gruesome tales of the physical and psychological assaults 'nonces' can expect to receive from other prisoners or, more rarely, during the collective 'score settling' and retributive justice that are a universal feature of prison riots (Carrabine 2004; Sampson 1994; Sabo *et al.* 2001). In most British prisons, sexual offenders accordingly have two choices. They can try to 'front it out' on the wing, but this will require the adoption of elaborate and always tenuous strategies by which to 'pass' (Schwaebe 2005), either by lying about their index offence, protesting their innocence, or maintaining some other 'viable identity' which will, to some degree, compensate for their crime.[13] Alternatively, they can elect to be relocated away from non-sexual offenders. When protective segregation is urgently required, this may necessitate a temporary move to the existing establishment's segregation unit; otherwise, sexual offenders can reside permanently on a discrete Vulnerable Prisoners' Unit (VPU) – meaning here, 'vulnerable' to the risk of harassment and assault from other prisoners – or a specialist 'sex offenders only' prison.[14] This was widely considered to 'the only sensible solution' (Steve, GTC) to mainstream prisoners' ostentatious rejection of sexual offenders, but is still an imperfect response. VPUs may additionally house prisoners whose personality or mental health problems (often drug- or gambling-related) debts, previous criminal justice occupation, gang affiliation, or reputation as an informant renders them a target for reprisals, but who will nevertheless consider themselves to be 'superior to bacons,[15] especially kiddie fiddlers; they really are the lowest of the very low' (Nigel, Grendon). Prisoners housed within establishments exclusively concerned with sexual offending, but for whom physical violence is within their repertoire of behaviours, may also still attack their peers. Ironically then, the offenders who are considered the most 'dangerous' by the public are simultaneously the 'weakest' and most 'vulnerable' within prison.

At Grendon,[16] however, men who have been convicted of sexual offences or crimes that were sexually motivated[17] are expected to be able to engage in therapy and participate in communal activities alongside residents serving sentences for other (non-sexual) offences. One community, currently A-wing,[18] has since the late 1980s evolved[19] to cater exclusively for residents who have sexually or physically abused or killed children and/or committed exceptionally vicious sexual (or, less frequently, sexually motivated) offences against adults, but its members can still associate socially with other Grendonites around the prison. As previous chapters have explored, all residents are expected to contribute to the maintenance of a safe, non-violent environment, and to renounce any imported and acquired beliefs that 'nonce bashing', either rhetorically or physically, is desirable behaviour. Indeed, the minority of interviewees who admitted to 'abusing the nonces' in previous prisons and/or (for they were not necessarily the same men) to feeling 'not entirely happy' about living alongside sexual offenders now, were accordingly adamant they would never mistreat a TC resident on the basis of his offence.[20] They expressed a willingness to work with any offender who was seen to be remorseful, honest, and sincere in his attempts to change, and voiced their sense of responsibility for ensuring that their own and other residents' attitudes and behaviours did not render the TC unsafe for, or inhospitable to, sexual offenders, who might then prematurely leave therapy. As Bill (Grendon) pondered: 'If I give a nonce a really bad time and he leaves here – he's left because of me bullying him basically – and some day, I pick up the newspaper and find he's re-offended, am I partly to blame for that?'

The integration of sexual and sexually motivated offenders that occurs at Grendon is therefore remarkable in comparison to other high-security and category B prisons.[21] Both offenders against children and women interviewed for this research unequivocally reported feeling protected at Grendon and welcomed the social inclusiveness and normalization or de-othering this enabled:

> When you go to education or gym, you're not ridiculed because of your offence … [Other residents] may not always talk to you, or have deep meaningful conversations, some of them, but they won't actually abuse you or attack you and they will work alongside you. It's totally different to the system where you're under constant risk of attack or having shit parcels thrown at you.
>
> (Grendonite who had sexually abused children)

> I find it good here. People are fine with me; I've never not felt safe. Sometimes people might not like my offence and that, but they respect my determination to try and change and work on it and yeah, I get some good encouragement and advice … When you're on a VPU, it's like the prison *creates* problems for you because there's a target for people, 'Oh, it's the nonce wing; it's them lot'; like we're different because we have to be kept from everyone else. But here, we're all equal.
>
> (Grendonite who had raped a woman)

> There's no comparison with the system; you don't have to be on edge, you can take part in everything … Most of the lads treat me no different to anyone else. I mean, you'll always get a few idiots who will just totally blank[22] you but that's about it. Most people, if they think you're here for the right reasons, don't have a problem with you. And if anyone does say anything, you just wing them – simple. That soon shuts 'em up!
>
> (Grendonite who had raped and murdered a woman)

> I feel very safe. There was a time when I didn't, when I first arrived, but now I do. I think now that was my own paranoia, holding me back; I was wary of people's reactions so, you know, I isolated myself a bit … There's none of that feeling of trepidation, you know what I mean, of constant unease, you get in other prisons.
>
> (Grendonite who had murdered his wife)

The limits of 'de-othering': A-wing and intra-offence distinctions

Whilst safety was afforded to all, however, some othering of sexual offenders at Grendon remained. The consensus amongst non-sexual offenders was that whereas men who had raped women could fully integrate into and be accepted by their community, because their offence was 'more understandable'; men who had offended sexually (though not necessarily physically) against children probably could not. Their crimes were thought to be 'particularly stomach-churning' and raised legitimate therapeutic concerns about the transference their presence would occasion amongst men who themselves had been abused in childhood and who might then feel compelled to 'act out' violently. The community would therefore be neither safe psychologically and emotionally for men who had been abused, nor safe physically for men who had abused:

> I don't think I could sit here and listen to a man saying how he fantasizes over messing with children. I'd find that very difficult and for men who'd been abused, how would they cope with that? That could be quite dangerous; you might see some backlash … And I think paedophiles have got deeper mental issues, if you like? I mean, someone that goes out and rapes a woman has got serious problems, obviously, but, I suppose, to want to have sex with women, it's more understandable because at least it's normal, but *children?* I don't think 99 out of 100 people could understand that and as inmates, we've got the whole anti-nonce thing going on as well, so I think you need [A]-wing for paedophiles.
>
> (Wesley, Grendon)

The apparently utterly 'alien' quality of 'the paedophile' was therefore thought by some to necessitate a separate community in which perceived 'deeper mental issues' could be explored without the risk of exposing other offenders – including those who had raped adults – to these 'issues'. Interestingly, this distinction was also propounded by sexual offenders: interviewees who had abused children mostly thought that a specialist community was desirable, whilst those who had offended against women mostly preferred to reside on an integrated community. A-wing interviewees, however, recognized and regretted the de facto VPU status this afforded their community, and revealed themselves to be highly conflicted about the overall value of exiling the rehabilitative endeavours of most Grendonite sexual offenders to one community.

Thus, a specialist wing allows sexual offenders to discuss without inhibition and in detail their sexual fantasies and favoured triggers for sexual arousal and masturbation, including the use of pornography, and to revisit emotionally and enact through role play their offence(s) (Akerman 2010; Ware *et al.* 2010). Like all TC residents, because 'therapy doesn't stop when the group ends' (Nigel, Grendon), community members are expected to be constantly alert to and to challenge 'telltale signs and traits in each other' (Roger, Grendon), but amongst sexual offenders, these 'traits' and offence paralleling behaviours may include attempts to groom sexually other residents or to defend or trivialize sexist and misogynistic values as culturally normative; the significance of which non-sexually motivated and unreconstructed hypermasculine offenders might not fully appreciate (see further Bond and Steptoe-Warren 2010). Thornton *et al.*'s (1996) research, conducted when Grendon offered the cognitive-behavioural SOTP alongside psychotherapy, concluded that sexual offenders made the most pronounced rehabilitative progress on offence-specific factors on the specialist wing. This finding may reflect the, ideally, rehabilitative reinforcement provided by out-of-group discussions amongst men who share an understanding of the aetiological and experiential characteristics of sexual and sexually motivated offending, and who are therefore best placed to encourage the mutual consultation on, rehearsal and modelling of, pro-social alternative perspectives (Frost and Connolly 2004). Interviewees on A-wing also acknowledged that disclosing the often highly disturbing content of their fantasies and the eroticized recitation of their offences risked psychologically incapacitating non-sexual offenders (and prison staff) who did not wish to or could not process such material. Conversely, they could be uncomfortable with the, to them, sometimes distasteful and inexplicable nature of other forms of criminal activity:

> [A]-wing is definitely needed. I wouldn't feel comfortable on any other wing. I would feel very self-conscious; I would be afraid of opening up fully, of things being said behind my back … I don't think it would be fair that someone with no knowledge of sex offences has to sit and listen to what I've done and I don't particularly want to hear about their offending. Apart from my sex offending, I've got no criminal values whatsoever and to be honest, I find those sort of behaviours really annoying.
>
> (Tim, Grendon)

> It's turned into a VPU and it shouldn't have done. We should be part of the whole prison because really, if you can't have full integration here, where could you? Having said that, I couldn't have done the work that I'm doing anywhere else, on another community or in the system. Say, if I'm struggling over something and need to talk about it, in the system, I wouldn't say that I was in fantasy and I was masturbating because the response would be, 'Oh fucking hell, so am I, my hand's falling off!' Porn is normal in the system; it's quite normal for people to be extremely derogatory about their offences, their attitude to it. Rapists in particular, they'll come straight off SOTP, where, you know, they've sat there, saying all the right things, back to the wing and start telling totally inappropriate jokes which are *extremely* offensive … That doesn't happen here, except with very new guys who really don't know anything better … So,

> on this wing, we take sexual offending very seriously; everything is looked at in great detail and you can talk frankly. So for me, it's necessary. I wouldn't have got the support or engagement that I have had elsewhere. So [A]-wing needs to exist; it's sad, but it does.
>
> (Peter, Grendon)

Residents of the 'sex offenders only' community, however, also implied they were hindered in pursuing identity reconstruction because their therapy was directed towards a single-minded focus upon sex offending 'as if that's the be all and end all of who I am' (Colin, Grendon). Some A-wing residents made conscious efforts to resist their imposed 'master status' (Becker 1963) by declining to label themselves as a 'child molester' or 'rapist'. The fact that they found it necessary to uncouple the perceived equation between one what did and who one is, however, was telling: 'armed robbers' and 'murderers' on other communities were neither given by staff nor self-selected these social identities. Other residents denounced what they perceived to be the blinkered determination of A-wing staff to frame *all* their 'issues' through the prism of sex, sexuality, and sexual deviancy, and thus to reinterpret or, indeed, 'nihiliate', alternative, resident-led explanations of behaviours. One resident exasperatedly complained, for example, that his group facilitator 'insisted' his frequent sexually descriptive swearing pointed to some 'hidden meaning or intention'; yet, such language passed without comment upon the other communities: 'Just because I say fuck, it doesn't mean I'm planning to do it! It's just a word; it doesn't *mean* anything! … She goes on and on about sex and then has the nerve to say that *I'm* preoccupied with sex!' (fieldnotes). Another recounted how a prison officer had entered his cell as he was watching a television wildlife programme in which two animals were copulating, and he was then 'picked up on' his viewing preferences in his small group:

> I raped and buggered my victim and battered her half to death: I'm not interested in fucking lions! But on here, you're not allowed to do anything that isn't 'really' about sex. It *infuriates* me. I wouldn't have to put up with this crap on another community.

These sentiments cohere with Lacombe's (2008) contention that the responsibilizing content and focus of correctional treatment encourages 'the "making up" of the sex offender into a species entirely consumed by sex' (ibid.:56). Men who are trying to change their conception of who they are and work towards prospective desistance are surely less likely to be able to do so if they are excessively reduced to one aspect of their personality and lifestyle – here, sexual functioning – which risks denying their essential normality and similarity to other people. In this sense, residing on a community that is 'consumed by sex' only furthers the othering of the sexual offender. The resident who had internalized notions that sexual offending is akin to alcoholism, a 'disease that I will always have to be on my guard about', was therefore presuming that his capacity to offend was an enduring part of his psychological make-up, which other (physically violent) residents, more focused upon strengths-based capability building and the Pygmalion effects that were driving their identity reconstruction (Maruna *et al.* 2009), did not.

The de-othering of sexual offenders at Grendon is thus partial and profoundly paradoxical: the ideals of the TC demand egalitarianism and communalism, yet the prison is complicit in perpetuating notions of 'otherness' by confining the therapy, and much of the social lives, of one category of offenders to a specialist community. Residents differentiated between sexual offenders, sexually motivated offenders, and 'normal' offenders, and between those who victimized children and those who victimized adults. Such distinctions, of course, only mirror the circumvention of risk and tacit reaffirmation of othering in mainstream VPUs, but it is curious that Grendon, which in all other respects actively pursues the strategic reversal and revisioning (Rhodes 2010) of system ways of imprisonment and rehabilitation, disappointingly fails to challenge the prison's normative expectations in relation to the most stigmatized of offenders and subordinated of masculinities. The limits of de-othering thus reveal the limits to TC 'permissive' and egalitarian ideals within the prison, but perhaps also the divergence between criminological theorizing on the criminogenic properties of othering and the realities of operational practice which must prioritize prisoner safety. Certainly, some A-wing residents praised the merits of, and acceptance and understanding they had found within, specialist 'sex offender only' therapy. The reasons why such offence-specific therapy groups could not be facilitated on otherwise socially integrated communities, however, remains unclear.

Hypermasculinity revisited: the hierarchy of offending reconsidered

The perception that men who had offended against children were less suitable for 'ordinary' generic communities was not universally supported. A minority of senior residents across all Grendon communities supported a fully heterogeneous mix of residents, citing both ideological principle and, more instrumentally, the valuable insights and therapeutic benefits that they perceived sexual offenders contributed to 'regular cons about criminal values and victim empathy' (Winston, Grendon):

> [A-wing] is contrary to the ethos of TCs; I was very surprised to find they had that sort of VPU here and I don't agree with it at all. Sex offenders provide a *massive* aspect of challenge in the community. Most of them were straight-goers[23] in every other aspect of their life, especially paedophiles, so their challenges to people like me are very valuable, very humbling really, because they're not labouring under strong criminal values. They're not interested in drugs or glorifying robberies or whatever; they

> cut right through some of the macho crap – I mean, in the system, if you're an armed robber, you're one of the boys, they give you a medal for it! ... So I welcome sex offenders. We need more of them on here; we need that mix for the unique challenge they bring.
>
> (Luke, Grendon)

As Luke's comments also indicate, certain prisoners are rhetorically rewarded by their peers for the hypermasculine quality of their offending. This reflects what is known as the hierarchy of offending: a 'pecking order' which elevates to the pinnacle of the professional premier league those offences and offenders most consistent with autonomous, confident hypermasculinity: the professionalized acquisition of 'serious money' and material goods; meticulously organized, executed, and protected 'commercial interests'; and the use of instrumental violence and controlled aggression. Such 'hard men', of course, are never sexually attracted to children, and have no need to rape in order to achieve regular sexual satisfaction and a sense of mastery and control over their lives. Indeed, they are more frequently wedded to the reproduction of the patriarchal social order, in which 'their' women and children require protection *from* 'deviant' men *by* 'real' men. Consequently, it is the perpetrators of secretive, shame-ridden sexual offending and the expressive, unrestrained rage of the spurned lover, who are relegated to the lower echelons of non-league criminal amateurism. This is one element of the inmate code that remains remarkably impervious to changing mores, across time and continents (Sapp and Vaughn 1990; Winfree *et al.* 2002; Crewe 2009).

A popular prison pastime for 'regular cons' is therefore to luxuriate in the reassuring notion that there is always some scapegoat 'deviant' against whom one favourably compares; someone whose offending is morally inferior – more harmful and less 'worthwhile' – than one's own. For Grendonites and, to a lesser degree, GTC residents, however, working with and living alongside sexual and sexually motivated offenders in their small groups and communities, such a position rapidly became insupportable.

Most obviously, the assimilation of sexual offenders into the prison enabled the demystification of 'bacons as a breed apart; like they're from a totally different planet to the rest of us' (Ravi, Grendon). Even residents who described themselves as 'tolerant' pre-TC and stated that privately, they had never subscribed to the hierarchy of offending, had rarely *been able* to become acquainted with sexual offenders at other establishments. The combination of the physical and psychological apartheid supported by prison organizational practice, and the inmate code's unequivocal expectations about how a 'con' should behave towards 'nonces' – when 'for your own safety, you can't risk being labelled a nonce lover' (Johnny, Grendon) – effectively ensured their otherness. It could therefore come as a tremendous surprise to these men to learn that the 'rapist' on their group with whom they reciprocally engaged in the psychotherapeutic explorations of their life story, or the 'child molester' with whom they chatted over tea and biscuits at the chapel drop-in, was not some mythical 'monster' or 'beast' but a man, like any other, like them:

> Up until here, my views on beasts was as harsh as anybody's … [But now] I'm on a group with a rapist and I see that he's genuinely here to make amends and change, and see why he did what he did, and he's open to questions, same as I am. He's not a monster; he's just like anyone else. And if being here is going to help him go out and not do that again, and I can be a part of that, then, you know, I'm happy to work with him.
>
> *Why* is *there such antagonism to sex offenders in the system?*
>
> There's a slim part of it that's revulsion. The most part of it is a macho thing – you're not even classed as a *real* man as a sex offender in the system; you're an animal. And it's partly peer pressure: you're expected to join in attacking them, given the chance. I mean, if you're friends with a rapist, you're more or less as open to attack as they are.
>
> (Wesley, Grendon)

> [A resident] is in for rape but I've got to know him and made that decision for myself that he's a good person, so we're mates. He's the kind of guy I would go for a drink with on the outside. He's not a monster, you know? And I'm thinking, wow! I'm sort of surprised that I like someone like that, but one thing I've come to realize about people who have committed sex offences is that they are normal.
>
> (Joe, Grendon)

Residents were therefore free to like or dislike, enjoy the company or not, of other men, based on nothing more than the personal affinity and shared interests that underpin any friendship. Their common ideological and cultural identity – that of a TC resident, committed to therapy and hopeful of lasting change – could overcome the constraints of 'system thinking' about 'nonces'. They had neither to fear the risk of being 'tarred with the same brush' (Shane, Grendon), as if criminogenic proclivities were contagious; nor the influence of the inmate code which dictates that one should avoid even the most casual of pleasantries with these penal pariahs, lest civility be thought to equate with approval. They were members now of a different club, following the different rules of the TC way, including those pertaining to socially permissible friendships.

Moreover, and particularly for those whose small group contained one or more sexual offenders, working collaboratively on each other's 'issues' tended to produce the startling insight that many of these 'issues' were remarkably similar. This is not to deny the specificity of certain risk factors for sexual offences; nor the ocean of intent that separates the man who thinks about sexually 'taking advantage' of a woman (see below) and the man who does translate his primitive drives and inner conflicts into an act of rape. The precise proximal and distal reasons why, for example, one sexually abused child becomes a sexual abuser in adulthood whilst another becomes a robber, or why one 'angry young man' becomes a rapist and another a drug dealer, can also only be located in the depths of individual psychopathology and inclination. Difficulties, however, with attachment, intimacy, and trust resulting from dysfunctional parenting and/or personal relationships; with regulating one's emotional responses to (perceived or actual) rejection, stressful situations, or the more mundane but cumulatively debilitating 'whips and scorns of time'; and with habitually relying upon some external coping mechanism to suffocate one's internal distress, unexpressed anger, and unmet emotional needs – all these problems were repeatedly uncovered in group therapy and across offender 'type':

> I wouldn't know that someone in for rape could have something in common with me but that's what I'm learning: it's all emotional stuff, it's all what's gone on that turns us to the way we are. Nothing just happens. Everything you do has meaning and there are men here with different problems to me, but, in other ways, we're all quite similar … We've all fucked up and have made a mess of things, and we've all done wrong and created victims. That's a very uncomfortable truth to get your head around, know what I mean, that takes a while, but it's making me look at myself differently and question all sorts of things.
>
> (Tony, Grendon)

As Tony also suggests, however, accepting the similarity of one's 'issues' could prompt a critical and ruminative reappraisal of one's crime and, concomitantly, of oneself, not least when this related to conceptions of (hyper) masculinity. One interviewee, for example, recounted a recent group session in which the (male) therapist had stated that many of the residents were 'child abusers on some level' by, for example, absenting themselves as fathers through their imprisonment; or by killing or assaulting the fathers of other children, who were then vicariously traumatized; or by dealing drugs to men too incapacitated to parent properly. He discussed with me, with evident anxiety, whether it really was 'fair comment' that his own neglect of his 'babymums' and offspring 'on the out', and his 'terrifying' early morning arrest by armed police officers in front of his young stepchildren, was 'a form of emotional abuse'. Whilst 'not as bad, obviously', he wondered whether his expressed 'hatred' for his group member who had committed incest was really displacement of his own self-loathing for the harm he had caused his children. In his attempts to provide economically for them through armed robbery and other 'big man crimes', he had to face the 'devastating' realization that he had failed them emotionally, as a father and 'the man of the house'. Some interviewees also acknowledged – though nearly always by reference to other community members – how 'perhaps' 'getting a girl drunk to boost your chances' or 'taking advantage' when she was 'off her trolley' could be 'very close to rape'; which their work with men convicted of that offence forced them to contemplate:

> Don't get me wrong, it's a struggle at times when you sit on groups and you've got to listen to *nasty* details; I'm thinking, how can you do that to another human being? It's very hard to try and understand what was going on for [a resident convicted of rape]. But then, me and him were talking the other day, this was at dinner time, about lads' nights out on the town … [and] it got me thinking about the way I've behaved sometimes when I've been out with my mates. Men do push the boundaries with women sometimes; if there's a chance of a leg over, they do push it. Because there is not a red-blooded male on this planet, when they see an attractive woman, doesn't go, 'Cor, I fancy a bit of that!' Obviously, I would *never* rape a woman, *never*, but men do have a nasty tendency to see women as a means to an end; I'm sure you know what I'm talking about. So the attitudes lads can have – they're not much different to the fellas in here for rape. That's quite scary, and not nice to own up to, you know?
>
> (Nate, Grendon)

Indeed, it was those residents who had committed extremely violent, weapon(s)-assisted assaults and robberies who could be particularly alert to the connections between their offences and those of men who had raped. Money and sex were now appreciated as the prima facie benefits of acquisitive and sexual crime, but which distracted from the 'hidden meanings' buried beneath the surface of the presenting symptoms. The armed robber and the rapist – normally dwelling on opposite rungs of the hierarchical ladder – could therefore acquire and entertain a sophisticated understanding that they shared an interest in privileging their need for power, domination, and control over another,[24] in part to disguise and recompense for their own disassociated fears of hypermasculine vulnerability, inadequacy, and impotence. Whether the 'weapon' of choice was a sawn-off shotgun or a penis, both possessors thereof sought the aggrandizement of the self through the negation of another, and inflicted upon their victim, or the deceased victim's family, incalculable, life-impairing trauma:

> Just 'cos my victim was a man and I fucking shot him, is that better than raping a woman? No, course it ain't. Does it make me more of a man than a fella whose weapon is his dick, to be blunt? No, course it don't. But it's only here I've learned that. I've spent years in the system nonce bashing every chance I got, telling myself I'm so much better than them, but I ain't; in some ways, I'm *worse*. My victim is dead; if you left your victim alive, that's got to be better. Course, if someone had said that to me in the system, I'd have knocked 'em clean out!
>
> (Winston, Grendon)

> I struggle with sex offenders but they have issues, don't they? … To say they're sick is rubbish. They do it because they want to, because they get pleasure from it, because they enjoy the power and control, end of. Like any criminal, like me … The lad on my group, he's very similar to me in many ways. Why he done his crime, it's the power trip; he thought he was this and that and could do what he fucking wanted … That ain't really no different to what I done, know what I mean? Rape fucking disgusts me but when you're sitting in there and talking about it, you're working out why he done his crime and why I done mine, and you see there's loads of the same shit going on.
>
> (Don, Grendon)

The comforting certainties about the 'moral' polarity between the violent and the sexually violent offender accordingly crumbled as the awful truth about the neutralizing, minimizing, inmate stratification system was laid bare:

> You know what I'm realizing about the hierarchy? That it's just about making yourself feel better; kidding yourself that you're not a bad person really. Because if I can tell myself that my crime's not half as bad as his crime, then that means I've not got half the problems he has.
>
> (Andrew, Grendon)

> None of us are oozing with empathy; none of us are blameless. But in the system, you act like you're personally outraged, like some vigilante, 'cos obviously, you're such a nice guy by comparison! But really, it's bollocks; it's all just pretence. Anything to protect your own defence mechanisms and save yourself from actually looking at what *you've* done and the pain *you've* caused.
>
> (Chris, Grendon)

> I don't look at the crime now; I look at the person. I try not to hang on to the beliefs what have held me back all my life. And what were they? They were only fuelled, like everyone else, by criminal values: 'Nonces are the worst, fucking do them.'
>
> *And did you 'do them'?*
>
> Oh yeah! I've been a right bastard to them. It's one of the highlights of your day that is – abusing the nonces! Not proud of it now, but slashings, burn outs,[25] these are normal in the system. But now, I don't look on them as no different to anyone else. It does me good to have them around me … Even for a hardened criminal like me, I've had to listen to some terrible things here. But a rapist, their victim is still alive but mine isn't, so who am I to say that I'm a better person? Because here, you're encouraged to look at yourself, harshly, rather than worrying about where you sit in the pecking order. I could never have done that before.
>
> (Dominic, Grendon)

The deconstruction of hypermasculinity was therefore additionally advanced at Grendon by including some sexual and sexually motivated offenders on all communities, whose presence effectively ensured that the purposeful othering of 'bacons' as completely 'alien', unknowable, and inferior to all other offenders and, moreover, other men, became unsustainable. In the system, the invisibility and 'subordination' of 'nonces' is institutionally perpetuated by their exile to the penal hinterland of VPUs and 'sex offender only' prisons, which unwittingly serves both to confirm their 'unacceptability' and to legitimize the normative (penal) social order of inter-male domination and hypermasculine values and discourses. In psychotherapeutic parlance, it is sexual offenders who are quite literally 'split off' from other offenders, and the VPU that is forced to function as the receptacle for all 'normal' offenders' disowned and displaced feelings of self-loathing, anxiety, and anger. In the TC, however, residents were given the opportunity to learn to differentiate the offender from the offence, to accept that every serious violent offender has 'done wrong and created victims', and thus to discover that they had much in common with, and could learn much from, sexual and sexually motivated offenders.

TC residents' radical and interpretative assertions of commonality across serious offending will not be palatable to many 'ordinary' offenders who, with arguable merit, one may think, justify their contempt of 'nonces' by claiming 'moral distinctions' between 'survival' offences and offences committed for personal gratification (Crewe 2009). Indeed, attitudes to sexual offenders in the TC can be seen to represent the defining test of therapeutization: it was only those residents who had wholeheartedly committed themselves to the TC way who espoused these changed perceptions of sexual offenders and of their own offending. This socialized abandonment of 'system thinking' *even* about 'nonces' may be thought to represent the kind of concealed social control that critics argue always flows through TCs, by collectively encouraging or psychologically coercing residents into accepting the TC's ideologically driven stance on assimilation. Certainly, it reflected the influence of so-called 'culture carriers': senior residents whose acquired knowledge and internalized acceptance of TC rules and practices passes, through verbal instruction and by lived example, from one generation of residents to the next. Such Grendonites, then, not only conveyed to newer arrivals that integration was the norm but, in some cases, sought to persuade their peers that integration *should* be the norm. GTC residents, by contrast, had no experience of sexual (as opposed to sexually motivated) offenders on their community and, without this established tradition, consequently had no expectation that they should 'tolerate', or would be able to work constructively with, sexual offenders.

What Grendonites said they gained from working with 'nonces', however, was the ability to render obsolete the ordering of the moral gravity of offences, with its almost impossible micro-calculations of which crime of serious personal violence is 'worse' and in which circumstances. Instead, they recognized the need to focus on and take responsibility for 'what *you've* done and the pain *you've* caused', rather than trying to externalize and project their feelings of shame, guilt, distress, fear, and self-disgust onto others. Within these parameters, it became impossible for residents to sustain an 'honourable', hypermasculine self- and social image when confronted with the thematic similarities between crimes which also, if not equally, disempower and degrade their victims; and between the enacted misogynistic values of men convicted of rape, and the discursively endorsed notions of 'laddism' and culturally embedded myths about rape, rapists, and rape victims (Burt 1980, 1983; Malamuth 1981; Briere and Malamuth 1983).

The re-evaluation of hypermasculine values and practices the TC invites could therefore produce significant changes to men's sense of self *as a man*. Kimmel (2001:275, emphasis preserved) contends that 'masculinity is a *homosocial* enactment … we want other men to grant us our manhood'. By changing the ground rules by which prison masculinities are usually performed, TC residents agreed to approve – to grant the status of 'manhood' to – alternative, desistance-friendly abilities and qualities: the capacity to access and express 'soft' emotions, to be or find 'who *you really are*', and to form new understandings of respect, criminal status, and the attractions of power and control over others, in its various manifestations. These men no longer had to be afraid that their vulnerability and 'failure' to cope with and conceal their problems would be adversely judged. This emboldened them to have the courage and 'manly' assurance to allow multiple masculinities to emerge, to learn to liberate themselves from the imprisonment of 'macho masks', and to invert some of the hierarchies of power amongst men. Combined with the safety normally assured by the TC's 'no violence' rule, sexual offenders could then enjoy a level of normalizing inclusivity usually unavailable to them in secure prisons. Performative hypermasculinity amongst men was revealed for what it fundamentally is: an attempt to hide and displace onto others one's core vulnerability. Accordingly, 'the façades of being macho', which conventionally dictate homosocial relations in prisons and contribute to criminogenic attitudes, were largely overcome.

7 Pursuing change the TC way and beyond

> I've become here the person I've always wanted to be; the person that's always been there underneath but was scared to come out and got covered up with all the bollocks of my lifestyle and attitudes … I am the person now I was always meant to be, but who got lost somewhere along the way.
>
> (Neil, Grendon)

A treatment method as complex and multifaceted as the therapeutic community is difficult to anatomize for the different processes and mechanisms potentially at work. Academics and practitioners from diverse disciplinary backgrounds all have their own, equally valid, ways of understanding 'what happens' in a TC. This book, written by a criminologist and informed by serving residents' perspectives, presents one such alternative but complementary explanation of TCs' enablement of change; an explanation that highlights progressive improvements to residents' present and prospective self-concept, 'storied self' (McAdams 1996), and expectations. The empirical 'grounded theory' of the TC way of offender rehabilitation and imprisonment presented here derives from the author's semi-ethnographic research in three prison-based TCs and qualitative interviewing of 60 residents; a method and experience of research recounted and reflected upon in Chapter 2. The book's key findings cohere with recent theoretical and empirical developments in understanding desistance from crime. These emphasize the importance of purposive and agentic changes to the offender's personal identity and self-narrative, so that, for example, the 'old' self is redefined and repositioned as a bridge, rather than a barrier, to the emergence of a 'better' 'replacement self' (Giordano *et al.* 2002), who is committed to a 'redemption script' (Maruna 2001) and prepared for a crime-free future. My research therefore lends support to the argument that even the most serious of offenders can 'change *for the better*' (Robinson and Crow 2009:3, emphasis preserved), and one way in which this can be achieved is by either re-identifying with 'the real me … allowing that decent person to come through' (Michael, Grendon), or rediscovering 'the old me, before I went wrong' (Nigel, Grendon), or even 'finding the me that I always wanted to be, but was never allowed to be' (Natalie,

Send). Such identity reconstruction and narrative reframing is uniquely advanced in prison-based TCs because, in contrast to residents' experiences of mainstream cognitive-behavioural interventions or system imprisonment, the TC creates, through prolonged engagement in psychodynamic psychotherapy and a '24/7' culture of observation and enquiry, opportunities to develop, practise, and have reaffirmed by a supportive community, ways of thinking about oneself and one's capabilities positively and of behaving towards and relating to other people pro-socially.

The story arc of this book, then, has been that people who enter a prison-based TC can find in this 'different' penal environment and the 'different' rehabilitative method it offers, ways in which to start to become someone 'different'. As Chapter 1 explained, the TC has always challenged the received wisdom about how treatment, in psychiatric or penal settings, can be most effectively delivered. More specifically, prison-based TC culture consciously transcends and renounces the system 'way' of imprisonment and, in so doing, fundamentally disputes both populist and academic representations of what life is – and by implication, 'naturally' has to be – like in prison. Chapter 3 accordingly detailed how new arrivals were immediately exposed to institutional indicators of 'difference': informal and more egalitarian relationships with prison staff, the reciprocated use of first names, the 'freeing' of communication, early involvement in the day-to-day running of the community, and, at Grendon, the integration of some sexual offenders. Prisoners who could successfully negotiate the simultaneously obvious and subtle processes of therapeutization began to redefine their identity towards that of *residents* living in a therapeutically literate social *community,* and started to believe that, even after many years of offending or previously unsuccessful attempts at rehabilitation, 'I don't have to be that person no more; I *can* change' (James, Grendon).

The experience and expression of constructive, trusting, and genuinely caring attachments to other community members, facilitated by community living and unusual (in the penal environment) practices such as 'open-door' wing offices and communal dining, was explored in Chapter 4. Residents gained through group therapy emotional insight into their lives and the ability to link experiences cognitively, and benefited from the cathartic disclosure of pain-filled life histories in which 'the *true meaning*' (Charles, Grendon) of their offending was revealed over time. They discovered the universality (Yalom 1995:5–7) of their seemingly intractable and 'shameful' and 'unacceptable' problems, impulses, and fantasies, and the commonalities in residents' personal and offending histories, which resulted in the reassuring recognition that 'I'm *not* the only one. It makes you feel more normal' (Richie, GTC). In helping and supporting each other, as auxiliary therapists and participants in the group psychotherapy process, residents found that their self-esteem improved, and their understanding of their own and others' problems deepened.

Chapter 5 highlighted the unique opportunities afforded to TC residents for democratized participation in and accountable decision making about the management of their community. The TC regime demanded from its residents 'some *real* responsibility, which, let's be honest, is a novelty for most of us!' (Steve, GTC), *for* oneself, one's peers, and the therapeutic integrity and cohesiveness of one's community, rather than the responsibilization *of* prisoners in the mainstream. In the well-functioning, norm-creating, self-policing TC, residents had no reason to fear, or to seek to protect themselves against, the pervasive underbelly of violence, exploitation, and the treachery that the 'trappings of the system – drugs, booze, mobile phones' (Bill, Grendon) customarily attract; nor any reason to resist or seek to subvert the 'rules' collectively agreed by and for the protection of the community. Moreover, amongst 'cons who can't be conned', their scrutiny of each other's behaviour was as unsentimental as it was searching. All of the most therapeutically successful challenges emanated from other residents, who reinterpreted 'grassing' as therapeutic feedback 'to help someone with his behaviours and to keep the community safe' (Steve, GTC). These positive experiences of responsibility enabled residents to develop, or pro-socially re-develop, new interpersonal, communication, and organizational skills, which fundamentally challenged some of the self-limiting, esteem-depleting ideas they had held about themselves, and encouraged them to question, then jettison, the crime-supporting, culpability-minimizing 'beliefs what have held me back all my life' (Dominic, Grendon).

The tangible sense of safety, normative compliance, and self-control this 'social plus' model of crime prevention engineered, combined with the emotional honesty and openness therapy promoted, encouraged men to emerge from behind the hypermasculine, hyper-vigilant, invulnerable masks they had felt compelled to adopt in other secure prisons, as Chapter 6 explored. Grendon, with its peaceful, if partial, integration of sexual (and other so-called 'vulnerable') offenders, also drew its men into rethinking some of the motivations behind their offending; while learning from senior, therapeutically perceptive residents encouraged all residents to afford appraisal respect to those who achieved change and could model for TC novices 'better' ways to respond to, manage, and cope with their 'issues'.

This concluding chapter begins by documenting residents' self-assessments of their prospects for life beyond the TC. The themes of the preceding chapters are then drawn together to present an explanation of how change can be achieved in the penal counter-culture that is the prison-based TC.[1]

Desistance in process: proceed with caution

Giving up habitual criminal offending, like the renunciation of any 'bad habit', is often a demanding personal challenge. It is also, as the desistance literature abundantly illustrates, a process – a gradual, incremental, often faltering process – and 'relapses' back into crime have been known to occur many years after last reconviction. For this reason, it is arguably only after a person's death that one can pinpoint with any confidence a time after which the ex-offender truly did become an ex-offender (though even then, having no further reconvictions does not necessarily equate with no further re-offending). Accounts of desistance are therefore always, whilst the desister remains alive, inherently incomplete.

To borrow from the 'journey' metaphor many interviewees spontaneously adopted when discussing their therapeutic progress, most resident participants in this research were keenly aware they were still in transit towards change, with only a minority of senior residents possessed of the self-assurance to declare themselves as having truly arrived as a rehabilitated ex-offender. This research therefore does not claim that the TC had definitely enabled change which did eventually result in a non-offending, productive, and peaceable life upon release. Indeed, apart from the blunt instrument of reconviction studies, very little is known about the transferability and durability of TC treatment effects beyond the TC. Whilst one hesitates to repeat the customary, and potentially self-serving, refrain of researchers that 'more research is needed', further qualitative longitudinal research *is* sorely needed to determine what happens to TC graduates in general, and in particular whether the kind of improvements to residents' personal identities that this research identified were sustained following graduates' transfer to other (less supportive) prisons and after release. Moreover, given the hesitant and gradual nature of desistance, it is perhaps unrealistic to expect prison-based TCs to be able to demonstrate that they, and they alone, provided the magic bullet, the radical intervention, by which a damaged and damaging offender irrevocably ceased to be so, and a lifetime of law-abiding conformity was embraced. One can, however, identify turning points (Sampson and Laub 1993) or hooks for change (Giordano *et al.* 2002) in an offender's life, favourable to giving up crime, and an evidence base of already achieved and externally verifiable change, which bodes well for the future. That is the partial desistance, the desistance in process, which this research uncovered.

When asked directly about their prospects for desistance post-release, 40 per cent of the resident participants in this research were 'certain' they would 'definitely not' re-offend 'ever'. Of these six women and 18 men, 17 were serving indeterminate sentences, although only two presented their emphatic renunciation of crime as resulting at least in part from the deterrent effect of the dire personal consequences they knew would follow should they be reconvicted: 'It's simply not an option because I would die in prison' (Bill, Grendon); or even, 'I'll be on a life licence so I can't really afford to offend again. Plus, I really wouldn't dare commit another crime because my mum would kick my fucking head in!' (Callum, Grendon). The majority directly credited their confidence that they had changed to the life-transforming, life-enhancing '*real* rehabilitation' they had undergone in the TC and the pro-social reinvention of the self this had enabled. They had few or no qualms about transferring back to mainstream prisons, as they would import with them the 'lessons learned … [and] the skills you need to avoid trouble' (Shane, Grendon); and could provide a reasoned explanation as to why offending was no longer consistent with or 'fitted' into the 'new me' they had created and the new life they now envisaged for themselves:

> I think that it's now very unlikely that I will re-offend in any way. If I hadn't been here, I think I would still have been a sky-high risk, regardless of what I was saying to the Parole Board or anybody else who wanted to hear it. Because you can do all the courses you like, and, you know, be nice to the screws and stay under their radar [chuckles], but that's not *real* rehabilitation; that's just doing what you need to do to get out. Because if you haven't done the underlying work, if you haven't pulled yourself apart to see who you are, and why you've been the way you have and *really* worked, day after day, at being someone better, then you're not going to be any different when you're out. So while I still feel vulnerable in some ways and I've still got my fears and concerns, I'm certain I won't re-offend. I'm just not the person I was, and the person I am now, isn't interested in the kind of things that land you in prison.
>
> (Neil, Grendon)

> I told myself from very early days inside that I wouldn't be coming back again … But I think the difference was then, I just wanted to believe it; wanted it to be true, but didn't have the ability to make it a certainty. And here, it's about learning to make it a certainty: having more awareness, being able to deal with things, to think in stressful situations – that's what we learn to do here. So I feel equipped now to go out there and not offend again, to be *certain* of that rather than just wanting it to be okay.
>
> (Michael, Grendon)

A further 47 per cent of interviewees were 'cautiously optimistic' that their rehabilitation was genuine and robust: they did 'not want to' re-offend at all, and were 'almost certain' they would not. This less than perfect self-assessment of their ability to desist *entirely* from crime in the future, whatever circumstances they encountered, may seem at odds with residents' glowing descriptions of the 'better person' they had become in the TC. Their hesitancy simply reflected, however, their awareness of a range of contingencies and, in particular, substantial social difficulties commonly associated with resettlement (or, as it is known in the United States, re-entry), which might derail their resolve to 'go straight' (see, for example, Social Exclusion Unit 2002; Clancy *et al.* 2006; May *et al.* 2008). Securing permanent accommodation, viable and stable employment, and meaningful personal relationships; being required to return to live in a location where one's former criminal reputation still lingers, and wherein former 'business associates' might not respect or support the ex-offender's proclamation of a 'new' identity; maintaining addiction-free, physical and mental well-being; and overcoming poverty and debt, social isolation, and the stigma sometimes attached to those whom the community remains reluctant to 'restore'; these are all substantial, enduring, and very real difficulties for many released prisoners which cannot simply be wished away by the assumption of a new identity:

> I want to say that I won't ever re-offend but that's not realistic, is it? … I choose not to take drugs in here, and in TC, I've got every bit of support I could ever need not to. But on the out, there's just me … I really want things to be different but I need to get a support network out there, rehab or self-help or something like that, because I know if I can get some support, there's a 99 per cent chance I can stay clean and away from crime.
>
> (Shelley, Send)

> Obviously I can't say that I'm *never* going to come to prison again, like I can never say that I'm never going to do drugs again, but I've made a decision that I don't want to. And I'm going to do whatever is in my power to keep out of jail and to not take drugs or drink alcohol again. I don't want to be around those people that would pull me back down; I don't want to be the person I was ever again. So I'm pretty sure that I won't re-offend but if I do, it wouldn't be for violent crime. I do know that.
>
> (James, Grendon)

James's statement that any re-offending would be for a less serious offence was commonly repeated by other interviewees. The possibility that they might commit an acquisitive (property) crime but not one which involved interpersonal violence represented for many a significant qualitative improvement in the nature of their offending; a nuanced indicator of reduced risk to others which quantitative reconviction figures cannot always capture. The ability residents said they had gained to manage and contain violent impulses and 'difficult' emotions within the periodically highly charged TC environment, to identify and comprehend the source of their 'issues', and to care for and be empathetic towards others, had changed the type of offences they could conceive of themselves as committing: 'I can't hurt anyone now, because I understand what that hurt feels like … Once you do, you know, it changes everything' (Muktar, Grendon). Equally, men who had exclusively committed sexual offences against children also believed that their residency had fundamentally changed their attitudes to and challenged their delusions about their offending:

> I'm *really* committed to not re-offending. I've got lots of coping strategies that I didn't have previously, and a much deeper understanding of my problems. I feel a lot better about myself as a person and feel able to cope better with my fantasies, and I know now what damage my abuse does.

> I've had it literally shoved right in my face that I was doing tremendous harm. You can't pick and choose what you listen to and you can't hide from the harm you've done here. I've had to look at my whole personality and change the bits I don't like and enhance the bits that I do like. I've done that and now I want to go out and lead a fulfilling life without re-offending … I can't say that I definitely, 100 per cent will not offend again but I feel very sure I won't. As much as I will struggle with my attraction to children, I can't kid myself now about the harm I've caused, and would cause if I ever re-offended, so that's a big difference to before.
>
> (Leslie, Grendon)

This group of 'pretty sure' residents also expressed reservations not just about the problems they might encounter upon release, but upon their return to (ideally, lower security category) mainstream prisons to complete their sentence. At best, they matter-of-factly accepted that 'the system has absolutely *nothing* to offer me after here' (Tim, Grendon), and viewed their transfer back to mainstream imprisonment warily, as a potential obstacle to their continued ownership of a 'new me' and a malignant force against which they would have to battle just to maintain the progress they had made in the TC.[2] In particular, some interviewees, especially those serving indeterminate sentences, expressed the concern that identifying themselves or being identified as a TC graduate would 'put a price' on their head, because prisoners who had no interest in rehabilitation would seek to undermine TC graduates' claims to change by trying to provoke or tempt them into 'trouble'. Demonstrating their newly gained insightfulness, however, these residents also portrayed such prisoners as possessed of a fear of change, which drove their need to believe that other offenders cannot and do not change: they denied their own capacity for change by seeking to destroy change in others. This prompted the mental preparation of an avoidance strategy, whereby they would seek to safeguard their rehabilitation by evading the contamination of those who would undermine them. Wesley (Grendon) spoke for many when he predicted that:

> I'll have to probably isolate myself going back into the system because what they teach you here, and the way they teach you to be, you can't be like that in the system. It's just not feasible, unless you can find some like-minded people to be with.

The probable accuracy of these comments is underlined by the experiences of 40 former Grendonites who were re-interviewed after their transfer to other prisons by Genders and Player (1995). Whilst 80 per cent of these men continued to feel that they had benefited from their TC experience and 60 per cent believed that their residency had reduced their risk of re-offending, 60 per cent also reported some difficulties in readjusting to the system and conventional prison culture. This problem seemed to be particularly acute for 'vulnerable prisoners' (n = 16), of whom nine said that having enjoyed the liberation of the TC, to find themselves once again under threat of violence and relegated to pariah status in the system, rendered the completion of their sentence there *more* difficult. Few ex-residents felt able to credit their present establishment with assisting in the nurturance of their developmental progression; indeed, the majority 'had effectively put their lives on "hold", and suspended much of what they had learned at Grendon' (ibid.:175).

The remaining 13 per cent (all men) of my sample comprised mostly of residents with less than one's year residency, who presented themselves as travelling towards what they 'hoped' or 'thought' would be the destination of desistance, *if* they continued to make progress with their therapy. Echoing their peers, they too believed that any future re-offending would be less serious and more infrequent than previously, with some itemizing the 'only' 'minor' offending they could envisage themselves committing as including opportunistic (but non-contact) 'petty' theft, handling stolen goods, or tax evasion and benefit fraud (working 'cash in hand' while 'signing on'). No one was fully *intending* to commit violent or sexually violent crime again, nor portrayed themselves as hapless victims of fate, entirely unable to determine their future. Chris's (Grendon) self-assessment of his prospects was representative of these residents:

> I think if I go a little bit more deeper in my therapy, and stay on that path, I think people with that kind of understanding just naturally don't offend. I don't think you can offend when you're fully aware of what you're doing, to you and other people ... I hope that what I'm learning here will keep me on the right path. I could fall backwards, or I could keep walking forwards. I won't be doing [my index offence] again, that's for sure, but little things, maybe ... I don't want to fall back, but it will just take courage, I suppose, to keep going forwards, to keep learning. I've got a good character. I had a bad time there for a little while, but I've rediscovered what I'd lost here. So it will depend on me.

TC residents therefore displayed an agentic determination and a passionate belief in themselves to 'go straight' or, at minimum, 'straighter' than ever before. Such confidence may appear to some readers to be naively optimistic; it may seem too easy to make such predictions when one is cocooned in prison and hence removed to a significant extent from the criminogenic temptations of life 'on the out'. Certainly, the reconviction statistics amongst former prisoners from across the prison estate consistently tell another, less encouraging, tale; and claims to have created a temporary 'escape' identity in prison – such as a student, lawyer, or sportsman, for example (Jewkes 2002) – and unilateral declarations of 'reform' or, at least, an expressed desire 'not to return' to prison, are commonplace. What, then, accounts for residents' extraordinary confidence in their (eventual) rehabilitation, and why might their declarations of long-lasting change be thought credible?

First, it mattered to residents that the prison-based TC was 'different', because this provided them with an operational and cultural framework within which to pursue their aspirations to become someone 'different'. As a distinct and numerically limited group of residents living within a custodial community, they experienced their environment as more decent and less damaging than 'normal' prisons because of the TC's pronounced and pervasive ethic of care and ethos of change (Stevens 2011). Residents found in the TC 'a kind and caring atmosphere with everyone looking out for each other' (Belinda, Send), a 'positive feel to the place' (Dominic, Grendon), and 'a humane environment' (Raymond, GTC); with, at Grendon, as the MQPL survey has established, the highest quality of life of any secure establishment in the Anglo-Welsh prison system (Newton 2006; Shefer 2010b). To neo-abolitionists, discourses around decency and humanity in prison risk legitimizing and theorizing 'the prison' into acceptability: the term 'humane imprisonment', they argue, represents 'an oxymoronic juxtaposition of incompatible objectives' (Toch 2006:1). There is no such thing, however, as 'the prison' as a monolithic dispenser of pain and 'discipline' (Foucault 1977). Although the fundamental characteristics of imprisonment – the inherent coerciveness of detention and innate pains of imprisonment (Sykes 1958) – are unchangeable, prisons are experienced as more or less coercive, more or less painful, more or less self-limiting, depending upon the culture of each establishment and the political context within which the prisons of any given country operate. 'Prisons can be moral communities and can be experienced as such' (Liebling, assisted by Arnold 2004:474), not least when prisoners' intrinsic humanity is affirmed, and their capacity for '*real* rehabilitation' and '*real* responsibility' is respected. The TC created for its residents a less painful experience *in prison* and produced a greater moral performance *as a prison*.

Central to residents' more favourable assessments of the TC as a prison was their perception that TCs are exceptionally committed to the enablement of rehabilitation: 'Grendon is a rehabilitative changing house! Everything that you need to change is here' (Johnny, Grendon). For prisons to aspire to be 'serious about decency, then [they've] got to be serious about rehabilitation' (Mark, Grendon); yet it was a depressing subtext of this research that TC residents had negligible faith in system imprisonment as an instrument of rehabilitation. They routinely and roundly condemned the closed prisons of England and Wales as not merely unable to 'deliver' rehabilitation through 'superficial' cognitive-behavioural OBPs – not least, because 'fundamentally, the average con doesn't *want* to change; I know, I used to be the average con' (Nate, Grendon) – but as institutions infinitely more suited to promoting a furtherance and enhancement of criminal behaviours and criminogenic cultures. TC residents were adamant that they had simply not encountered, in 'normal' prisons, a social and learning environment that robustly challenged the determinism of their own low expectations of themselves and others and uncovered the reasons behind their offending, nor a culture that was supportive and facilitative of change:

> The rehabilitation is absolutely shite in most prisons. I've been to prison nine times, so where's the rehabilitation in that? Them offending behaviour programmes, they're pathetic, they're superficial. My issues go deeper than all that cognitive stuff. This is the first time I've done something that is *really* helping me.
>
> (Don, Grendon)

> There is nothing rehabilitating *ever* about system prisons, nothing in the world. You learn how to be *more* devious, how to dodge MDTs, how to manipulate; you learn how to survive ... If you want rehabilitation, this is the place, this is the real deal. We're all trying to change here, so we're all in the same boat, but in the system, change is a swear word! People there don't want to change and if you're their mate, they don't want you to change neither 'cos that would make them look bad, wouldn't it?
>
> (Robbie, Grendon)

Residents' overtly discursive signage of differentiation, then – their blunt disparagement and perhaps, at times, oversimplified demonization of the system, its inmate culture, and reliance upon cognitive-behavioural OBPs, as opposed to the progressive TC way and its deployment of psychodynamic psychotherapy – nurtured a symbolically significant sense of 'collective internal definition' (Jenkins 2004:82), and a social identity which constituted 'an act of power' (Laclau 1990:33, cited in Hall 2000:18). As Jenkins (2004:79, emphasis preserved) observes, 'Logically, *in*clusion entails *ex*clusion, if only by default ... Defining "us" involves defining a range of "thems" also.' In being required to 'do *everything* differently' (Ross, GTC), even to the extent of mastering an exclusionary jargon of 'being grouped', 'specials', use of 'therapy speak', and so on, and, at Grendon, taking on the identity-confirming moniker of Grendonites, TC residents came to perceive of themselves as an 'us'; as members of a superior 'special kind' of penal club, to which they invariably came to feel intense loyalty and about which they shared proprietorial concern. This 'us' contrasted with, and encouraged the repudiation of, all the 'thems' of the system, including *their own* 'old' former offender identity and all that it had implied.

A second factor in enabling desistance in process was that residents were encouraged, through their democratized engagement in and responsibility for their community, to assume a repertoire of self-esteem enhancing and capacity-building roles – community member, auxiliary therapist, decision maker, disciplinarian, rule-enforcer, peacemaker, social host, educator, mentor, role model – and to demonstrate qualities – caring, empathetic, supportive, analytical, responsible, reliable, trustworthy, safety-conscious, organized, admirable – almost wholly unavailable to offenders incarcerated within deficits-focused mainstream prisons. Prisoners cannot be told to show concern for others or to take responsibility for themselves without any meaningful opportunities to do so. Equally, people who have previously behaved uncaringly and irresponsibly, towards society and towards themselves, do not suddenly become caring and responsible by imprisoning them within a regime in which 'kindness is seen as weakness' (Robbie, Grendon) and the ability to exercise some control over and effect changes to one's daily life is highly curtailed. The opportunity to do both in the TC allowed for the discovery that 'you can do things, good things, worthwhile things, that you never thought you could do' (Ben, GTC) and thus produced the Pygmalion effect of higher expectations of prisoners resulting in their higher performance (Maruna *et al.* 2004). Residents' endeavours to change were refocused from their perceived 'deficits' to their newly claimed or rediscovered 'strengths', and the positive contribution, through 'community service' and as co-therapists, they made to the lives of others. Over time, as the congruent good lives model of offender rehabilitation proposes (for example, Ward *et al.* 2007), the 'good things' of which individual residents were shown to be capable nurtured profound improvements to their self-worth, self-confidence, and self-efficacy. Moreover, the resulting re-envisaged identity and re-imagined future was not claimed unilaterally by the individual but was, as it must be, confirmed by the 'looking glass' held up by his or her peers or social visitors and their recognition of change:

> I don't think I'll be coming back to prison no more 'cos I've changed. Sometimes it's hard to measure how well you've done, ain't it, but my people outside, they knew me as the person I was and when I see them now, they say, 'You've changed so much' … I mean, I feel different anyway, but I'm *definitely* doing something right because my people say they can see the new me and they know me from old … I think I can take with me the changes I done here. I never had no hope before, never saw my life being no different, but now, I *am* like a new person; I *am* different, and my life outside will be too.
>
> (Lenny, Grendon)

The excavation and exploration of residents' life histories in group therapy, meanwhile, enabled them to understand how their past had influenced their present but need not dictate their future. The TC had provided them with the safe arena in which to 'go back to go forwards' (Manor 1994:252): to return oneself, mentally and emotionally, to 'the dark places in your life' (Josephine, Send) with all its attendant vulnerabilities and maladjusted coping mechanisms, in order to first truly feel and then alleviate the pains they had suffered, accept responsibility for the pains they had caused others to suffer, and progress towards a future in which, as many TC residents liked to say, they would create 'no more victims'. By positioning their offending within their whole life story, TC residents were enabled to transcend their imposed master status of 'offender' or 'prisoner', whose cognitive deficits and risk factors normally define the parameters of treatment. Instead, their self-presentation was that of a human being with a multifaceted life history and multi-dimensional needs and abilities, for whom the commission of criminal offences was only one – neither fundamental nor permanent – component of that identity. Such contextual and holistic understanding was not to deny the seriousness of the offence or the offender's responsibility for it; nor did it minimize the importance of risk assessment for the TC staff who must still recognize, record, and manage that risk. Forensic psychotherapy presumes, however, that understanding of and reflection upon why one has committed heinous offences is necessary if one is to escape from the trauma of one's past, heal one's damaged and damaging self-concept, and reposition one's prospective self-narrative to allow for a happier and personally meaningful future.

To reflect upon one's life in therapy, then, is to invite one's narrative identity to be challenged and changed as a consequence of that self-reflection. Residents' narrative plotlines exposed, situated, and hence humanized their actions, but also challenged the damaging and self-limiting notions some residents had unconsciously created and passively accepted about the inevitability of their life history, and the tentacular ability of crime to grasp hold of an individual and infiltrate every aspect of one's identity. 'Thieving, violence, was normal in my family' may have worked as an explanation for the resident's initiation into crime but within the scrutiny of the small group, the determinism it contained was challenged by any evidence that the resident was already deviating from the 'story' by which he or she had lived. Equally, conventional 'con' self-narratives, those hypermasculine, anti-authoritarian, crime-glorifying, risk-taking tales of criminal derring-do, sometimes intertwined with self-pitying justifications to the effect that 'life made me do it', could no longer be sustained when residents disclosed to the group incidents of trauma and need, remorse and shame, and the re-evaluation and regret they prompted. It is no coincidence that it is these redrafted scripts, and not stories of bravura and minimization, that often correlate with accounts of desistance.

The narrative could therefore be reframed to reflect the adoption of a new normality within the new normative milieu of the TC, and its implications for narrative emplotment beyond the TC explored. This process was experienced by some residents as an explicitly reconstructive endeavour, in which they perceived the purpose of therapy as 'like a jigsaw puzzle, with all of these pieces on the table, and I've got to put them in, one by one, to make the full picture of my life' (Jenny, Send). Previously, the cognitive and affective factors, and hidden motivations of the choices they had made, including to offend, had been invariably mysterious *to them*. These men and women had been, in their own self-assessment, 'closed off' to their emotions, 'in denial' about their lives, and 'unknown', partially or completely, even to themselves. The work of the small group exposed this opaque internal world to the light of therapeutic insight, prompting the disclosure of the resident's both felt and intellectualized past, the 'psychological truths' (McAdams 1993:12) it contained for the story teller, and thus the potential for a re-storied, reconstructed self. As one senior GTC resident explained:

> I needed to cry out and feel sad and I needed to feel this hate for myself and to feel the shame and guilt and to give that child that I was, a voice. Being here has enabled me to cry … I can see now how everything in my life stems from what happened to me as a child and how all the mistakes I've made, and masking everything with drugs and alcohol, and the murder I committed, all are related to *not* being able to deal with emotions before … I like myself now. I have much more peace of mind. I feel able now to draw a line under the past and move on. I'm not carrying around all that self-hatred any more, and it's completely changed the way I see myself – and other people, because I've learned to trust people again here … I've discovered who I am.

The cumulative effect of the TC experience was therefore fundamentally to change the ways in which residents understood themselves, their offending and their life history, and thought about their life beyond prison. Over time, residents could sew together the constituent parts of their life into the kind of cohesive 'redemption script' Maruna (2001) identified amongst his desisters, which both made sense of the past and made plausible a desistance-focused future. The new, or rediscovered, or reclaimed and newly endorsed identities, functions, and characteristics that residents accumulated gradually empowered them to erect a psychological boundary between the system inmate they were, the TC resident they are, and the 'better person' they aspired to become. Just as Maruna's desisters and persisters revelled in polarized cognitive understandings of their lives, so the research participants in this study cognitively distanced 'the person I was' from 'the person I am now' and wanted to remain:

> Before GTC, I was kind of lost and really broken … I've changed so much. I honestly don't believe I will ever offend again because I'm not that person now. I've found a better person here.
>
> (Ben, GTC)

> I'm a straight-goer now. I could never say that before. I fucked everything up for myself, time after time. But now, I don't want no shady dealings, know what I mean? I'm not interested; it just ain't what I'm about any more. I've changed. I'm a different man now and there's no going back.
>
> (Winston, Grendon)

> I got a beautiful letter off my youngest yesterday and she said, 'I don't know what they're doing to you there but I hope they keep doing it, because you're different.' TC can work, if you want it to. You're allowed to change in here, they want you to change. I always knew there was someone else underneath, not just the person who used drugs and violence and got into trouble, but she got lost a long time ago. And here, I've found her again. I've been able to let go the woman I was, and go right back to find me again, the real me.
>
> (Louise, Send)

To think of oneself as a 'better person' gives rise to a third factor which explains TC residents' new-found confidence: hope. As conceptualized by Snyder (1994, 2002; Snyder *et al.* 1991), hope is a positive motivational state based on three interdependent components: goals, agency thinking, and pathways thinking. In other words, it requires the will (motivation and determination) to reach one's desired goal and belief that one is capable of achieving that goal combined with identified (psychological and practical) ways, plans, or routes by which to reach that goal. Such hope is therefore not merely wishful thinking or blind optimism, but an aspiration that is based on one's sense of competency or self-efficacy and is married to a plausible method.

The importance of hope to offenders has not yet been widely recognized by criminologists or criminal justice practitioners. This is despite a small but persuasive body of research which indicates that higher levels of hope for and belief in one's ability to desist is associated with lower reconviction rates (Maruna 2001; Burnett and Maruna 2004; LeBel *et al.* 2008; Martin and Stermac 2010), and which asserts the importance of the generation and enhancement of hope to rehabilitative work with sexual offenders (Marshall *et al.* 2005; Moulden and Marshall 2005). Notably, Ros Burnett (1992) compared 130 persistent imprisoned property offenders' pre-release self-reports of whether they wanted, and thought themselves able, to 'go straight', with their post-release self-reported offending after different periods of time. She found a strong correlation between these men's estimates of their likelihood of re-offending and actual re-offending, which suggests that offenders could both predict their own susceptibility to recidivism reasonably accurately and that the extent of their hope for the future might have a positive impact upon their successful resettlement. Ten years later, Burnett and Maruna's (2004) reconviction study of the same sample found that the average cohort member had since acquired a further six convictions and served another 27 months in prison. Re-examination of Burnett's original data also revealed that high levels of hope prior to release continued to correlate with successful post-prison desistance and appeared to assist the would-be desister to cope better with the resettlement problems that they invariably encountered, as long as these exogenous problems were neither too severe nor too numerous. Burnett and Maruna (2004:399) therefore concluded that 'self-confidence in one's ability to change seems to be a necessary, if not sufficient, condition for an individual to be able to desist from crime', because the sense of hope, autonomy, and self-efficacy they enjoyed protected them from the fatalistic 'doomed to deviance' mindset (Maruna 2001) frequently adopted by persisters.

For the residents in this study, their TC experiences had, in Synder's term, strengthened their agency thinking: their initial desire or perceived need to change, their confidence to believe that they could change, and, in time, their hope that the changes they had made and seen confirmed by others could be sustained beyond the TC. Their positive expectations for change were constantly reinforced by staff members who were 'very into therapy and change' (Nick, Grendon) and through the formal recording of therapy targets and treatment gains, and by being witness to change in others, which in turn reinforced and reaffirmed for all residents the plausibility of change, the cultural acceptability and desirability of change, and the demonstrable attainability of change: 'You can actually see people changing. I've seen people change so much in the time I've been here and that gives me hope for myself' (Andrew, Grendon). Hope, for these serious and generally recidivist imprisoned offenders, was a hitherto almost entirely unknown phenomenon. In the custodial sentences these residents had already served and the correctional interventions they had previously 'successfully' completed, *prior* to re-offending again, nothing had occurred to foster any hope for change or, indeed, any plausible, evidence-based grounds for hope. All earlier attempts at rehabilitation had neither produced any significant impact upon their willingness or ability to desist from crime, nor fundamentally challenged their estimation and expectations of themselves and of others; let alone invited existential meditations upon who they really were and might dare to imagine they could become. 'Personal development' had been measured only in terms of the progression of a criminal career and acquisition of additional criminal 'skills sets'; whilst prison had been 'an inconvenience' which they 'hoped' to avoid only by escaping detection for their offending, not through any belief that they could actually (choose to) desist from offending.

To hear these residents narrate the ways in which they had changed in the TC and describe their belief that these changes were 'for real' was therefore powerfully affecting: they were desperados no more. Hopelessness had been replaced by hope, and low self-esteem by self-confidence and self-efficacy. The TC had enabled them to conjoin their motivation to change with a method of change; a method that was uniquely able to inspire in them and communicate to them the genuine possibilities for other selves and other futures. Rather than aimlessly, despondently, 'doing time', these residents considered they were '*making* time … trying to create something positive for the future' (Michael, Grendon), and finding 'meaning' in their TC experience, whereby their prospects for a happy ending to their personal script became entirely plausible and achievable. They had found, as successful desisters do, a 'forward'-focused momentum towards change (Farrall 2002; Farrall and Calverley

2006) which allowed them to envisage for themselves a 'becoming' identity as a desister beyond the TC:

> I believe I've changed with all my heart ... I wouldn't stay here and do this hard work if I didn't know that change was possible. The staff, they say all the time that they believe everybody can change. I know I can change; I have changed. I have such hope now. I can feel it in my heart.
>
> (Dominic, Grendon)

> I can see that I *am* changing; I am seeing a nicer person coming out, so I know I'll get there eventually. I do feel positive, very positive, about where I'm heading ... I'm not going to make the same mistakes I always done. Every time I come out of prison before, I've had fuck all to look forward to and was *worse* – it's weird, Alisa, it really is: you can get far, far worse in prison than whatever you was on the out 'cos it's what you have to do to survive. But here, although it's hard work and it's head fucking, it's good because you can change, you can have that hope for yourself. It's a powerful place.
>
> (Stewart, Grendon)

> It's very painful here: sometimes I wish I was back in dispersal; it's simpler there, if that's the right word. But for people who are damaged like me, I think you can do some good work here and next time, I can go out of prison and not create any more victims – and I mean that sincerely, I'm not just trying to fob you off with nice words. Last time, I re-offended within 48 hours. I don't believe I'll be doing that again. There's some meaning in this work, some hope for change and normality here, if you want to find it.
>
> (Keith, Grendon)

It is not therefore fanciful to propose that when TC residents were able to enumerate the ways in which they had changed, and were enabled to rehearse new roles and capabilities in the TC that reinforced that progress towards change, they could create their own self-fulfilling prophecy and embed it within the reconstructed narrative identity actual desisters have been found to achieve. A desistance-friendly future was possible because there were already specific indicators of change in the TC: in residents' therapeutic discoveries and emotional disentanglement from their 'old' self, the pro-social roles they assumed and associated normative capabilities and qualities they internalized, and the daily 'living-learning' situations they successfully negotiated; upon all of which they received constructive feedback and validation from supportive fellow community members. Participants based their predictions of future re-offending not only upon their own evaluations of how they had changed, but had these changes confirmed by others; thereby solidifying their ambitious expectations and feeding their re-scripted, prospective self-narrative and re-established identity. In short, then, interviewees had created the necessary 'cognitive shifts' (Giordano *et al.* 2002) to revise fundamentally the ways in which they identified themselves and, in so doing, had become less likely to revert to an 'old' offending self and more likely to choose to retain the preferred 'new me'.

The prison-based TC: 'different', but underused and undervalued

Wilson and McCabe (2002:290) once asked whether Grendon 'needs "the system" to be as awful as it is, so as to be able to maintain an obvious difference between itself and other prisons'. This research suggests that it is not that TCs need the system to be 'awful', but they do need to be – and to continue to be allowed to be – different. To put it another way, if TCs are to be the Prison Service's 'jewel in the crown', then they also need to be the thorn in its side. Mixed metaphors notwithstanding, Grendon and the TC units offer a vision of how prisons could 'look and feel' if small and inclusive communities, supportive, mutually respectful, individualized staff–prisoner relationships, '*real* responsibility', and '*real* rehabilitation' were the foundations of the prison experience in all prisons; and thus TCs inevitably invite unfavourable comparison with and 'criticism of practically every other prison in the service' (Jones 2004b:5). I make this observation not in order to provoke speculation upon what a neo-abolitionist agenda for wholesale revolution of the penal system might encompass, nor whether it should or could ever be possible, in any meaningful way, to remake mainstream prisons in the image of TCs or, at least, to import elements of TC best practice to mainstream prisons to help make the latter the 'least worst' they can be. Indeed, the Anglo-Welsh TC prison has, to date, evidently had no real impact at all upon the institution of 'the prison', but has merely been tolerated as an eccentric, and relatively unthreatening, aberration to the norm. Rather, my contention is that the 'thorniness' of TCs is most evident in its embrace of 'difference' *and* that this 'difference' is integral, not incidental, to offender rehabilitation, the TC way. For it is this difference, in culture and rehabilitative method, in the combination of interpersonal, symbolic, and situational factors, that creates and shapes an alternative penal environment, and so permits, socially produces, and incrementally nurtures amongst serious offenders an emerging internal sense of difference.

This difference is thus the TC's rehabilitative strength, but it is also its weakness, politically. Being a rehabilitative and penal outsider places TCs in an inherently precarious position, always at risk of being, at best, undervalued by the mainstream and, at worst, submerged into the mainstream. The TC is not well understood. The complexity of its model of change reflects the multiple perspectives, from multiple disciplines, of the ways in which it may 'work', but only adds to confusion about how it works, not least in comparison with the much more theoretically straightforward and simpler to understand cognitive-behavioural model.

Moreover, Grendon's original designation as an 'experimental psychiatric prison' and subsequent and continuing self-identification as a national resource for men identified as psychopathic or severely personality disordered has created a continuing perception amongst 'normal' prisoners and mainstream prison staff that TCs are suitable *only* for those 'suffering' from such disorders or, even more pejoratively, at least in prison culture, for 'nonces and grasses, nutters, the weak, the vulnerable' (Paul, Grendon). As a result of this lack of understanding, TCs have never been used to the extent that they might be. The estimates of unmet psychiatric need amongst male and female prisoners (Gunn *et al.* 1991; Maden *et al.* 1994) have not translated into long waiting lists for the 538 places available, and TCs remain extremely marginal to the efforts of the Anglo-Welsh penal system to contain and change people convicted of criminal offences: less than 1 per cent of all prisoners in England and Wales enter a prison-based therapeutic community.

True, TCs are not designed for the 'average' prisoner. They attract long-term prisoners who have committed serious offences, many of whom will have recognized psychological problems. The difficulties of recruitment at Send TC are due in part to the very limited number of women in prison at any one time who are serving a sentence of sufficient length to qualify for the TC programme. Moreover, in order to apply for entry, prisoners have to want to change or, on some level, and however grudgingly, recognize the need to change, and be willing to 'deal with emotions, not just how you think about things' (Andrew, Grendon). This alone distinguishes TC applicants from the bulk of short-term offenders who view prison as 'an occupational hazard' and a revolving door through which they expect to pass many times, perhaps amassing cognitive-behavioural OBP completions along the way, whilst remaining fundamentally unchallenged and unaltered by the experience. Yet, the small number of CJS followers in this research who heeded the advice of correctional professionals to apply to the TC suggests that more referrals could be made if, in particular, offender managers were more alert to, and accurately aware of, what the TC offers. Even the enthusiasts in this sample had generally gleaned only minimal information about the regime prior to application, chiefly through the verbal 'prison grapevine', and most interviewees had very little accurate understanding of or meaningful knowledge about what TC treatment actually involves (Stevens, forthcoming). Although TCs have themselves made considerable efforts to market their services to other prisons, there is still no national strategy in place to prompt suitable referrals to TCs through the sentencing planning process, contrary to the repeated recommendation of HM Chief Inspector of Prisons (2009, 2010, 2011). One has to wonder why this is, and how many people in prison, who could benefit from TC treatment, are being denied an opportunity for '*real* rehabilitation' as a result.

The lack of understanding about the prison-based TC also reflects their status as inherently contradictory institutions, subject to inherently contradictory forces. They detain people in custodial conditions against their will, yet only accept men and women who apply to enter and who must, if they are to remain, reiteratively adhere to and participate in the policing of collectively endorsed rules and codes of behaviour. They provide a method of rehabilitation that is 'extremely demanding and very painful at times' (Raymond, GTC) but situate this demanding, painful treatment within 'a very decent nick' (Dominic, Grendon). They encourage their residents to build on their strengths in the present, and prospects for a good life in the future, yet do so by demanding complete and self-immolating exposure of all the failings and disasters, for oneself and others, of the past.

TC prisons are part of the prison estate, but stand apart in their culture and rehabilitative method. Grendon must conform to the instructions for and requirements of 'similar' category B prisons, yet there is no other prison, of any category, that is wholly similar in purpose to Grendon; nor does any other category B prison contain so many violent, indeterminate sentenced, men with diagnoses of personality disorder and psychopathy. TC units depend upon the patronage of a host mainstream prison for their very existence and survival, and thus can be particularly susceptible to new governors' preferences and, perhaps, apprehensions about the 'foreign body' (Lewis 1997:8) in their midst, and new regional managers' priorities. It is certainly much easier, when faced with financial or administrative pressures, to close a TC unit, with minimal fuss and little publicity, than an entire prison.

TCs recruit from the system and nearly always return their graduates to that same system that they have, in many cases, just spent several years denigrating and decrying for its criminogenic effects. Grendon is recognized as 'a model of good prison practice and a leader in the treatment of severe personality-disordered offenders' whose funding should be maintained, if not increased (House of Commons Home Affairs Committee 2005:73, para. 240), yet imposed financial cutbacks and a reduction in uniformed and clinical staff, including fewer officer facilitators, seriously impacted upon the provision of therapy at Grendon and 'threatened the viability of the entire therapeutic regime' (HM Chief Inspector of Prisons 2009:5; see also Genders and Player 2010). Demands for 'efficiency' and 'resource savings', even to the extent of undermining the core practices required of an effective, and ethical, psychotherapeutic regime, reveal a fundamentally poor appreciation of the rehabilitative value of Grendon and the TC units, and how and why they need to be 'different' from the system to achieve what they do. TCs, more than most prisons, are particularly sensitive to any decrease in their funding which results in a reduction of the amount of time, and the number of informal opportunities, available to residents to build constructive, caring, trusting relationships with other community members, and for staff to observe for developmental needs, offence paralleling behaviour and, more positively, evidence of progression amongst residents. Regular social interaction is therefore not a luxury which can be sacrificed without consequence to satisfy fiscal imperatives, but an essential component of the TC regime. Without it, residents cannot gain 'living-learning experiences' (Jones 1968:106), and staff and residents are hampered in their efforts to create and continuously renew a safe and sustainable 'culture of enquiry' (Main 1946, cited in Dolan 1998:410) and 'secure base' (Bowlby 1988), upon which the entire edifice of successful psychotherapeutic work rests. As one Grendon therapist speculated:

> I'm always saying, as long as the therapy continues, because that is the most powerful bit. If you don't get quite as much time out of cell as before and the canteen goes, nevertheless, the therapy continues. But actually, I have to recognize that the great fear is that TCs will be shut down, not because someone in London decides we don't work any more but simply because of indifference and neglect … If [managers] keep chipping away at the regime, I don't know, but I wonder if there may be a threshold and once you cross over that, you've no longer got viable therapy and a fully functioning TC, and then [Grendon] just becomes an adjunct to a normal prison … I'm sure that's a long way off, I hope so, but – I don't know. I could see how it could happen.

The important implication about 'difference', then, is this. People who apply to and remain in prison-based TCs are not like 'the average con', live within a counter-culture penal environment and by a counter-culture inmate code, pursue an unusual type of rehabilitation, and perform alternative roles and acquire alternative characteristics to that normally permissible and congruent with the inmate and offender identity in the mainstream. These differences within the TC create the conditions in which aspirations for, and the blossoming of, difference within the individual can occur, and therefore are central to residents' acquisition of a 'new, improved' self-concept and prospective self-narrative. Whilst mainstream prisons could certainly do more to become, as Wilson and McCabe (2002: 290) put it, less 'awful', by emulating some of the values and practices of care, decency, and responsibility associated with therapeutic communities (Bennett and Shuker 2010), the prison-based TC *is* 'different' to mainstream prisons and must be permitted and enabled to remain so.

Concluding remarks

> I don't know, I'm giving you all these different sides of me. I don't sound very nice but I can be nice, you know? I just can't believe I'm sat here saying all this to you. You must think, what a twat! But you know, where I come from, being nice gets you fuck all, do you know what I mean?
>
> *Of course. And I really appreciate you being so honest with me.*
>
> But that's this place, it teaches you to look at yourself, honestly; all the sides of you, all the bits that are nasty, and then you can choose to leave them behind. Yeah, I come from a rough area but I still chose to do those things, and now, I don't. I want a better life for myself 'cos *I'm* a better person now. I look back at myself and think, what the fuck was

> I thinking? [laughs] I've moved so far forward here. This place helps you become someone better. I can't thank it enough for all it's done for me.
>
> (Francis, GTC)

The research for this book is based upon serving residents' accounts of their TC experiences. I asked interviewees to talk to me, in as much or as little self-revelatory detail as they wished, about what they felt that they had gained from, and suffered during, their TC residency. Arguably, this emphasis upon residents' experiences, garnered from a sample of extreme self-selection, has resulted in a book that has concentrated too much on the best aspects of the TC way. An intentionally non-random sample of residents unintentionally produced a cohort of people wherein long-term TC persisters were over-represented, and one might well expect that people who not only elected to join but to remain in a TC and, furthermore, to volunteer to share their intensely personal experiences with an external researcher, would be at least reasonably upbeat about a rehabilitative programme to which they had committed so much of their time and energies. Certainly those for whom the TC appears to 'work' do become extraordinarily positive about its redemptive powers, to an extent that must strain the patience of the more sceptical or, at least, more world-weary commentators upon offending, offenders, and offender rehabilitation. What I describe as a club, others might call cult-like.[3] The criticisms that have been levelled at TCs generally, about the limits to democratized involvement, the potential for covert social control, and the tendency to interpret all 'deviancy' through the prism of a traumatic past and personal pathology, were rarely raised by participants in this research (and infrequently observed by this researcher), with the focus for residents' discontent, especially at Grendon, unequivocally directed towards the Prison Service and NOMS, their persistent under-resourcing of TCs, and the damaging and ill-informed modifications to the regime this can necessitate.

Yet, there is no denying the sincerity of the men and women who participated in this study and who were adamant that the TC had helped them to 'become someone better'. For all of the uncertainties surrounding TCs – to what extent they work, how they work, and, in darker moments, concerns about whether they will endure – one cannot ignore that, for some people, the prison-based TC, with its self-esteem enhancing, strengths-based, and hope-inducing rehabilitative regime, can provide the hook for change upon which to hang a new, transformed version of oneself. Grendon can rightly claim to be the only prison in England and Wales that has demonstrated empirically that its regime reduces the likelihood of reconviction by around one-fifth to one-quarter, amongst residents who complete 18 months or more of therapy (Marshall 1997; see also Taylor 2000), whilst TCs generally have amply evidenced an ability to improve people's psychological functioning, promote behavioural change in prison, and reduce those dysfunctional attitudes and affects that can be supportive of crime (inter alia, Newton 1998, 2010; Shuker and Newton 2008; Birtchnell *et al.* 2009). The number of people who enter TCs – and, more to the point, continue with their therapy until some measure of 'success' is identifiable – each year is very small, but they tend to include some of the violent and sexually violent, exploitative and harmful, offenders whose rehabilitation is most pressing, if they are ever to reintegrate peaceably into society again. Of course, TCs do not, cannot, always 'work' with and for every offender; after all, nothing 'works' for every offender, in every circumstance. TCs can help people, however, who wish to be helped towards change and for whom nothing has helped previously. It is therefore to be hoped that this book has usefully contributed to explanations and understandings of the rehabilitative work and value of prison-based therapeutic communities, and thus to ensuring that TCs not only continue to survive, but are allowed to prosper.

Notes

Introduction: offender rehabilitation and therapeutic communities

1. Strategic management of forensic therapeutic communities is accordingly centrally located within NOMS, which since 2008 has been an executive agency of the Ministry of Justice.
2. All OBPs must undergo a process of accreditation (and regular re-accreditation) by the Correctional Services Accreditation Panel (CSAP), an expert advisory panel to the Ministry of Justice. Prison-based TCs must adhere not only to the accredited core model (HM Prison Service 2003), but also to generic TC service standards (Keenan and Paget 2008), which are assessed by audit and self- and peer-review (see Clark and Lees 2007; Royal College of Psychiatrists 2008).
3. This figure has been calculated from combining the data on programme completions of general, domestic violence, sex offender, and drug treatment programmes.
4. Psychotherapy encompasses any form of psychological 'talking therapy', as opposed to physical or pharmacological treatment, for mental illness and psychological and emotional problems (Clarkson 1994a).
5. The term psychodynamic encompasses psychoanalytic and all related perspectives and approaches which emphasize the critical importance of unconscious, instinctual and emotional, often conflicting, psychic motivations and fears, and their influence upon human behaviour (see further, inter alia, Clarkson and Pokorny 1994; Cordess and Cox 1996; Yalom 1995). It is important to distinguish, however, the prison-based TC, which draws upon psycho*dynamic* theory and practice in its work and uses *group* psychotherapy, from the type of *individual* 'reclining on couch' therapy, concerned with, amongst other things, free association, the interpretation of dreams and parapaxes (slips of speech), associated with the theories and traditions of classic (Freudian) psycho*analysis.* The majority of prison-based clinical staff are neither trained in nor work from psychoanalytic perspectives (Shuker 2010).
6. A 'slow, open' long-term therapy group is one whose membership, whilst fairly stable, accommodates new residents whenever space permits (Manor 1994).

1 Therapeutic communities and prisons

1. Clark (1965) distinguished between the TC 'proper', in which the democratic social environment is the main therapeutic tool, and establishments and regimes that adopt a more diluted or modified TC 'approach', involving more generalized psycho-social therapies and techniques.
2. A personality disorder is an enduring, pervasive, and inflexible pattern of inner experience and behaviour which causes clinically significant distress or functional impairment, particularly to interpersonal relationships. The most recent version of

the psychiatrists' bible, the *Diagnostic and Statistical Manual of Mental Disorders* (DSM-IV), lists 10 specific – frequently co-occurring – personality disorders, grouped into three descriptively similar clusters (American Psychiatric Association 1994). Whilst personality disorders are generally regarded as incurable, treatment can modify their behavioural expression (Dolan 1998). Coid *et al.*'s (2006) study suggests that 4.4 per cent of the UK *general* population suffers with at least one personality disorder.

3 Psychosis is a severe mental illness, characterized by impaired understanding of reality. Symptoms may include delusions, hallucinations, dramatically inappropriate mood, and marked personality change. It can be contrasted with the much more common neurosis: a relatively benign, though personally discomforting, mental disorder, such as anxiety or depression (Gelder *et al.* 1983).

4 La Pâquerette is situated, rather bizarrely, within Switzerland's largest remand (and perpetually overcrowded) prison, Champ-Dollon, but is due to relocate to a new centre, Curabilis, in November 2013 (Département de la sécurité, de la police et de l'environnement 2011; Mansour 2011).

5 Synanon was founded by Charles ('Chuck') Dederich, a recovered alcoholic. Its original Utopian, communitarian ideals, and Dederich's charismatic leadership, attracted many 1960s 'lifestylers' and satellite facilities, managed by ex-addicts, were swiftly established across the United States. From the 1970s onwards, however, allegations increasingly surfaced in the media about the surreal, isolationist, abusive, cult-like practices of Dederich's now proclaimed 'independent nation' and 'church'. Following his 1980 convictions for soliciting assault and conspiracy to murder, Dederich was forced to relinquish managerial control of Synanon, from which both he and his organization never recovered (Kennard and Roberts 1983; Manning 1989; Kooyman 2001).

6 A version of this chapter first appeared as Stevens (2010) 'Introducing forensic democratic therapeutic communities', in R. Shuker and E. Sullivan (eds) *Grendon and the Emergence of Forensic Therapeutic Communities: Developments in Research and Practice.* I gratefully acknowledge the publishers, Wiley, for permission to reuse some of this material.

7 Moral treatment was a model of humane care for the mentally ill, most famously established in England in 1796 by Quakers at the (still surviving) York Retreat. Its revolutionary recognition of the individuality of the patient and the relationship between illness and social and environmental factors is widely credited with a lasting influence upon psychiatry.

8 London's Tavistock Clinic was, and remains (as the Tavistock and Portman), a world leader in the clinical practice of and professional training in psychoanalytic and psychotherapeutic approaches to mental health.

9 This condition would now be recognized as post-traumatic stress disorder.

10 Also known as neurocirculatory asthenia, effort syndrome was first identified amongst soldiers fighting the American Civil War. The condition was considered to be psychosomatic since the symptoms sufferers reported, including breathlessness, palpitations, chest pain, postural giddiness, and persistent fatigue, had no discernible medical cause (Jones 1968; Crisp 2001).

11 At the time of Jones's arrival in 1947, his workplace was the Belmont Hospital's Industrial Neurosis Unit for the long-term unemployed, 'social misfits', and 'drifters'. Both the functionally redefined unit and the hospital were subsequently renamed (Jones 1968). It was Jones who invited Rapoport and his team of social anthropologists to conduct research at the Unit, resulting in the influential *Community as Doctor* and identification of core TC values and qualities (Rapoport 1960).

12 The application and extension of psychiatric knowledge to social organization, interpersonal relationships, and group dynamics (Jones 1968).

13 This movement denounced psychiatry as a coercive agent of social control and preserver of the status quo, and argued that mental illness is a deliberately stigmatizing social construct designed to regulate culturally acceptable conduct. Its legacy is contested but certainly its advocates 'effectively politicised the psychiatric field … creating a space within and around it in which subsequent critical projects, such as the user movement, could emerge' (Crossley 1998:887).
14 As implemented by the British (Conservative) government, community care conveniently married a political preoccupation with reducing state intervention and welfare with ideological disavowal of long-term hospital-based psychiatric treatment. The policy seemed to equate residential care per se with institutionalization; an ill-informed overreaction to the latter which wilfully ignored the carefully crafted principles of democratic TCs (Roberts 1997b).
15 The Anglo-Welsh penal system classifies all convicted male prisoners from category A (high) to D (low). Categorization is primarily determined by the risk the prisoner poses of escaping, and of the harm he could cause to the public should he do so, but a higher-security categorization can also be applied when the prisoner threatens order and control within the prison. Category A prisoners can only be held in high-security prisons, none of which operate a TC.
16 Women were never admitted to Grendon but young offenders ('Borstal boys') were accommodated on three, then two, communities until 1989 (Gray 1973a).
17 DSM-IV regards anti-social personality disorder as descriptively interchangeable with psychopathy and sociopathy (see below), but specifically, psychopathy is associated with a constellation of affective, interpersonal, and behavioural characteristics including lack of empathy and remorse, pathological lying, egocentricity, superficial charm, grandiosity, manipulation, impulsivity and irresponsibility, and a parasitic, deviant lifestyle (American Psychiatric Association 1994; Hare 1996; Blackburn 2007). Considerable debate has ensued about whether and to what extent psychopathy is amenable to treatment, and how successful (psychiatric and prison-based) TCs are with this client group (inter alia, Jones 1982; Ogloff *et al.* 1990; Salekin 2002). Definitional issues about TCs can confuse the assessment, however. Salekin's review of treatment modalities for psychopathy, for example, included Rice *et al.*'s (1992) damning study of a Canadian 'therapeutic community', but the regime the researchers depicted bore no resemblance to the defining ideology and culture of a genuine democratic TC (Warren 1994), and their conclusions accordingly represent 'a travesty of science' (Thomas-Peter 2006:37).
18 This American term never gained currency with British psychiatry, which has preferred the similar constructs of psychopathy and anti-social personality disorder.
19 Cooke *et al.* (2005a, 2005b) subsequently revised their recommended diagnostic cut-off score to 28. Their contention that there should be some metric adjustment to reflect alleged cross-cultural differences, so that the North American cut-off score may not represent the same intensity of the disorder in Europe, is strongly disputed (Bolt *et al.* 2007).
20 See Cullen and Mackenzie (2011) for a full account of the creation and, at times, difficult development and precarious survival of Dovegate 'therapeutic prison'.
21 It is interesting to compare the fate of the Max Glatt Centre with La Pâquerette, whose durability vindicates the assertion of the authors of an early evaluation of its regime that 'a remand prison can maintain a therapeutic setting inspired by community therapeutic [*sic*] principles' (de Montmollin *et al.* 1986:33).
22 In fact, no more than eight men resided in the BSU at any one time (Stephen 1988).
23 Internal locus of control measures the extent to which an individual accepts personal responsibility for his or her behaviour and regards life experiences as controllable and (largely) predictable (Rotter 1966; Phares 1976).

2 Conducting research in prisons: tightrope walks and emotion work

1. The choice of wording is deliberate. Feminist research ethics have highlighted the importance of minimizing the power dynamic inherent to the traditional research relationship, which 'treats people as mere objects, there for the researcher to do research "on"' (Stanley and Wise 1983:170).
2. I use the term semi-ethnography in recognition that it is impossible for any 'free world' researcher, who spends only a finite period of time 'inside' and can 'escape' at will, to experience fully the realities of imprisonment or become completely immersed in the social world of the prison. Owen (1998:20–22) prefers 'quasi-ethnography' for similar reasons.
3. At the time of the research, I was a doctoral student at the Centre for Criminology, University of Oxford. I soon stopped describing myself in this way, however, as many people thought 'doctoral student' meant I was training to be a physician. Instead, my chosen identity was that of an independent researcher or criminologist.
4. I was neither offered nor needed keys at GTC and Send, where I could spend the entire day on the unit.
5. The problems I encountered chiefly occurred on two palpably tense Grendon communities, both of which, I was subsequently to learn, were wrestling with 'drug issues'. In hindsight, my persistent 'hanging about' must have been an immense irritation to officers preoccupied with more pressing matters than research.
6. With the wisdom the enlarged perspective of time brings, I now wonder whether TC prisons are more suspicious and less liberal than a 'normal' prison in this respect, precisely because the enquiring therapeutic culture encourages staff to question *why* people are talking (again), and what about, and what such 'friendliness' 'means'. I did encounter instances of what I experienced as gendered paternalism at Grendon (see also Genders and Player 1995); although admittedly, as Loraine Gelsthorpe (1990:96) and her female colleague found during their fieldwork in mainstream prisons, 'Suspicion of us as women … was hard to distinguish from suspicion of us as researchers.'
7. 'Weren't no cop': was no good.
8. This designation includes psychotherapists, forensic psychologists, and complementary therapists.
9. Two interviewees declined to be tape recorded. At Gartree, the security department initially refused me permission to use a tape recorder but reversed this decision after I had conducted two interviews. These four resident interviewees allowed me to take verbatim notes instead, which I further augmented immediately upon completion of the interview.
10. Where quotations have been edited for length, this is indicated by three dots.
11. This was a highly contentious issue at the time of the Grendon fieldwork. Prison officers' right to take industrial action varies internationally (Ministry of Justice 2008a).
12. Researchers always need to learn the specific jargon or argot of the prison(s) in which they are working (Sparks *et al.* 1996). I swiftly realized that immersion in a therapeutic environment would additionally result in some fluency in 'therapy speak'; not least since residents come to think, and share those thoughts, within these paradigmatic understandings of their 'issues' and the TC way of addressing them.

3 New beginnings: commencing change the TC way

1. The only prisoners who are automatically disbarred from entry to the TC are those who are assessed as requiring the highest security conditions or are on the 'escape list' (that is, they have previously tried to escape custody); have insufficient time left

to serve to complete 18 months of therapy; deny their offence or are pursuing an appeal against conviction; are presently using (and admit to using) recreational drugs or are reliant upon prescribed psychotropic medication; or are at risk of self-harm or suicide. They must also be possessed of at least average intelligence and an ability to express themselves verbally.

2 In particular, German offenders who fall under the remit of Das Gesetz zur Bekämpfung von Sexualdelikten und anderen gefährlichen Straftaten 1998 (The Sexual and other Dangerous Criminal Offences Act), can be ordered to receive treatment within a social therapeutic prison.

3 'ETS': Enhanced Thinking Skills.

4 'PED': parole eligibility date.

5 'Nonces and grasses': British prison slang for sexual offenders and informants, respectively. 'Nonce' reputedly denotes that these offenders are 'not on normal communal exercise' alongside other prisoners.

6 'B cats': category B prisons.

7 'Puff': cannabis.

8 'Plunge him up … mug *me* off': stab him for disrespecting me.

9 'Tool': (home-made) weapon.

10 'Down the block': in segregation.

11 'CSCP': Cognitive Self-Change Programme.

12 'Stick one on you': punch you.

13 'ESOTP': Extended Sex Offender Treatment Programme.

14 'Their book': programme manual.

15 'Bus': escort van.

16 'Ruck': fight.

17 'It weren't going off': arguing with each other without this resulting in a fight.

18 'An IEP': incentives and earned privileges. The IEP scheme allows prisoners to 'earn', through consistent good behaviour, additional material privileges such as extra social visits and association or eligibility for in-cell television and the ability to spend more private cash. Josephine was referring to written warnings, the accumulation of which within a specified time frame will lead to a reduction in the IEP level the prisoner enjoys.

19 The Prison and Probation Ombudsman provides, amongst other things, an adjudication service between prisoners and establishments. The Ombudsman upheld the right of a serving prisoner, Colin Gunn, to require staff to address him formally, as he preferred. See 'Call me Mister', Letters to the editor, *Inside Time*, December 2010.

20 'Screws': prison officers. Although some participants distinguished between 'system screws' and TC *officers* (see further Chapter 4), 'screw' mostly appeared to be used without derogatory intent and merely as traditional prison parlance. Similarly, residents often referred to themselves and their peers as inmates and 'cons', rather than prisoners.

21 In psychoanalysis, counter-transference is the unconscious displacement by analysts (here, prison staff) of their emotional reactions to their clients and to the clients' transference of feelings onto them (Clarkson 1994b).

22 Personal communication with Richard Shuker, HMP Grendon, 2011.

23 Sullivan's (2005) study of Grendon drop-out rates confirmed that there had been an increase in men RTU'd from the assessment wing, which she attributed to increasing use of clinical assessment tools for suitability. Conversely, there was no discernible increase in drop-outs from main therapy wings, and no evidence to suggest that men were being progressed more rapidly, and without suitable preparation, from the assessment wing to a community.

24 'Pad': cell.

25 '48': at GTC, a form giving 48 hours' notice of intention to leave.

26 These changes included the loss of the prison shop, dedicated officer-facilitator posts, and some evening and weekend association time, while chronic staff shortages sometimes resulted in cancellation of therapy groups and a progressively increasing backlog of therapy and progress reports. These problems were noted in a 2009 inspection (HM Chief Inspector of Prisons 2009) and their effect on the regime critiqued in Genders and Player (2010). The most recent inspection (HM Chief Inspector of Prisons 2011) reports some improvements to the regime, notably that groups were only rarely cancelled, but continued to caution that Grendon's funding remains under pressure.

27 In his report on the English prison disturbances of April 1990, Lord Justice Woolf (1991) recommended that in-cell sanitation (lavatories and washbasins) be installed throughout the penal estate by February 1996. As of September 2011, 1,973 cells across nine prisons, including Grendon, are still dependent during lock-up upon 'nightsan': an electronic unlocking system that allows one prisoner, per landing, out of his cell for a few minutes to use the lavatory (Hansard 2011). A lidded bucket is issued as 'an emergency measure' (ibid.), though more 'informal and unpleasant expedients' are also relied upon by some prisoners (IMB 2010:8).

28 'Fess up': confess.

4 Care, trust, and support

1 This alliance is 'probably the most essential relationship modality operative in psychotherapy', which indicates people's willingness to continue to engage in the psychotherapeutic relationship, despite any resulting distress (Clarkson 1994b:31).

2 'Apps': applications.

3 A personal officer is a named officer who holds additional responsibilities for specified prisoners and who should interact regularly with those prisoners. One might therefore expect personal officers to be obvious attachment figures, but this was not necessarily so.

4 Spring Hill is a category D (open) prison, sited opposite Grendon, and governed by the same management team.

5 As I noted in the introduction to this book, my participants invariably sought to distinguish unequivocally between TC and system imprisonment in discussing their intra-individual experiences. This research was not explicitly comparative, however, and can make no claims about mainstream staff–prisoner relationships. The Prison Service's 'decency agenda' (a focus upon treating prisoners with respect and care) has undoubtedly had a humanizing effect upon some aspects of staff culture, and other recent research (notably, Liebling, assisted by Arnold 2004; Crewe 2009; Liebling *et al.* 2011) accordingly presents a more complimentary and complex picture of mainstream staff–prisoner relationships than that painted by most of my TC participants.

6 Prior to 1994, prison officers were sometimes arbitrarily assigned to Grendon. These 'conscripts' could, unsurprisingly, be highly resistant to and critical of the TC regime – see, for example, one such officer's account of 1960s Grendon as 'the easiest nick in the country … mollycoddling … nothing more or less than a pantomime' (Parker 1970:78–90).

7 'Censoriousness': 'criticism of those in power for not following, in their behaviour, principles that are established as correct within the social system in question' (Mathiesen 1965:23).

8 'The dilemma': the irresolvable tension between wanting 'deep involvement' with another, and fearing the hurt that could result from a friendship formed in an inherently transitory and volatile environment (Cohen and Taylor 1972:75–78).

9 This question was posed before those about relationships with TC officers and residents. There is therefore no reason to suppose that participants felt, even subconsciously, that their answer should relate to care or attachments to others.

10 'Put my papers in': to request a transfer.
11 These graphic images were used by veterans of pre-decency agenda imprisonment to convey that officers could now 'do you more damage with their pen than their fists' (Neil, Grendon), while psychologists 'smile to your face, then stab you in the back' (Johnny, Grendon).
12 Most participants used the words 'mate' and 'friend' interchangeably, but where they did make a clear distinction, a friend was superior: 'Mates and friends are very different. A mate is someone you can have a laugh with and talk about general things. A friend is someone you can rely on and talk about deep, personal things and he won't judge you; he's just there for you' (Richie, GTC).
13 'Having the screws over': deceiving the officers; getting away with prohibited or illegal activity.
14 'Gaffs': prisons.
15 Unproductive, unresolved shame which results in an all-pervasive sense of worthlessness, failure, and 'a rupture of the self with the self ... the feeling of being isolated and alone in a complete sense' (Bradshaw 1988:10).
16 'Twist you up': physically manipulate a prisoner through institutionally approved 'control and restraint' techniques.
17 There were, of course, limits to this access: sometimes residents were required to leave the office and the door was closed, so that officers could discuss other residents or complete sensitive work. The greater trust shown to *residents* by officers did not mean that officers' occupational mistrust of *prisoners* was, or indeed, ever could be, absent.
18 The other three are the efficient delivery and collection of mail, a reliable supply of hot water, and the provision of social visits.
19 Interestingly, Woolf (1991:127, para. 4.115[3]) concluded from his consideration of the regime and serious disturbance at Glen Parva Young Offenders' Institution that dining in association, at least amongst sentenced prisoners, could be achieved safely and was 'a desirable objective'. Several – resident and officer – participants also suggested that the 'flashpoint' argument was an ex post facto rationalization and interpretation of the decision to reclaim communal space, given that any occasion that allows inmates to congregate is potentially dangerous: 'It's just a convenient excuse. [The Prison Service] got rid because they wanted the space to cram more inmates in! The private prisons do it, so why can't they? We never had no problems at [a contracted-out prison], 'cos really, it's no different to association' (Shane, Grendon). Besides private prisons, custodial institutions for juveniles and young offenders also usually provide dining rooms or areas.
20 'Leaving dinners': a celebratory meal held for a resident who has completed therapy and is progressing to another (usually, lower security category) establishment.

5 Responsibility, accountability, and safety

1 The take-up of these schemes varies between categories of prison, but are most common in adult men's training prisons and the female estate. However, only 'a tiny fraction of prisoners in each prison' are able to participate (Edgar *et al.* 2011:18).
2 'Nicking': strictly, being charged with an offence against Prison Rules, but often used to refer to the actual adjudication.
3 Although residents seek the support of community members for these applications, only a governor can authorize recategorizations and ROTLs.
4 At GTC, residents deployed a reflection vote to indicate their feelings to staff about the acceptability or otherwise of a particular 'issue', but did not actually vote on

whether the resident should be expelled from the community. For ease of narrative, I refer here only to commitment votes, but the reader should assume the substantive discussion includes reflection votes.

5 Grendon has long championed the use of 'social evenings' or, latterly, 'social afternoons'. Residents from each of the five therapy wings invite members of the public who have a professional interest in the TC (other prison staff, judges, academics, or politicians, for example) or in individual residents' rehabilitation (such as home probation officers) to tour the community, talk informally with community members, and enjoy a buffet supper paid for by residents.

6 His psychotherapist reported: 'He was almost in tears one day when something had gone wrong with one of the lights in the tank and he thought he was responsible for fixing that … So it changed his views on looking after creatures that are not as highly functioning as human beings, and he did it very well.'

7 'To create': make trouble.

8 'Positives': indications of recent drug use, obtained from (random and targeted) mandatory or voluntary tests.

9 Self-report studies variously suggest that between half and three-quarters of all prisoners have misused drugs *during* their sentence (Keene 1997; Hucklesby and Wilkinson 2001; Boys *et al.* 2002; Bullock 2003); figures that cannot be reconciled with the officially recorded rate of positive results from random MDTs, which fell from 24.4 per cent in 1996–97 to 7.1 per cent in 2010–11 (Ministry of Justice 2011a). There were 14,356 reported 'assault incidents' in prison in 2010 (Ministry of Justice 2011c) – approximately 40 per day – and two homicides in the reporting year 2010–11 (Prisons and Probation Ombudsman 2011). Edgar *et al.*'s (2003) prodigious five-year enquiries into prisoner victimization, however, found that 19 per cent of adult male prisoners and 30 per cent of young male offenders had been physically assaulted by their peers at least once in the previous month, and 26 per cent of men and 44 per cent of these young offenders had similarly been threatened with violence. Even then, since these figures were for the number of individuals who reported being victimized, and not the number of incidents of their victimization, the authors stressed that this was 'a minimum estimate'.

10 This is particularly the case at Grendon, where the layout of the communities does not follow the Benthamite panoptican-style design common to many prisons in which all landings are visible to staff from one central point on the ground floor. Rather, concrete ceilings separate the floors, so staff working in the ground floor wing office or community and therapy rooms cannot observe the residential areas without climbing the stairs to each floor.

11 'Stick it on': to inform or confront.

12 'Threes': third floor.

13 The only direct accusation of bullying I encountered occurred at one Grendon community meeting, where one resident wanted to wing another for 'bullying' for calling him 'a cockroach' and refusing to socialize with him. The community voted against construing this incident as bullying, with one member noting: 'We've murdered and raped and used guns on people and he's upset about being called names?' (fieldnotes).

14 'The pod': small kitchen on the community.

15 Printed pornographic material is permitted in prisons, but not films in any format, and there is a general prohibition against 'unacceptably' 'hardcore' pornography, the definition of which is determined locally.

16 'Notes in the box': placing notes addressed to staff in the wing postbox; a time-honoured way for prisoners to inform surreptitiously by providing staff with information when posting, or appearing to post, external mail.

17 To clarify, Bowlby's (1969) attachment theory views attachment as innate. It should not be confused with Hirschi's (1969) understanding of attachment as resulting

from successful socialization and as a contributor to the 'virtuous circle' which, Hirschi argued, facilitates conformity and social control.

18 'Bang at it': (frequently) taking drugs.
19 'Pinned': pupils are constricted; a reliable indicator of recent opiate use.
20 'Weed': cannabis.
21 'Arrange parcels': organize the smuggling of contraband into the prison.
22 'Mashed': in turmoil.

6 Vulnerability, unmasking, and 'de-othering'

1 Hegemony, from the Greek word for chieftain, was appropriated by Gramsci (1971) to explain the relationship between social dominance, power, and stability. Hegemonic masculinity refers to a seemingly consensual but patriarchally legitimated and structurally embedded configuration of gender practice. It represents a culturally idealized notion of masculinity, against which femininity and all alternative 'subordinate' and 'marginalized' masculinities are measured: homosexual and ethnic minority men, and those non-hegemonic but 'complicit' masculinities that benefit from the patriarchal dividend (Connell 1987, 1995). The concept became hugely influential within the sociology of masculinity and critical gender research but subsequently attracted criticism for its imprecision, essentialism, and obfuscation of Gramsci's original thesis (Collier 1998; Jefferson 2002; Hall 2002; Hearn 2004). For my purposes, I accordingly prefer the less conceptually laden term, hypermasculinity (Mosher and Tompkins 1988; Toch 1998).
2 'Dispersals': high-security prisons. This nickname arises because in these prisons, category A prisoners are 'dispersed' alongside category B prisoners.
3 Male residents repeatedly distinguished between 'hard' and 'soft' men, without the slightest embarrassment at – or perhaps even consciousness of – the possible sexual connotations. Canaan's (1998) ethnographic research with pugnacious young men contended that 'the concept of hardness' provided the idiom by which their (hyper) masculinity could be constructed and articulated, and that 'this masculinity is located in and symbolized by the hard state and heterosexual orientation of their genitals' (ibid.:184).
4 Contrary to the experience in the United States, man-on-man anal rape is thought to be rare in British prisons (Banbury 2004; O'Donnell 2004). One of the 50 male participants in this research disclosed to me his experiences of being raped in prison.
5 'The numbers': placing oneself on Rule 45 (protective segregation).
6 There is no equivalent superordinate version of femininity against which all women are measured, and all expressions of femininity remain 'subordinated' to hegemonic masculinity. Even the power hierarchies that do exist between women – Connell (1987:187) gives the examples of mother–daughter relationships and single-sex girls' schools, and to which he might have added women's prisons – are more muted and lack many of the thematic and exclusionary pressures of hypermasculinity. Accordingly, most of the discussion in this chapter bears no direct comparison with (imprisoned) women's experiences.
7 'Jack Jones': rhyming slang for 'own'.
8 'An iron': homosexual. Homosexual interviewees reported that Grendon was, in their experience, the only prison where they could safely 'come out' to, and live without fear alongside, heterosexual men.
9 As a woman amongst men, I was thankfully spared these discussions. The kind of misogynistic and sexually judgemental comments made about mainstream female officers to Ben Crewe (2006b), for example, almost certainly would not have been shared with a female researcher, either at all or with as much candour, in any men's prison. Conversely, a male researcher would probably not have been treated to the

witty, self-deprecating, conspiratorial anecdotes about 'the multiple ways in which men can be such dicks!' (Dave, Grendon) that I was. The point is that male and female researchers asking men about prison masculinities are likely to receive qualitatively different answers.

10 'Dispersal walk': swaggering 'like a right cocky bastard, chest puffed out; strutting about like you've got a permanent hard on!' (Sandeep, Grendon).
11 'Call it on': provoke confrontations.
12 'Giving it all that': enacting the hypermasculine performance.
13 This option is confined to men who raped adults. Potential substitute identities include 'the wing joker' or 'jailhouse lawyer', and may be adopted by other non-hypermasculine men to atone for their 'deficiencies' (Sim 1994).
14 VPUs and offence-specific prisons do not exist in the female estate. Sexual offending amongst women is extremely rare: of women sentenced to immediate custody in 2007, just 1.4 per cent had committed sexual offences (Ministry of Justice 2008b). Typically, female 'vulnerable prisoners' are those who have been complicit in or, more unusually, wholly responsible for, the death or physical abuse of their own child. Such women may be still spurned and occasionally assaulted, but the incessant safety precautions that envelope male sexual offenders are unnecessary.
15 'Bacons': rhyming slang ('bacon bonce') for 'nonce'.
16 There were no sexual offenders at GTC during my fieldwork. This reflected the general offending profile of Gartree's population, though residents also voiced their anxiety that if the GTC were to accommodate 'nonces', it would only augment its reputation as *already* 'full of wrong 'uns' (Richie, GTC). A number of residents, however, had committed sexually motivated murder (see note below).
17 Sexually motivated offences are those which contain a sexual element rather than being of an overtly sexual nature. Whilst this term could include offences such as burglary – when sexual gratification is gained from illicitly 'penetrating' a woman's bedroom, for example – the sexually motivated participants in this study had all been convicted of the murder or manslaughter of a former, present, or desired sexual partner.
18 At the time of my research, this community was located on G-wing. To avoid confusion, interviewees' references to G-wing have been amended to A-wing.
19 This specialist role occurred more by accident than design. In 1987, G-wing was requisitioned for a mass exodus of vulnerable prisoners from across the south-west of England. These men were initially kept strictly segregated from the rest of the prison, and had their own staff group, provided by HMP Albany on the Isle of Wight. As Albany's officers were recalled to their parent establishment, however, they were replaced by Grendon staff and thus a decision was taken to return G-wing to a functioning therapeutic community which would meet its existing residents' needs by specializing in sexual offending (Gomersall 1991; personal communication with Geraldine Akerman, HMP Grendon, 2011).
20 In August 2010, Robert Coello, a man convicted of sexually abusing a child, was murdered in his cell on a (offence non-specific) Grendon community by a fellow resident: the first such homicide in the prison's history. Evidence presented at the subsequent criminal trial suggested that his killer had expressed his distaste at being required to share the community with such an offender. As shocking as this appalling crime was, it should be understood as a truly exceptional incident. When I conducted research at Grendon in 2006, there was some resistance from residents and staff to placing sexual offenders against children on integrated communities, but the prospect that a Grendonite would seriously, let alone fatally, injure a sexual offender because he was a sexual offender was, at that time, unimaginable.
21 Peaceful, or at least tolerant, integration appears to be more frequently attained in category C and D establishments, where 'sensible' prisoners do not want to jeopardize their prospects for release by assaulting sexual offenders 'on principle'.

22 'Blank': ignore.
23 'Straight-goers': 'law-abiding, functional people, holding down normal jobs' (Tony, Grendon).
24 I resisted the temptation to point out to residents that their hard-won psychotherapeutic understanding of the 'meaning' of sexual offences tallied perfectly with long-espoused feminist theorizing (Brownmiller 1975; MacKinnon 1987; Kelly and Radford 1987; Scully 1990). This was one 'f word' I feared was just too shocking to utter!
25 'Burn outs': setting fire to a prisoner's cell, often with the expressed aim of ensuring that person's relocation from the wing.

7 Pursuing change the TC way and beyond

1 In its summation of key research findings and implications, this chapter draws intermittently from material that first appeared as Stevens (2012) '"I am the person now I was always meant to be": Identity reconstruction and narrative reframing in therapeutic community prisons', in the journal *Criminology and Criminal Justice.* I gratefully acknowledge the publishers, Sage, for permission to reuse some of this material.
2 Future TC graduates may benefit from more support than that available to my interviewees, following the recent introduction of 'psychologically informed planned environment' (PIPE) pilots in two men's and two women's prisons, jointly funded by the Department of Health and NOMS. The PIPE units aim to consolidate changes achieved elsewhere, including TCs, and thus will offer a long overdue 'step-down' service for residents moving on to other prisons.
3 Or, as a former governing governor of Grendon observed, there are conceptual and organizational similarities between sects and TCs, and members of both may enjoy 'an intensely emotional, personal and life-changing experience amounting to "conversion"' (Bennett 2006:135).

References

Adler, A. (1924) *The Practice and Theory of Individual Psychology.* London: Kegan Paul.

Adshead, G. (2004) 'Three degrees of security: Attachment and forensic institutions', in F. Pfäfflin and G. Adshead (eds) *A Matter of Security: The Application of Attachment Theory to Forensic Psychiatry and Psychotherapy.* London: Jessica Kingsley.

Ainsworth, M. (1967) *Infancy in Uganda: Infant Care and the Growth of Love.* Baltimore, MD: Johns Hopkins University Press.

Ainsworth, M., Blehar, M., Waters, E. and Wall, S. (1978) *Patterns of Attachment: A Psychological Study of the Strange Situation.* Hillsdale, NJ: Erlbaum and London: Halsted Press.

Akerman, G. (2010) 'Undertaking therapy at HMP Grendon with men who have committed sexual offences', in R. Shuker and E. Sullivan (eds) *Grendon and the Emergence of Forensic Therapeutic Communities: Developments in Research and Practice.* Chichester: Wiley-Blackwell.

Allen, F. (1981) *The Decline of the Rehabilitative Ideal: Penal Policy and Social Purpose.* New Haven, CT: Yale University Press.

American Psychiatric Association (1994) *Diagnostic and Statistical Manual of Mental Disorders* (DSM-IV), 4th edn. Washington, DC: American Psychiatric Association.

Andrews, D. (1995) 'The psychology of criminal conduct and effective treatment', in J. McGuire (ed.) *What Works: Reducing Reoffending: Guidelines from Practice and Research.* Chichester: Wiley.

Andrews, D. and Bonta, J. (1994) *The Psychology of Criminal Conduct.* Cincinnati, OH: Anderson.

Andrews, D., Zinger, I., Hoge, R., Bonta, J., Gendreau, P. and Cullen, F. (1990) 'Does correctional treatment work? A clinically relevant and psychologically informed meta-analysis', *Criminology* 28 (3): 369–404.

Ansbro, M. (2008) 'Using attachment theory with offenders', *Probation Journal* 55 (3): 231–44.

Arnold, H. (2005) 'The effects of prison work', in A. Liebling and S. Maruna (eds) *The Effects of Imprisonment.* Cullompton: Willan Publishing.

Atkinson, P. and Silverman, D. (1997) 'Kundera's immortality: The interview society and the invention of self', *Qualitative Inquiry* 3 (3): 304–25.

Banbury, S. (2004) 'Coercive sexual behaviour in British prisons as reported by adult ex-prisoners', *Howard Journal of Criminal Justice* 43 (2): 113–30.

Barnes, M. and Berke, J. (1971) *Two Accounts of a Journey through Madness.* London: MacGibbon and Kee.

Baron, C. (1987) *Asylum to Anarchy.* London: Free Association Books.

Bartholomew, K. (1990) 'Avoidance of intimacy: An attachment perspective', *Journal of Social and Personal Relationships* 7 (2): 147–78.

Bauman, Z. (1993) *Postmodern Ethics.* Oxford: Blackwell.

Becker, H. (1958) 'Problems of inference and proof in participant observation', *American Sociological Review* 23 (6): 652–60.

——(1963) *Outsiders: Studies in the Sociology of Deviance.* New York: Free Press and London: Collier Macmillan.

——(1967) 'Whose side are we on?', *Social Problems* 14 (3): 239–47.

Belknap, I. (1956) *Human Problems of a State Mental Hospital.* New York: McGraw-Hill.

Benedict, H. (1992) *Virgin or Vamp: How the Press Covers Sex Crime.* New York: Oxford University Press.

Bennett, J. (1981) *Oral History and Delinquency: The Rhetoric of Criminology.* Chicago, IL: University of Chicago Press.

Bennett, P. (2006) 'Governing a humane prison', in D. Jones (ed.) *Humane Prisons.* Abingdon: Radcliffe.

Bennett, P. and Shuker, R. (2010) 'Improving prisoner–staff relationships: Exporting Grendon's good practice', *Howard Journal of Criminal Justice* 49 (5): 491–502.

Berger, P. and Luckmann, T. (1967) *The Social Construction of Reality: A Treatise in the Sociology of Knowledge.* London: Penguin.

Bernheim, J. and de Montmollin, M-J. (1990) 'A special unit in Geneva', in R. Bluglass and P. Bowden (eds) *Principles and Practice of Forensic Psychiatry.* Edinburgh: Churchill Livingstone.

Bion, W. (1961) *Experiences in Groups and Other Papers.* London: Tavistock Publications.

——(1970) *Attention and Interpretation: A Scientific Approach to Insight in Psychoanalysis and Groups.* London: Tavistock Publications.

Birtchnell, J. and Shine, J. (2000) 'Personality disorders and the interpersonal octagon', *British Journal of Medical Psychology* 73 (4): 433–48.

Birtchnell, J., Shuker, R., Newberry, M. and Duggan, C. (2009) 'An assessment of change in negative relating in two male forensic therapy samples using the Person's Relating to Others Questionnaire (PROQ)', *Journal of Forensic Psychiatry and Psychology* 20 (3): 387–407.

Blackburn, R. (2007) 'Personality disorder and psychopathy: Conceptual and empirical integration', *Psychology, Crime & Law* 13 (1): 7–18.

Bloor, M. (1986) 'Social control in the therapeutic community: Re-examination of a critical case', *Sociology of Health and Illness* 8 (4): 305–24.

Blumenthal, S., Gudjonsson, G. and Burns, J. (1999) 'Cognitive distortions and blame attribution in sex offenders against adults and children', *Child Abuse and Neglect* 23 (2): 129–43.

Bolt, D., Hare, R. and Neumann, C. (2007) 'Score metric equivalence of the Psychopathy Checklist–Revised (PCL-R) across criminal offenders in North America and the United Kingdom: A critique of Cooke, Michie, Hart, and Clark (2005) and new analyses', *Assessment* 14 (1): 44–56.

Bond, N. and Steptoe-Warren, G. (2010) 'A qualitative exploration of offence paralleling behaviour: A prison-based democratic therapeutic community resident's perspective', in M. Daffern, L. Jones and J. Shine (eds) *Offence Paralleling Behaviour: A Case Formulation Approach to Offender Assessment and Intervention.* Chichester: Wiley.

Bosworth, M. (1999) *Engendering Resistance: Agency and Power in Women's Prisons.* Aldershot: Dartmouth.

——(2001) 'The past as a foreign country? Some methodological implications of doing historical criminology', *British Journal of Criminology* 41 (3): 431–42.

——(2007) 'Creating the responsible prisoner: Federal admission and orientation packs', *Punishment & Society* 9 (1): 67–85.

Bottomley, K., Liebling, A. and Sparks, R. (1994) *Barlinnie Special Unit and Shotts Unit: An Assessment.* Scottish Prison Service Occasional Paper no. 7. Edinburgh: Scottish Prison Service.

Bottoms, A. and McClintock, F. (1973) *Criminals Coming of Age: A Study of Institutional Adaptation in the Treatment of Adolescent Offenders.* London: Heinemann.

Bottoms, A., Hay, W. and Sparks, R. (1990) 'Situational and social approaches to the prevention of disorder in long-term prisons', *Prison Journal* 70 (1): 83–95.

Bottoms, A., Shapland, J., Costello, A., Holmes, D. and Muir, G. (2004) 'Towards desistance: Theoretical underpinnings for an empirical study', *Howard Journal of Criminal Justice* 43 (4): 368–89.

Bourdieu, P. (2000) 'The biographical illusion', in P. du Gay, J. Evans and P. Redman (eds) *Identity: A Reader.* London: Sage and The Open University.

Bowlby, J. (1969) *Attachment and Loss, Volume I: Attachment.* London: The Hogarth Press and the Institute of Psycho-Analysis.

——(1973) *Attachment and Loss, Volume II: Separation, Anxiety and Anger.* London: The Hogarth Press and the Institute of Psycho-Analysis.

——(1979) *The Making and Breaking of Affectional Bonds.* London: Tavistock Publications.

——(1980) *Attachment and Loss, Volume III: Loss, Sadness and Depression.* London: The Hogarth Press and the Institute of Psycho-Analysis.

——(1988) *A Secure Base: Clinical Applications of Attachment Theory.* London: Routledge.

Boyle, J. (1977) *A Taste of Freedom.* London: Pan Books.

——(1984) *The Pain of Confinement: Prison Diaries.* Edinburgh: Canongate.

Boys, A., Farrell, M., Bebbington, P., Brugha, T., Coid, J., Jenkins, R., Lewis, G., Marsden, J., Meltzer, H., Singleton, N. and Taylor, C. (2002) 'Drug use and initiation in prison: Results from a national prison survey in England and Wales', *Addiction* 97 (12): 1551–60.

Bradshaw, J. (1988) *Healing the Shame that Binds You.* Deerfield Beach, FL: Health Communications.

Braithwaite, J. (1989) *Crime, Shame and Reintegration.* Oxford: Oxford University Press.

Briere, J. and Malamuth, N. (1983) 'Self-reported likelihood of sexually aggressive behaviour: Attitudinal versus sexual explanations', *Journal of Research in Personality* 17: 315–23.

British Medical Journal (1990) 'Obituary: T. F. Main', *British Medical Journal* 300 (6741): 1718.

Broekaert, E., Vandevelde, S., Soyez, V., Yates, R. and Slater, A. (2006) 'The third generation of therapeutic communities: The early development of the TC for addictions in Europe', *European Addiction Research Journal* 12 (1): 1–11.

Brown, G. and Walker, J. (2010) 'Prison language as an organizational defence against anxiety', in S. Wilson and I. Cumming (eds) *Psychiatry in Prisons: A Comprehensive Handbook.* London: Jessica Kingsley.

Brownmiller, S. (1975) *Against our Will: Men, omen and Rape.* New York: Simon and Schuster.

Bruner, J. (1990) *Acts of Meaning*. Cambridge, MA: Harvard University Press.

Bullock, T. (2003) 'Changing levels of drug use before, during and after imprisonment', in R. Ramsay (ed.) *Prisoners' Drug Use and Treatment: Seven Research Studies.* Home Office Research Study 267. London: Home Office Research, Development and Statistics Directorate.

Bumby, K. and Hansen, D. (1997) 'Intimacy deficits, fear of intimacy, and loneliness among sexual offenders', *Criminal Justice and Behavior* 24 (3): 315–31.

Burnett, R. (1992) *The Dynamics of Recidivism: Report to the Home Office Research and Planning Unit*. Oxford: Centre for Criminological Research, University of Oxford.

——(2000) 'Understanding criminal careers through a series of in-depth interviews', *Offender Programs Report* 4 (1): 1–15.

——(2004) 'To re-offend or not to re-offend? The ambivalence of convicted property offenders', in S. Maruna and R. Immarigeon (eds) *After Crime and Punishment: Pathways to Offender Re-Integration*. Cullompton: Willan Publishing.

Burnett, R. and Maruna, S. (2004) 'So "prison works", does it? The criminal careers of 130 men released from prison under Home Secretary, Michael Howard', *Howard Journal of Criminal Justice* 43 (4): 390–404.

——(2006) 'The kindness of prisoners: Strengths-based resettlement in theory and in action', *Criminology and Criminal Justice* 6 (1): 83–106.

Burston, D. (1996) *The Wing of Madness: The Life and Work of R. D. Laing*. Cambridge, MA: Harvard University Press.

Burt, M. (1980) 'Cultural myths and supports for rape', *Journal of Personality and Social Psychology* 38 (2): 217–30.

——(1983) 'Justifying personal violence: A comparison of rapists and the general public', *Victimology: An International Journal* 8 (3–4): 131–50.

Butler, M. (2008) 'What are you looking at? Prisoner confrontations and the search for respect', *British Journal of Criminology* 48 (6): 856–73.

Butler, M. and Drake, D. (2007) 'Reconsidering respect: Its role in Her Majesty's Prison Service', *Howard Journal of Criminal Justice* 46 (2): 115–27.

Byrne, C. and Trew, K. (2008) 'Pathways through crime: The development of crime and desistance in the accounts of men and women offenders', *Howard Journal of Criminal Justice* 47 (3): 238–58.

Camp, S. and Gaes, G. (2005) 'Criminogenic effects of the prison environment on inmate behavior: Some experimental evidence', *Crime and Delinquency* 51 (3): 425–42.

Campbell, R. (2001) *Emotionally Involved: The Impact of Researching Rape.* New York and London: Routledge.

Campbell, S. (2003) *The Feasibility of Conducting an RCT at HMP Grendon*. Home Office Online Report 03/03. London: Home Office.

Campling, P. (2001) 'Therapeutic communities', *Advances in Psychiatric Treatment* 7: 365–72.

Canaan, J. (1998) 'Is "doing nothing" just boys' play? Integrating feminist and cultural studies perspectives on working-class young men's masculinity', in K. Daly and L. Maher (eds) *Criminology at the Crossroads: Feminist Readings in Crime and Justice.* New York and Oxford: Oxford University Press.

Cann, J., Falshaw, L., Nugent, F. and Friendship, C. (2003) *Understanding What Works: Accredited Cognitive Skills Programmes for Adult Men and Young Offenders.* Home Office Research Findings 226. London: Home Office.

Carlsson, C. (2012) 'Using "turning points" to understand processes of change in offending: Notes from a Swedish study on life courses and crime', *British Journal of Criminology* 52 (1): 1–16.

Carrabine, E. (2004) *Power, Discourse and Resistance: A Genealogy of the Strangeways Prison Riot*. Aldershot: Ashgate.

Carroll, L. (1974) *Hacks, Blacks, and Cons: Race Relations in a Maximum Security Prison*. Lexington, MA: Lexington Books.

Caudill, W. (1958) *The Psychiatric Hospital as a Small Society*. Cambridge, MA: Harvard University Press.

Clancy, A., Hudson, K., Maguire, M., Peake, R., Raynor, P., Vanstone, M. and Kynch, J. (2006) *Getting Out and Staying Out: Results of the Prisoner Resettlement Pathfinders*. Bristol: Policy Press.

Clark, D. (1965) 'The therapeutic community: Concept, practice and future', *British Journal of Psychiatry* 111 (479): 947–54.

——(1998) 'Current Research'. Unpublished internal report. London: Planning Group, HM Prison Service.

——(1999) 'Social psychiatry: The therapeutic community approach', in P. Campling and R. Haigh (eds) *Therapeutic Communities: Past, Present and Future*. London: Jessica Kingsley.

Clark, D. and Lees, J. (2007) 'Auditing of Prison Service accredited interventions', in M. Parker (ed.) *Dynamic Security: The Democratic Therapeutic Community in Prison*. London: Jessica Kingsley.

Clarkson, P. (1994a) 'The nature and range of psychotherapy', in P. Clarkson and M. Pokorny (eds) *The Handbook of Psychotherapy*. London and New York: Routledge.

——(1994b) 'The psychotherapeutic relationship', in P. Clarkson and M. Pokorny (eds) *The Handbook of Psychotherapy*. London and New York: Routledge.

Clarkson, P. and Pokorny, M. (eds) (1994) *The Handbook of Psychotherapy*. London and New York: Routledge.

Clay, J. (2001) *Maconochie's Experiment*. London: John Murray.

Clemmer, D. (1958) *The Prison Community*, 2nd edn. New York: Holt, Rinehart and Winston. First published 1940.

Coffey, A. (1999) *The Ethnographic Self: Fieldwork and the Representation of Identity*. London: Sage.

Cohen, S. and Taylor, L. (1972) *Psychological Survival: The Experience of Long-Term Imprisonment*. Harmondsworth: Penguin.

Coid, J., Yang, M., Tyrer, P., Roberts, A. and Ullrich, S. (2006) 'Prevalence and correlates of personality disorder in Great Britain', *British Journal of Psychiatry* 188 (5): 423–31.

Collier, R. (1998) *Masculinities, Crime and Criminology: Men, Heterosexuality and the Criminal(ised) Other*. London: Sage.

Collins, H. (1997) *Autobiography of a Murderer*. London: Macmillan.

Commissioners of Prisons (1963) *Report for 1962*. London: Her Majesty's Stationery Office.

Connell, R. (1983) *Which Way is Up? Essays on Sex, Class and Culture*. London and Sydney: Allen and Unwin.

——(1987) *Gender and Power: Society, the Person and Sexual Politics*. Cambridge: Polity Press.

——(1995) *Masculinities*. Cambridge: Polity Press.

Cooke, D. (1989) 'Containing violent prisoners: An analysis of the Barlinnie Special Unit', *British Journal of Criminology* 29 (2): 129–43.
——(1991) 'Violence in prisons: The influence of regime factors', *Howard Journal of Criminal Justice* 30 (2): 95–109.
——(1997) 'The Barlinnie Special Unit: The rise and fall of a therapeutic experiment', in E. Cullen, L. Jones and R. Woodward (eds) *Therapeutic Communities for Offenders.* Chichester: Wiley.
Cooke, D. and Michie, C. (1999) 'Psychopathy across cultures: North America and Scotland compared', *Journal of Abnormal Psychology* 108 (1): 58–68.
Cooke, D., Michie, C., Hart, S. and Clark, D. (2005a) 'Assessing psychopathy in the UK: Concerns about cross-cultural generalisability', *British Journal of Psychiatry* 18 (4): 335–41.
——(2005b) 'Searching for the pan-cultural core of psychopathic personality disorder', *Personality and Individual Differences* 39 (2): 283–95.
Cooley, C. (1902) *Human Nature and the Social Order.* New York: Schocken Books.
Cooper, D. (1967) *Psychiatry and Anti-Psychiatry.* London: Tavistock Publications.
——(1980) *The Language of Madness.* Harmondsworth: Penguin Books.
Corbin, J. and Strauss, A. (2008) *Basics of Qualitative Research: Techniques and Procedures for Developing Grounded Theory,* 3rd edn. Los Angeles, CA, and London: Sage.
Cordess, C. and Williams, A. H. (1996) 'The criminal act and acting out', in C. Cordess and M. Cox (eds) *Forensic Psychotherapy: Crime, Psychodynamics and the Offender Patient.* London: Jessica Kingsley.
Cordess, C. and Cox, M. (eds) (1996) *Forensic Psychotherapy: Crime, Psychodynamics and the Offender Patient.* London: Jessica Kingsley.
Cortoni, F. and Marshall, W. (2001) 'Sex as a coping strategy and its relationship to juvenile sexual history and intimacy in sexual offenders', *Sexual Abuse: A Journal of Research and Treatment* 13 (1): 27–43.
Cowburn, M. (2005) 'Confidentiality and public protection: Ethical dilemmas in qualitative research with adult male sex offenders', *Journal of Sexual Aggression* 11 (1): 49–63.
Coyle, A. (1987) 'The Scottish experience with small units', in A. Bottoms and R. Light (eds) *Problems of Long-Term Imprisonment.* Aldershot: Gower.
——(2002a) *A Human Rights Approach to Prison Management: Handbook for Prison Staff.* London: International Centre for Prison Studies.
——(2002b) *Managing Prisons in a Time of Change.* London: International Centre for Prison Studies.
Crawley, E. (2004) *Doing Prison Work: The Public and Private Lives of Prison Officers.* Cullompton: Willan Publishing.
Crewe, B. (2005a) 'Codes and conventions: The terms and conditions of contemporary inmate values', in A. Liebling and S. Maruna (eds) *The Effects of Imprisonment.* Cullompton: Willan Publishing.
——(2005b) 'Prisoner society in the era of hard drugs', *Punishment & Society* 7 (4): 457–81.
——(2006a) 'Prison drug dealing and the ethnographic lens', *Howard Journal of Criminal Justice* 45 (4): 347–68.
——(2006b) 'Male prisoners' orientations towards female officers in an English prison', *Punishment & Society* 8 (4): 395–421.
——(2009) *The Prisoner Society: Power, Adaptation and Social Life in an English Prison.* Oxford: Oxford University Press.

Crewe, B. and Maruna, S. (2006) 'Self-narratives and ethnographic fieldwork', in D. Hobbs and R. Wright (eds) *Sage Handbook of Fieldwork*. London: Sage.

Crisp, A. (2001) 'Cardiology – history', in S. Lock, J. Last and G. Dunea (eds) *The Oxford Companion to Medicine,* 3rd edn. Oxford: Oxford University Press.

Crossley, N. (1998) 'R. D. Laing and the British anti-psychiatry movement: A socio-historical analysis', *Social Science & Medicine* 47 (7): 877–89.

Cullen, E. (1993) 'The Grendon reconviction study, part 1', *Prison Service Journal* 90: 35–37.

——(1994) 'Grendon: The therapeutic community that works', *Therapeutic Communities: The International Journal for Therapeutic and Supportive Organizations* 15 (4): 301–11.

——(1997) 'Can a prison be a therapeutic community: The Grendon template', in E. Cullen, L. Jones and R. Woodward (eds) *Therapeutic Communities for Offenders.* Chichester: Wiley.

——(1998) *Grendon and Future Therapeutic Communities in Prison*. London: Prison Reform Trust.

Cullen, E., Jones, L. and Woodward, R. (eds) (1997) *Therapeutic Communities for Offenders.* Chichester: Wiley.

Cullen, E. and Mackenzie, J. (2011) *Dovegate: A Therapeutic Community in a Private Prison and Developments in Therapeutic Work with Personality Disordered Offenders.* Hook, Hampshire: Waterside Press.

Darwall, S. (1977) 'Two kinds of respect', *Ethics* 88 (1): 36–49.

Davidson, L., Chinman, M., Kloos, B., Weingarten, R., Stayner, D. and Tebes, J. K. (1999) 'Peer support among individuals with severe mental illness: A review of the evidence', *Clinical Psychology: Science and Practice* 6 (2): 165–87.

de Boer-van Schaik, J. and Derks, F. (2010) 'The Van der Hoeven Clinic: A flexible and innovative forensic psychiatric hospital based on therapeutic community principles', in R. Shuker and E. Sullivan (eds) *Grendon and the Emergence of Forensic Therapeutic Communities: Developments in Research and Practice.* Chichester: Wiley-Blackwell.

de Leon, G. (ed.) (1997) *Community as Method: Therapeutic Communities for Special Populations and Special Settings.* Westport, CT: Greenwood.

——(2000) *The Therapeutic Community: Theory, Model, and Method.* New York: Springer.

de Montmollin, M-J., Zimmermann, E., Bernheim, J. and Harding, T. (1986) 'Socio-therapeutic treatment of delinquents in prison', *International Journal of Offender Therapy and Comparative Criminology* 30 (1): 25–34.

de Ruiter, C. and Trestman, R. (2007) 'Prevalence and treatment of personality disorders in Dutch Forensic Mental Health Services', *Journal of the American Academy of Psychiatry and the Law* 35 (1): 92–97.

de Zulueta, F. (1993) *From Pain to Violence: The Traumatic Roots of Destructiveness.* London: Whurr Publishers.

Dean, J. and Whyte, W. Foote (1969) 'How do you know if the informant is telling the truth?', in G. McCall and J. Simmons (eds) *Issues in Participant Observation: A Text and Reader.* London: Addison-Wesley.

Deci, E. and Ryan, R. (1985) *Intrinsic Motivation and Self-Determination in Human Behavior.* New York: Plenum.

——(2000) 'The "what" and "why" of goal pursuits: Human needs and the self-determination of behavior', *Psychological Inquiry* 11 (4): 227–68.

Département de la sécurité, de la police et de l'environnement (2011) *Prison de Champ-Dollon: Rapport d'Activités 2010*. Republique et Canton de Genève: Département de la sécurité, de la police et de l'environnement.

Dhami, M., Ayton, P. and Loewenstein, G. (2007) 'Adaptation to imprisonment: Indigenous or imported?', *Criminal Justice and Behavior* 34 (8): 1085–1100.

Dietz, E., O'Connell, D. and Scarpitti, F. (2003) 'Therapeutic communities and prison management: An examination of the effects of operating an in-prison therapeutic community on levels of institutional disorder', *International Journal of Offender Therapy and Comparative Criminology* 47 (2): 210–23.

DiIulio, J. (1987) *Governing Prisons: A Comparative Study of Correctional Management*. London: Collier Macmillan and New York: Free Press.

Dolan, B. (1998) 'Therapeutic community treatment for severe personality disorders', in T. Millon, E. Simonsen, M. Birket-Smith and R. Davis (eds) *Psychopathy: Antisocial, Criminal and Violent Behavior*. New York: Guilford Press.

Downie, A. (2004) 'Thinking under fire: The prison therapeutic community as container', in D. Jones (ed.) *Working with Dangerous People: The Psychotherapy of Violence*. Abingdon: Radcliffe Medical Press.

Drieschner, K., Lammers, S. and van der Staak, C. (2004) 'Treatment motivation: An attempt for clarification of an ambiguous concept', *Clinical Psychology Review* 23 (8): 1115–37.

Dünkel, F. and Johnson, E. (1980) 'Introduction of therapy into Tegel prison: Evaluation of an experiment', *International Journal of Comparative and Applied Criminal Justice* 4 (2): 233–47.

East, W. N. (1932) *Report of the Commissioners of Prisons and the Directors of Convict Prisons for 1931*, Cmnd. 4295. London: His Majesty's Stationery Office.

East, W. N. and Hubert, W. (1939) *The Psychological Treatment of Crime*. London: His Majesty's Stationery Office.

Ebaugh, H. (1988) *Becoming an Ex: The Process of Role Exit*. Chicago, IL: University of Chicago Press.

Eccles, A. and Marshall, W. (1999) 'Relapse prevention', in W. Marshall, D. Anderson and Y. Fernandez (eds) *Cognitive-Behavioural Treatment of Sexual Offenders*. Chichester: Wiley.

Edgar, K. and Newell, T. (2006) *Restorative Justice in Prisons: Making it Happen*. Winchester: Waterside Press.

Edgar, K., Jacobson, J. and Biggar, K. (2011) *Time Well Spent: A Practical Guide to Active Citizenship and Volunteering in Prison*. London: Prison Reform Trust.

Edgar, K., O'Donnell, I. and Martin, C. (2003) *Prison Violence: The Dynamics of Conflict, Fear and Power*. Cullompton: Willan Publishing.

Einat, T. and Einat, H. (2000) 'Inmate argot as an expression of prison subculture: The Israeli case', *Prison Journal* 80 (3): 309–25.

Elliott, A. (2001) *Concepts of the Self*. Cambridge: Polity Press.

Elliott, D. and Menard, S. (1996) 'Delinquent friends and delinquent behavior: Temporal and developmental patterns', in J. Hawkins (ed.) *Delinquency and Crime: Current Theories*. Cambridge: Cambridge University Press.

Emerson, R. and Pollner, M. (2001) 'Constructing participant/observation relations', in R. Emerson (ed.) *Contemporary Field Research: Perspectives and Formulations*, 2nd edn. Prospect Heights, IL: Waveland Press.

Farrall, S. (2002) *Rethinking What Works with Offenders: Probation, Social Context and Desistance from Crime*. Cullompton: Willan Publishing.

Farrall, S. and Bowling, B. (1999) 'Structuration, human development and desistance from crime', *British Journal of Criminology* 39 (2): 253–68.

Farrall, S. and Calverley, A. (2006) *Understanding Desistance from Crime: Emerging Theoretical Developments in Resettlement and Rehabilitation*. Maidenhead: Open University Press.

Farrall, S., Sharpe, G., Hunter, B. and Calverley, A. (2011) 'Theorizing structural and individual-level processes in desistance and persistence: Outlining an integrated perspective', *Australian and New Zealand Journal of Criminology* 44 (2): 218–34.

Farrant, F. and Levenson, J. (2002) *Barred Citizens: Volunteering and Active Citizenship by Prisoners*. London: Prison Reform Trust.

Faulk, M. (1990) 'Her Majesty's Prison Grendon, Underwood' [sic], in R. Bluglass and P. Bowden (eds) *Principles and Practice of Forensic Psychiatry*. Edinburgh: Churchill Livingstone.

Federal Department of Justice and Police (2011) *Briefing on Ongoing and Completed Pilot Schemes in the Swiss Penal System*. Berne: Federal Office of Justice.

Feeley, M. and Simon, J. (1992) 'The new penology: Notes on the emerging strategy of corrections and its implications', *Criminology* 30 (4): 449–74.

——(1994) 'Actuarial justice: The emerging new criminal law', in D. Nelken (ed.) *The Futures of Criminology*. London: Sage.

Feldbrugge, J. (1990) 'The Van Der Hoeven Clinic, Utrecht', in R. Bluglass and P. Bowden (eds) *Principles and Practice of Forensic Psychiatry*. Edinburgh: Churchill Livingstone.

Finney, A. (2006) *Domestic Violence, Sexual Assault and Stalking: Findings from the 2004/2005 British Crime Survey*. Home Office Online Report (12/06). London: Home Office.

Fonagy, P., Leigh, T., Steele, M., Steele, H., Kennedy, R., Mattoon, G., Target, M. and Gerber, A. (1996) 'The relation of attachment status, psychiatric classification, and response to psychotherapy: Introduction to the special section on attachment and psychopathology: Part 1', *Journal of Consulting and Clinical Psychology* 64 (1): 22–31.

Foucault, M. (1977) *Discipline and Punish: The Birth of the Prison*. London: Allen Lane.

Foulkes, S. (1948) *Introduction to Group-analytic Psychotherapy: Studies in the Social Integration of Individuals and Groups*. London: W. Heinemann Medical Books.

——(1975) *Group-analytic Psychotherapy: Method and Principles*. London and New York: Gordon and Breach.

Fowler, A. (1997) 'Feltham's Albatross unit: The difficulties of small therapeutic communities for young offenders in the current economic climate', *Prison Service Journal* 111: 12–13.

Fox, K. (1999) 'Changing violent minds: Discursive correction and resistance in the cognitive treatment of violent offenders in prison', *Social Problems* 46 (1): 88–103.

Freilich, M. (ed.) (1970) *Marginal Natives: Anthropologists at Work*. New York: Harper and Row.

Freud, S. (1922) *Group Psychology and the Analysis of the Ego*. London: Hogarth.

Frost, A. and Connolly, M. (2004) 'Reflexivity, reflection, and the change process in offender work', *Sexual Abuse: A Journal of Research and Treatment* 16 (4): 365–80.

Gadd, D. and Farrall, S. (2004) 'Criminal careers, desistance and subjectivity: Interpreting men's narratives of change', *Theoretical Criminology* 8 (2): 123–56.

Gambetta, D. (2009) *Codes of the Underworld: How Criminals Communicate*. Princeton, NJ: Princeton University Press.

Garfinkel, H. (1956) 'Conditions of successful degradation ceremonies', *American Journal of Sociology* 61 (5): 420–24.

Garland, D. (1996) 'The limits of the sovereign state: Strategies of crime control in contemporary society', *British Journal of Criminology* 36 (4): 445–71.

——(1997) '"Governmentality" and the problem of crime: Foucault, criminology, sociology', *Theoretical Criminology* 1 (2) 173–214.

Gelder, M., Gath, D. and Mayou, R. (1983) *Oxford Textbook of Psychiatry.* Oxford: Oxford University Press.

Gelsthorpe, L. (1990) 'Feminist methodologies in criminology: A new approach or old wine in new bottles?', in L. Gelsthorpe and A. Morris (eds) *Feminist Perspectives in Criminology.* Buckingham: Open University Press.

Gelsthorpe, L. and Loucks, N. (1997) 'Magistrates' explanations of sentencing decisions', in C. Hedderman and L. Gelsthorpe (eds) *Understanding the Sentencing of Women.* Home Office Research Study 170. London: Her Majesty's Stationery Office.

Genders, E. (2003) 'Privatisation and innovation – rhetoric and reality: The development of a therapeutic community prison', *Howard Journal of Criminal Justice* 42 (2): 137–57.

Genders, E. and Player, E. (1995) *Grendon: A Study of a Therapeutic Prison.* Oxford: Clarendon Press.

——(2010) 'Therapy in prison: Revisiting Grendon 20 years on', *Howard Journal of Criminal Justice* 49 (5): 431–50.

George, R. (1971) *Grendon Follow-up 1967–68.* Grendon Psychology Unit Report Series A, No. 47. Grendon Underwood: HMP Grendon.

Giallombardo, R. (1966) *Society of Women: A Study of a Women's Prison.* New York: Wiley.

Giddens, A. (1990) *The Consequences of Modernity.* Cambridge: Polity Press.

——(1991) *Modernity and Self Identity: Self and Society in the Late Modern Age.* Stanford, CA: Stanford University Press.

Gideon, L. (2010) 'Drug offenders' perceptions of motivation: The role of motivation in rehabilitation and reintegration', *Journal of Offender Therapy and Comparative Criminology* 54 (4): 597–610.

Gilbert, M. (1997) 'The illusion of structure: A critique of the classical model of organization and the discretionary power of correctional officers', *Criminal Justice Review* 22 (1): 49–64.

Gilligan, C. (1982) *In a Different Voice: Psychological Theory and Women's Development.* Cambridge, MA: Harvard University Press.

Giordano, P., Cernkovich, S. and Holland, D. (2003) 'Changes in friendship relations over the life course: Implications for desistance from crime', *Criminology* 41 (2): 293–327.

Giordano, P., Cernkovich, S. and Rudolph, J. (2002) 'Gender, crime, and desistance: Toward a theory of cognitive transformation', *American Journal of Sociology* 107 (4): 990–1064.

Glaser, A. (1983) 'Therapeutic communities and therapeutic communities: A personal perspective', *International Journal of Therapeutic Communities* 4 (2): 150–62.

Glaser, D. (1969) *Effectiveness of a Prison and Parole System.* Indianapolis, IN: Bobbs-Merrill.

Glatt, M. (1985) 'The Wormwood Scrubs Annexe: Reflections on the working and functioning of an addict's therapeutic community within a prison', *Prison Care* November.

Glueck, S. and Glueck, E. (1940) *Juvenile Delinquents Grown Up*. New York: Commonwealth Fund.

Godderis, R. (2006) 'Dining in: The symbolic power of food in prison', *Howard Journal of Criminal Justice* 45 (3): 255–67.

Goffman, E. (1959) *The Presentation of Self in Everyday Life*. New York: Doubleday.

——(1961) *Asylums: Essays on the Social Situation of Mental Patients and Other Inmates*. New York: Anchor Books.

——(1963) *Stigma: Notes on the Management of Spoiled Identity*. Englewood Cliffs, NJ: Prentice-Hall.

——(1967) *Interaction Ritual: Essays on Face-to-Face Behavior*. New York: Anchor Books.

Gomersall, J. (1991) 'Monsters, beasts and animals: An account of the introduction and formation of HMP Grendon's Sex Offender Treatment Programme', *Prison Service Journal* 81: 22–24.

Goodey, J. (1997) 'Boys don't cry: Masculinity, fear of crime and fearlessness', *British Journal of Criminology* 37 (3): 401–18.

——(2000) 'Biographical lessons for criminology', *Theoretical Criminology* 4 (4): 473–98.

Graham, J. and Bowling, B. (1995) *Young People and Crime*. Home Office Research Study No. 145. London: Home Office.

Gramsci, A. (1971) *Selections from the Prison Notebooks*. London: Lawrence and Wishart.

Gray, N., Snowden, R., Brown, A. and MacCulloch, M. (2002) *Prevalence of Psychopathy and other Measures of Risk at HMP Grendon: An Investigation of Population Statistics*. Cardiff: School of Psychology, Cardiff University.

Gray, W. (1973a) 'The therapeutic community and evaluation of results', *International Journal of Criminology and Penology* 1: 327–34.

——(1973b) 'The English Prison Medical Service: Its historical background and more recent developments', in G. Wolstenholme and M. O'Connor (eds) *Medical Care of Prisoners and Detainees*. Amsterdam and London: Associated Scientific Publishers.

Greer, C. (2003) *Sex Crime and the Media: Sex Offending and the Press in a Divided Society*. Cullompton: Willan Publishing.

Grossman, K.E. and Grossman, K. (1991) 'Attachment quality as an organiser of emotional and behavioral responses in a longitudinal perspective', in C. Parkes, J. Stevenson-Hinde and P. Marris (eds) *Attachment Across the Life Cycle*. London: Tavistock/Routledge.

Gunn, J., Maden, T. and Swinton, M. (1991) 'Treatment needs of prisoners with psychiatric disorders', *British Medical Journal* 303 (6798): 338–41.

Gunn, J., Robertson, G., Dell, S. and Way, C. (1978) *Psychiatric Aspects of Imprisonment*. London: Academic Press.

Haigh, R. (1999) 'The quintessence of a therapeutic environment: Five universal qualities', in P. Campling and R. Haigh (eds) *Therapeutic Communities: Past, Present and Future*. London: Jessica Kingsley.

Hall, S. (2000) 'Who needs "identity?"', in P. du Gay, J. Evans and P. Redman (eds) *Identity: A Reader*. London: Sage and The Open University.

——(2002) 'Daubing the drudges of fury: Men, violence and the piety of the "hegemonic masculinity" thesis', *Theoretical Criminology* 6 (1): 35–61.

Hammersley, M. and Atkinson, P. (1995) *Ethnography: Principles in Practice*, 2nd edn. London: Routledge.

Hannah-Moffat, K. (2001) *Punishment in Disguise: Penal Governance and Federal Imprisonment of Women in Canada*. Toronto: University of Toronto Press.

——(2005) 'Criminogenic need and the transformative risk subject: Hybridizations of risk/need in penality', *Punishment & Society* 7 (1): 29–51.

Hansard (2011) *Written Statements: Monday 12 September 2011*. Available at: http://www.publications.parliament.uk/pa/ld201011/ldhansrd/text/110912-wms0001.htm [accessed 26 October 2011].

Hansen, H. and Lykke-Olesen, L. (1997) 'Treatment of dangerous sexual offenders in Denmark', *Journal of Forensic Psychiatry and Psychology* 8 (1): 195–99.

Hare, R. (1991) *Manual for the Hare Psychopathy Checklist – Revised*. Toronto: Multi-Health Systems.

——(1996) 'Psychopathy: A clinical construct whose time has come', *Criminal Justice and Behavior* 23 (1): 25–54.

Harper, G. and Chitty, C. (eds) (2005) *The Impact of Corrections on Re-offending: A Review of 'What Works'*, 3rd edn. Home Office Research Study No. 291. London: Home Office.

Harrison, T. (1999) 'A momentous experiment: Strange meetings at Northfield', in P. Campling and R. Haigh (eds) *Therapeutic Communities: Past, Present and Future*. London: Jessica Kingsley.

Hart, S., Michie, C. and Cooke, D. (2007) 'Precision of actuarial risk assessment instruments: Evaluating the "margins of error" of group v. individual predictions for violence', *British Journal of Psychiatry* 190 (Supplement 49): s60–s65.

Harvey, J. (2007) *Young Men in Prison: Surviving and Adapting to Life Inside*. Cullompton: Willan Publishing.

Hazan, C. and Shaver, P. (1994) 'Attachment as an organizational framework for research on close relationships', *Psychological Inquiry* 5 (1): 1–22.

Healey, B. (2000) *Grendon Prison: The History of a Therapeutic Experiment 1939–2000*. Wotton-under-Edge: HMP Leyhill.

Healy, D. (2010) *The Dynamics of Desistance: Charting Pathways through Change*. Cullompton: Willan Publishing.

Hearn, J. (2004) 'From hegemonic masculinity to the hegemony of men', *Feminist Theory* 5 (1): 49–72.

Hebenton, B. and Seddon, T. (2009) 'From dangerousness to precaution: Managing sexual and violent offenders in an insecure and uncertain age', *British Journal of Criminology* 49 (3): 343–62.

Heidensohn, F. (1985) *Women and Crime*. London: Macmillan.

Held, V. (2006) *The Ethics of Care: Personal, Political, and Global*. Oxford: Oxford University Press.

HM Chief Inspector of Prisons (2001) *Report on an Unannounced Inspection of HM Prison Wormwood Scrubs, 10–19 December 2001*. London: HM Inspectorate of Prisons.

——(2006) *Report on an Announced Inspection of HMP Send, 13–17 February 2006*. London: HM Inspectorate of Prisons.

——(2007) *Report on an Announced Inspection of HMP Birmingham, 19–23 February 2007*. London: HM Inspectorate of Prisons.

——(2008) *Report on an Unannounced Short Follow-up Inspection of HMP Send, 18–22 August 2008*. London: HM Inspectorate of Prisons.

——(2009) *Report on an Announced Inspection of HM Prison Grendon, 2–6 March 2009*. London: HM Inspectorate of Prisons.

——(2010) *Report on an Announced Inspection of HMP Send, 6–10 December 2010*. London: HM Inspectorate of Prisons.

——(2011) *Report on an Unannounced Short Follow-up Inspection of HMP Grendon, 15–17 August 2011*. London: HM Inspectorate of Prisons.

——(1999) *Suicide is Everyone's Concern: A Thematic Review by HM Chief Inspector of Prisons for England and Wales*. London: HM Inspectorate of Prisons.

HM Prison Service (2003) *Democratic Therapeutic Communities: Core Model Theory Manual*. London: HM Prison Service.

Hiller, M., Knight, K. and Simpson, D. (1999) 'Prison-based substance abuse treatment, residential aftercare and recidivism', *Addiction* 94 (6): 833–42.

Hirschi, T. (1969) *Causes of Delinquency*. Berkeley, CA: University of California Press.

Hobson, J. and Shine, J. (1998) 'Measurement of psychopathy in a UK prison population referred for long-term psychotherapy', *British Journal of Criminology* 38 (3): 504–15.

Hochschild, A. (1983) *The Managed Heart: Commercialization of Human Feeling*. Berkeley, CA and London: University of California Press.

——(2003) *The Managed Heart: Commercialization of Human Feeling, Twentieth Anniversary Edition, With a New Afterword*. Berkeley and London: University of California Press.

Hollway, W. and Jefferson, T. (2000) *Doing Qualitative Research Differently: Free Association, Narrative and the Interview Method*. London: Sage.

Holstein, J. and Gubrium, J. (2004) 'The active interview', in D. Silverman (ed.) *Qualitative Research: Theory, Method and Practice,* 2nd edn. London: Sage.

Home Office (1932) *Report of the Departmental Committee on Persistent Offenders*, Cmnd. 4090. London: His Majesty's Stationery Office.

——(1984) *Managing the Long-Term Prison System: The Report of the Control Review Committee*. London: Her Majesty's Stationery Office.

——(1985) *First Report of the Advisory Committee on the Therapeutic Regime at Grendon*. London: Her Majesty's Stationery Office.

Hood, R., Shute, S., Feilzer, M. and Wilcox, A. (2002) 'Sex offenders emerging from long-term imprisonment: A study of their long-term reconviction rates and of Parole Board members' judgements of their risk', *British Journal of Criminology* 42 (2): 371–94.

House of Commons Home Affairs Committee (2005) *Rehabilitation of Prisoners: First Report of Session 2004–05*, Volume 1. London: The Stationery Office.

House of Commons Justice Committee (2009) *Role of the Prison Officer*. London: House of Commons.

Howe, A. (ed.) (1998) *Sexed Crime in the News*. Sydney: The Federation Press.

Hua, H-F. (2005) 'The patterns of masculinity in prison sociology: A case study of one Taiwanese prison', *Critical Criminology* 13: 1–16.

Hubbard, G., Backett-Milburn, K. and Kemmer, D. (2001) 'Working with emotion: Issues for the researcher in fieldwork and teamwork', *International Journal of Social Research Methodology* 4 (2): 119–37.

Hucklesby, A. and Wilkinson, C. (2001) 'Drug misuse in prisons: Some comments on the Prison Service drug strategy', *Howard Journal of Criminal Justice* 40 (4): 347–63.

Hudson, K. (2005) *Offending Identities: Sex Offenders' Perspectives on their Treatment and Management*. Cullompton: Willan Publishing.

Hughes, E. (1962) 'Good people and dirty work', *Social Problems* 10 (1): 3–11.

Hyler, S. (1994) *Personality Diagnostic Questionnaire*, 4th edn. New York: New York State Psychiatric Institute.

IMB (Independent Monitoring Boards) (2010) *'Slopping out?' A report on the lack of in-cell sanitation in Her Majesty's Prisons in England and Wales*. IMB: London.

Inciardi, J., Martin, S. and Butzin, C. (2004) 'Five-year outcomes of therapeutic community treatment of drug-involved offenders after release from prison', *Crime and Delinquency* 50 (1): 88–107.

Inciardi, J., Martin, S., Butzin, C., Hooper, R. and Harrison, L. (1997) 'An effective model of prison-based treatment for drug-involved offenders', *Journal of Drug Issues* 27 (2): 261–78.

Irwin, J. (1970) *The Felon*. Berkeley, CA: University of California Press.

Irwin, J. and Cressey, D. (1962) 'Thieves, convicts and the inmate culture', *Social Problems* 10 (2): 142–55.

Irwin, J. and Owen, B. (2005) 'Harm and the contemporary prison', in A. Liebling and S. Maruna (eds) *The Effects of Imprisonment*. Cullompton: Willan Publishing.

Jacobs, J. (1977) *Stateville: The Penitentiary in Mass Society*. Chicago, IL: University of Chicago Press.

Jefferson, T. (2002) 'Subordinating hegemonic masculinity', *Theoretical Criminology* 6 (1): 63–88.

Jenkins, R. (2004) *Social Identity*, 2nd edn. London and New York: Routledge.

Jewkes, Y. (2002) *Captive Audience: Media, Masculinity and Power in Prisons*. Cullompton: Willan Publishing.

——(2005a) 'Loss, liminality and the life sentence: Managing identity through a disrupted lifecourse', in A. Liebling and S. Maruna (eds) *The Effects of Imprisonment*. Cullompton: Willan Publishing.

——(2005b) 'Men behind bars: "Doing" masculinity as an adaptation to imprisonment', *Men and Masculinities* 8 (1): 44–63.

——(2006) 'A prison tale: The role of empathy and emotion in the formulation of knowledge'. Paper presented at the Centre for Criminology, University of Oxford, 22 February 2006.

——(2012) 'Autoethnography and emotion as intellectual resources: Doing prison research differently', *Qualitative Inquiry* 18 (1): 63–75.

Johnson, R. (1996) *Hard Time: Understanding and Reforming the Prison*, 2nd edn. Belmont, CA: Wadsworth.

Jones, D. (ed.) (2004a) *Working with Dangerous People: The Psychotherapy of Violence*. Abingdon: Radcliffe Medical Press.

——(2004b) 'Introduction', in Jones, D. (ed.) *Working with Dangerous People: The Psychotherapy of Violence*. Abingdon: Radcliffe Medical Press.

——(ed.) (2006) *Humane Prisons*. Abingdon: Radcliffe Publishing.

Jones, L. (1988) *The Hospital Annexe: A Preliminary Evaluation Report*. Directorate of Psychological Services Report Series II No. 164. London: Directorate of Psychological Services, Home Office.

——(1997) 'Developing models for managing treatment integrity and efficacy in a prison-based TC: The Max Glatt Centre', in E. Cullen, L. Jones and R. Woodward (eds) *Therapeutic Communities for Offenders*. Chichester: Wiley.

Jones, M. (1952) *Social Psychiatry: A Study of Therapeutic Communities*. London: Tavistock Publications.

——(1953) *The Therapeutic Community: A New Treatment Method in Psychiatry*. New York: Basic Books.

——(1968) *Social Psychiatry in Practice: The Idea of the Therapeutic Community.* Harmondsworth: Penguin.

——(1976) *Maturation of the Therapeutic Community: An Organic Approach to Health and Mental Health.* New York: Human Sciences Press.

——(1980) 'Desirable features of a therapeutic community in a prison', in H. Toch (ed.) *Therapeutic Communities in Corrections.* Westport, CT: Greenwood Press.

——(1982) *The Process of Change.* Boston, MA: Routledge and Kegan Paul.

Josselson, R. and Lieblich, A. (eds) (1993) *The Narrative Study of Lives.* Newbury Park, CA: Sage.

Kane, S. (1998) 'Reversing the ethnographic gaze: Experiments in cultural criminology', in J. Ferrell and M. Hamm (eds) *Ethnography at the Edge: Crime, Deviance and Field Research.* Boston, MA: Northeastern University Press.

Katz, J. (1988) *Seductions of Crime: Moral and Sensual Attractions in Doing Evil.* New York: Basic Books.

Keenan, S. and Paget, S. (2008) *Service Standards for Therapeutic Communities,* 5th edn. London: Royal College of Psychiatrists' Research Unit.

Keene, J. (1997) 'Drug misuse in prison: Views from inside: A qualitative study of prison staff and inmates', *Howard Journal of Criminal Justice* 36 (1): 28–41.

Kelly, L. and Radford, J. (1987) 'The problem of men: Feminist perspectives on sexual violence', in P. Scraton (ed.) *Law, Order and the Authoritarian State: Readings in Critical Criminology.* Milton Keynes: Open University Press.

Kennard, D. (1996) 'Editorial: An education in sincerity and tolerance', *Therapeutic Communities: The International Journal for Therapeutic and Supportive Organizations* 17 (2): 71–73.

——(1998) *An Introduction to Therapeutic Communities.* London: Jessica Kingsley.

——(2004) 'The therapeutic community as an adaptable treatment modality across different settings', *Psychiatric Quarterly* 75 (3): 295–307.

Kennard, D. and Roberts, J. (1983) *An Introduction to Therapeutic Communities.* London: Routledge and Kegan Paul.

Kennedy, H. (1998) 'Women's Therapeutic Community Feasibility Study'. Unpublished report. London: Prison Service's Women's Policy Group.

Kimmel, M. (2001) 'Masculinity as homophobia: Fear, shame, and silence in the construction of gender identity', in S. Whitehead and F. Barrett (eds) *The Masculinities Reader.* Cambridge: Polity Press.

King, R. (2000) 'Doing research in prisons', in R. King and E. Wincup (eds) *Doing Research on Crime and Justice.* Oxford: Oxford University Press.

King, R. and Elliott, K. (1977) *Albany: Birth of a Prison, End of an Era.* London: Routledge and Kegan Paul.

King, R. and Liebling, A. (2008) 'Doing research in prisons', in R. King and E. Wincup (eds) *Doing Research on Crime and Justice,* 2nd edn. Oxford: Oxford University Press.

Kirk, J. and Miller, M. (1986) *Reliability and Validity in Qualitative Research.* Qualitative Research Methods Series, Volume 1. Newbury Park, CA, and London: Sage.

Kleinman, S. (1991) 'Field workers' feelings: What we feel, who we are, how we analyze', in W. Shaffir and R. Stebbins (eds) *Experiencing Fieldwork: An Inside View of Qualitative Research.* Newbury Park, CA: Sage.

Kleinman, S. and Copp, M. (1993) *Emotions and Fieldwork.* Qualitative Research Methods Series, Volume 28. Newbury Park, CA, and London: Sage.

Knight, K., Simpson, D., Chatham, L. and Camacho, L. (1997) 'An assessment of prison-based drug treatment: Texas' in-prison therapeutic community program', *Journal of Offender Rehabilitation* 24 (3): 75–100.

Kooyman, M. (2001) 'The history of therapeutic communities: A view from Europe', in B. Rawlings and R. Yates (eds) *Therapeutic Communities for the Treatment of Drug Users*. London: Jessica Kingsley.

Laclau, E. (1990) *New Reflections on the Revolution of our Time*. London: Verso.

Lacombe, D. (2008) 'Consumed with sex: The treatment of sex offenders in risk society', *British Journal of Criminology* 48 (1): 55–74.

Laing, R. D. (1960) *The Divided Self: A Study of Sanity and Madness*. London: Tavistock Publications.

——(1961) *The Self and Others: Further Studies in Sanity and Madness*. London: Tavistock Publications.

——(1966) *The Politics of Experience*. Harmondsworth: Penguin.

Laub, J. and Sampson, R. (2001) 'Understanding desistance from crime', in M. Tonry (ed.) *Crime and Justice: A Review of Research,* Volume 28. Chicago, IL, and London: University of Chicago Press.

——(2003) *Shared Beginnings, Divergent Lives: Delinquent Boys to Age 70*. Cambridge, MA: Harvard University Press.

Laws, D. R., Hudson, S. and Ward, T. (eds) (2000) *Remaking Relapse Prevention with Sex Offenders: A Sourcebook*. Thousand Oaks, CA, and London: Sage.

LeBel, T., Burnett, R., Maruna, S. and Bushway, S. (2008) 'The "chicken and egg" of subjective and social factors in desistance from crime', *European Journal of Criminology* 5 (2): 131–59.

Lees, J., Manning, N. and Rawlings, B. (1999) *Therapeutic Community Effectiveness: A Systematic International Review of Therapeutic Community Treatment for People with Personality Disorders and Mentally Disordered Offenders*. York: York Publishing Services.

——(2004) 'A culture of enquiry: Research evidence and the therapeutic community', *Psychiatric Quarterly* 75 (3): 279–94.

Leibrich, J. (1993) *Straight to the Point: Angles on Giving up Crime*. Otago, New Zealand: University of Otago Press.

Lemert, E. (1951) *Social Pathology*. New York: McGraw-Hill.

Lewin, K. (1935) *A Dynamic Theory of Personality: Selected Papers*. New York and London: McGraw-Hill.

Lewis, P. (1997) 'Sustaining therapeutic communities: The Grendon Experience', *Prison Service Journal* 111: 8–12.

Liebling, A. (1992) *Suicides in Prison*. London: Routledge.

——(1999) 'Doing research in prison: Breaking the silence?', *Theoretical Criminology* 3 (2): 147–73.

——(2001) 'Whose side are we on? Theory, practice and allegiances in prisons research', *British Journal of Criminology* 41 (3): 472–84.

——(2002) 'A "liberal regime within a secure perimeter"? Dispersal prisons and penal practice in the late twentieth century', in A. Bottoms and M. Tonry (eds) *Ideology, Crime and Criminal Justice: A Symposium in Honour of Sir Leon Radzinowicz*. Cullompton: Willan Publishing.

Liebling, A., assisted by Arnold, H. (2004) *Prisons and their Moral Performance: A Study of Values, Quality, and Prison Life*. Oxford: Oxford University Press.

Liebling, A., Price, D. and Shefer, G. (2011) *The Prison Officer*, 2nd edn. Cullompton: Willan Publishing.

Light, R. (1985) 'The Special Unit – Barlinnie prison', in J. Reynolds and U. Smartt (eds) (1995) *Prison Policy and Practice: Selected Papers from 35 years of the Prison Service Journal*. HMP Leyhill: Prison Service Journal.

Lipman-Blumen, J. (1984) *Gender Roles and Power*. Englewood Cliffs, NJ: Prentice-Hall.

Lipsey, M. (1992) 'Juvenile delinquency treatment: A meta-analytic inquiry into the variability of effects', in T. Cook, H. Cooper, D. Cordray, H. Hartmann, L. Hedges, R. Light, T. Louis and F. Mosteller (eds) *Meta-Analysis for Explanation: A Casebook*. New York: Russell Sage Foundation.

Lipton, D. (1998) 'Therapeutic community treatment programming in corrections', *Psychology, Crime & Law* 4 (3): 213–63.

——(2010) 'A therapeutic distinction with a difference: Comparing American concept-based therapeutic communities and British democratic therapeutic community treatment for prison inmates', in R. Shuker and E. Sullivan (eds) *Grendon and the Emergence of Forensic Therapeutic Communities: Developments in Research and Practice*. Chichester: Wiley-Blackwell.

Lloyd, C., Mair, G. and Hough, J. (1994) *Explaining Reconviction Rates: A Critical Analysis*. Home Office Research Study No. 136. London: Her Majesty's Stationery Office.

Loat, M. (2006) '"Sharing the struggle": An exploration of mutual support processes in a therapeutic community', *Therapeutic Communities: The International Journal for Therapeutic and Supportive Organizations* 27 (2): 211–28.

Lofland, J., Snow, D., Anderson, L. and Lofland, L. (2006) *Analyzing Social Settings: A Guide to Qualitative Observation and Analysis*, 4th edn. Belmont, CA: Wadsworth/Thomson Learning.

López-Viets, V., Walker, D. and Miller, W. (2002) 'What is motivation to change? A scientific analysis', in M. McMurran (ed.) *Motivating Offenders to Change: A Guide to Enhancing Engagement in Therapy*. Chichester: Wiley.

Lösel, F. (1995) 'The efficacy of correctional treatment: A review and synthesis of meta-evaluations', in J. McGuire (ed.) *What Works: Reducing Reoffending*. Chichester: Wiley.

Lösel, F. and Egg, R. (1997) 'Social-therapeutic institutions in Germany: Description and evaluation', in E. Cullen, L. Jones and R. Woodward (eds) *Therapeutic Communities for Offenders*. Chichester: Wiley.

McAdams, D. (1993) *The Stories We Live By: Personal Myths and the Making of the Self*. New York and London: Guilford.

——(1996) 'Personality, modernity, and the storied self: A contemporary framework for studying persons', *Psychological Inquiry* 7 (4): 295–321.

——(2006) *The Redemptive Self: Stories Americans Live By*. Oxford and New York: Oxford University Press.

McAdams, D. and de St Aubin, E. (1998) 'Introduction', in D. McAdams and E. de St Aubin (eds) *Generativity and Adult Development: How and Why we Care for the Next Generation*. Washington, DC: American Psychological Society.

McGuire, J. (ed.) (1995) *What Works: Reducing Reoffending: Guidelines from Practice and Research*. Chichester: Wiley.

——(ed.) (2002) *Offender Rehabilitation and Treatment: Effective Programmes and Policies to Reduce Re-Offending*. Chichester: Wiley.

MacKenzie, D. (2006) *What Works in Corrections. Reducing the Criminal Activities of Offenders and Delinquents*. Cambridge: Cambridge University Press.

Mackenzie, J. (1997) 'Glen Parva therapeutic community: An obituary', *Prison Service Journal* 111: 26.

——(2007) 'Changing a life sentence into a life', in M. Parker (ed.) *Dynamic Security: The Democratic Therapeutic Community in Prison*. London: Jessica Kingsley.

MacKinnon, C. (1987) *Feminism Unmodified: Discourses on Life and Law*. Cambridge: Harvard University Press.

McLure, L. (2004) 'Working with the unbearable', in D. Jones (ed.) *Working with Dangerous People: The Psychotherapy of Violence*. Abingdon: Radcliffe Medical Press.

McManus, J. (2007) 'The experience of officers in a therapeutic prison', *Prison Service Journal* 173: 21–26.

McMurran, M. and McCulloch, A. (2007) 'Why don't offenders complete treatment? Prisoners' reasons for non-completion of a cognitive skills programme', *Psychology, Crime & Law* 13 (4): 345–54.

McNeill, F. (2006) 'A desistance paradigm for offender management', *Criminology and Criminal Justice* 6 (1): 39–62.

Maden, T., Swinton, M. and Gunn, J. (1994) 'Therapeutic community treatment: A survey of unmet need among sentenced prisoners', *Therapeutic Communities: The International Journal for Therapeutic and Supportive Organizations* 15 (4): 229–36.

Main, M. and Solomon, J. (1986) 'Discovery of a new, insecure-disorganized/disoriented attachment pattern', in T. Brazelton and M. Yogman (eds) *Affective Development in Infancy*. Norwood, NJ: Ablex.

Main, T. (1946) 'The hospital as a therapeutic institution', *Bulletin of the Menninger Clinic* 10: 66–68.

——(1996) 'The hospital as a therapeutic institution', *Therapeutic Communities: The International Journal for Therapeutic and Supportive Organizations* 17 (2): 77–80.

Malamuth, N. (1981) 'Rape proclivity among males', *Journal of Social Issues* 37 (4): 138–57.

Malan, D. (1979) *Individual Psychotherapy and the Science of Psychodynamics*. Oxford: Butterworths Heinemann.

Manning, N. (1976) 'Innovation in social policy – the case of the therapeutic community', *Journal of Social Policy* 5 (3): 265–79.

——(1989) *The Therapeutic Community Movement: Charisma and Routinization*. London: Routledge.

Manor, O. (1994) 'Group psychotherapy', in P. Clarkson and M. Pokorny (eds) *The Handbook of Psychotherapy*. London and New York: Routledge.

Mansour, F. (2011) 'La Pâquerette, ou la prison autrement', *Le Temps*, 21 November.

Marshall, P. (1997) *A Reconviction Study of HMP Grendon Therapeutic Community*. Home Office Research Findings No. 53. London: Home Office Research and Statistics Directorate.

Marshall, W. (1993) 'The role of attachment, intimacy and loneliness in the etiology and maintenance of sexual offending', *Sexual and Marital Therapy* 8 (2): 109–21.

Marshall, W., Ward, T., Mann, R., Moulden, H., Fernandez, Y., Serran, G. and Marshall, L. (2005) 'Working positively with sexual offenders: Maximizing the effectiveness of treatment', *Journal of Interpersonal Violence* 20 (9): 1096–114.

Martin, K. and Stermac, L. (2010). 'Measuring hope: Is hope related to criminal behaviour in offenders?', *International Journal of Offender Therapy and Comparative Criminology* 54 (5): 693–705.

Martin, S., Butzin, C., Saum, C. and Inciardi, J. (1999) 'Three-year outcomes of therapeutic community treatment for drug involved offenders in Delaware: From prison to work release to aftercare', *Prison Journal* 79 (3): 294–320.

Martinson, R. (1974) 'What works? Questions and answers about prison reform', *Public Interest* 35 (Spring): 22–54.

Maruna, S. (2001) *Making Good: How Ex-Convicts Reform and Rebuild their Lives.* Washington, DC: American Psychological Association.

Maruna, S. and Farrall, S. (2004) 'Desistance from crime: A theoretical reformulation', *Kölner Zeitschrift für Soziologie und Sozialpsychologie* 43: 171–94.

Maruna, S. and LeBel, T. (2002) 'Revisiting ex-prisoner re-entry: A buzzword in search of a narrative', in S. Rex and M. Tonry (eds) *Reform and Punishment: The Future of Sentencing.* Cullompton: Willan Publishing.

Maruna, S., LeBel, T., Mitchell, N. and Naples, M. (2004) 'Pygmalion in the reintegration process: Desistance from crime through the looking glass', *Psychology, Crime & Law* 10 (3): 271–81.

Maruna, S., LeBel, T., Naples, M. and Mitchell, N. (2009) 'Looking-glass identity transformation: Pygmalion and Golem in the rehabilitation process', in B. Veysey, J. Christian and D. Martinez (eds) *How Offenders Transform their Lives.* Cullompton: Willan Publishing.

Mason, P., Mason, D. and Brookes, N. (2001) 'Therapeutic communities for drug-misusing offenders in prison', in B. Rawlings and R. Yates (eds) *Therapeutic Communities for the Treatment of Drug Users.* London: Jessica Kingsley.

Mathiesen, T. (1965) *The Defences of the Weak: A Sociological Study of a Norwegian Correctional Institution.* London: Tavistock Publications.

——(2006) *Prison on Trial*, 3rd English edn. Winchester: Waterside Press.

Matthews, R. and Pitts, J. (2000) 'Rehabilitation, recidivism and realism: Evaluating violence reduction programmes in prison', in V. Jupp, P. Davies and P. Francis (eds) *Doing Criminological Research.* London: Sage.

Matza, D. (1964) *Delinquency and Drift.* New York: Wiley.

——(1969) *Becoming Deviant.* Englewood Cliffs, NJ: Prentice-Hall.

May, C., Sharma, N. and Stewart, D. (2008) *Factors Linked to Reoffending: A One-year Follow-up of Prisoners who took part in the Resettlement Surveys 2001, 2003 and 2004.* Research Summary 5. London: Ministry of Justice.

May, J. (1979) *Committee of Inquiry into the United Kingdom Prison Services: Report*, Cmnd. 7673. London: Her Majesty's Stationery Office.

Mead, G.H. (1934) *Mind, Self, and Society: From the Standpoint of a Social Behaviorist.* Chicago, IL: University of Chicago Press.

Merton, R. (1957) *Social Theory and Social Structure.* Glencoe, IL: Free Press.

Messerschmidt, J. (1993) *Masculinities and Crime: Critique and Reconceptualization of Theory.* Lanham, MD: Rowman and Littlefield.

——(1997) *Crime as Structured Action: Gender, Race, Class, and Crime in the Making.* Thousand Oaks, CA: Sage.

Messner, M. (1992) 'Like family: Power, intimacy, and sexuality in male athletes' friendships', in P. Nardi (ed.) *Men's Friendships.* Newbury Park, CA, and London: Sage.

Miller, Q. (1982) *Preliminary Considerations of Psychological Test/Retest Scores and their Bearing upon Criminal Reconviction.* Grendon Psychology Unit Report Series D No. 13. Grendon Underwood: HMP Grendon.

Miller, S. (1952) 'The participant observer and "over-rapport"', *American Sociological Review* 17 (1): 97–99.

Miller, S. and Brown, J. (2010) 'HMP Dovegate's therapeutic community: An analysis of reconviction data', *Therapeutic Communities: The International Journal for Therapeutic and Supportive Organizations* 31 (1): 62–75.

Miller, S., Brown, J. and Sees, C. (2004) 'A preliminary study identifying risk factors in drop-out from a prison therapeutic community', *Journal of Clinical Forensic Medicine* 11 (4): 189–97.

Miller, S., Sees, C. and Brown, J. (2006) 'Key aspects of psychological change in residents of a prison therapeutic community: A focus group approach', *Howard Journal of Criminal Justice* 45 (2): 116–28.

Ministry of Justice (2008a) *Restrictions on Strike Action for Prison Officers in European Union Member Countries (EU) and Countries in the Organisation for Economic Co-operation and Development (OECD)*. London: Ministry of Justice.

——(2008b) *Offender Management Caseload Statistics 2007*. Ministry of Justice Statistics Bulletin. London: Ministry of Justice.

——(2010a) *The Correctional Services Accreditation Panel Report 2009–2010*. London: Ministry of Justice.

——(2010b) *Compendium of Reoffending Statistics and Analysis*. London: Ministry of Justice.

——(2010c) *Research Applications*. London: Ministry of Justice.

——(2011a) *National Offender Management Service Annual Report 2010/11: Management Information Addendum*. London: Ministry of Justice.

——(2011b) *Offender Management Statistics Quarterly Bulletin, April to June 2011, England and Wales*. London: Ministry of Justice.

——(2011c) *Safety in Custody 2010 England and Wales*. London: Ministry of Justice.

Misztal, B. (1996) *Trust in Modern Societies: The Search for the Bases of Social Order*. Cambridge: Polity Press.

Mitchell, O., Wilson, D. and MacKenzie, D. (2007) 'Does incarceration-based drug treatment reduce recidivism? A meta-analytic synthesis of the research', *Journal of Experimental Criminology* 3 (4): 353–75.

Mollerup, S., Jessen-Petersen, B. and Gabrielsen, G. (2005) *The Efficacy of Anti-hormone Therapy on Dangerous Sexual Offenders*. Copenhagen: Department of Prisons and Probation.

Morgan, D. (1992) *Discovering Men*. London: Routledge.

Morgan, S. (1999) 'Prison lives: Critical issues in reading prisoner autobiography', *Howard Journal of Criminal Justice* 38 (3): 328–40.

Morris, M. (2001) 'Grendon Underwood: A psychotherapeutic prison', in J. Williams Saunders (ed.) *Life within Hidden Worlds: Psychotherapy in Prisons*. London: Karnac.

——(2004a) *Dangerous and Severe – Process, Programme and Person: Grendon's Work*. London: Jessica Kingsley.

——(2004b) 'Psychopathy: The dominant paradigm', in D. Jones (ed.) *Working with Dangerous People: The Psychotherapy of Violence*. Abingdon: Radcliffe Medical Press.

——(2005) 'Therapeutic communities behind bars: Treatment and consent', *Therapeutic Communities: The International Journal for Therapeutic and Supportive Organizations* 26 (4): 355–65.

Morris, T. (1967) 'Research on the prison community', in Council of Europe (ed.) *Collected Studies in Criminological Research*, Volume 1. Strasbourg: European Committee on Crime Problems, Council of Europe.

Morris, T. and Morris, P., assisted by Barer, B. (1963) *Pentonville: A Sociological Study of an English Prison*. London: Routledge and Kegan Paul.

Mosher, D. and Tompkins, S. (1988) 'Scripting the macho man: Hypermasculine socialization and enculturation', *Journal of Sex Research* 25 (1): 60–84.

Moulden, H. and Marshall, W. (2005) 'Hope in the treatment of sexual offenders: The potential application of hope theory', *Psychology, Crime & Law* 11 (3): 329–42.

Myhill, A. and Allen, J. (2002) *Rape and Sexual Assault of Women: The Extent and Nature of the Problem*. Home Office Research Study 237. London: Home Office.

Nardi, P. (1992) '"Seamless souls": An introduction to men's friendships', in P. Nardi (ed.) *Men's Friendships*. Newbury Park, CA, and London: Sage.

National Audit Office (2006) *HM Prison Service: Serving Time: Prisoner Diet and Exercise*. London: The Stationery Office.

Neville, L., Miller, S. and Fritzon, K. (2007) 'Understanding change in a therapeutic community: An action systems approach', *Journal of Forensic Psychiatry and Psychology* 18 (2): 181–203.

Newburn, T. and Stanko, E. (1994) (eds) *Just Boys doing Business? Men, Masculinities and Crime*. London: Routledge.

Newell, T. and Healey, B. (2007) 'The historical development of the UK democratic therapeutic community', in M. Parker (ed.) *Dynamic Security: The Democratic Therapeutic Community in Prison*. London: Jessica Kingsley.

Newton, C. (1994) 'Gender theory and prison sociology: Using theories of masculinities to interpret the sociology of prisons for men', *Howard Journal of Criminal Justice* 33 (3): 193–202.

Newton, M. (1971) *Reconviction After Treatment at Grendon*. Chief Psychologist Report Series B, No. 1. London: Office of the Chief Psychologist, Prison Department, Home Office.

——(1973) *Progress of Follow-up Studies and Comparisons with Non-patients Carried out at HMP Oxford*. Grendon Psychology Unit Report, Series A, No. 15. Grendon Underwood: HMP Grendon.

——(1997) 'Changes in Test Scores during Treatment at Grendon'. Unpublished research paper. Grendon Underwood: HMP Grendon.

——(1998) 'Changes in measures of personality, hostility and locus of control during residence in a prison therapeutic community', *Legal and Criminological Psychology* 3 (2): 209–23.

——(2000) 'Psychological variables as dynamic risk factors for reconviction among residents in a prison therapeutic community', in J. Shine (ed.) *A Compilation of Grendon Research*. Grendon Underwood: HMP Grendon.

——(2006) 'Evaluating Grendon as a prison: Research into quality of life at Grendon', *Prison Service Journal* 164: 18–22.

——(2010) 'Changes in prison offending among residents of a prison-based therapeutic community', in R. Shuker and E. Sullivan (eds) *Grendon and the Emergence of Forensic Therapeutic Communities: Developments in Research and Practice*. Chichester: Wiley-Blackwell.

Newton, M. and Thornton, D. (1994) 'Grendon Reconviction Study, Part 1 Update'. Unpublished internal correspondence.

Niven, K., Holman, D. and Totterdell, P. (2010) 'Emotional influence and empathy in prison-based therapeutic communities', in R. Shuker and E. Sullivan (eds) *Grendon and the Emergence of Forensic Therapeutic Communities: Developments in Research and Practice*. Chichester: Wiley-Blackwell.

Noddings, N. (1984) *Caring: A Feminine Approach to Ethics and Moral Education*. Berkeley, CA: University of California Press.

O'Donnell, I. (2004) 'Prison rape in context', *British Journal of Criminology* 44 (2): 241–55.

O'Malley, P. (1992) 'Risk, power and crime prevention', *Economy and Society* 21 (3): 252–75.

Ogloff, J., Wong, S. and Greenwood, A. (1990) 'Treating criminal psychopaths in a therapeutic community programme', *Behavioral Sciences and the Law* 8 (2): 181–90.

Ortmann, R. (2000) 'The effectiveness of social therapy in prison – a randomized experiment', *Crime & Delinquency* 46 (2): 214–32.

Owen, B. (1998) *'In the Mix': Struggle and Survival in a Women's Prison*. Albany, NY: State University of New York Press.

Oyserman, D. and Markus, H. (1990) 'Possible selves and delinquency', *Journal of Personality and Social Psychology* 59 (1): 112–25.

Palys, T. and Lowman, J. (2001) 'Social research with eyes wide shut: The limited confidentiality dilemma', *Canadian Journal of Criminology* 43 (2): 255–67.

Parker, M. (ed.) (2007) *Dynamic Security: The Democratic Therapeutic Community in Prison*. London: Jessica Kingsley.

Parker, M. and Morris, M. (2004) 'Finding a secure base: Attachment in Grendon Prison', in F. Pfäfflin and G. Adshead (eds) *A Matter of Security: The Application of Attachment Theory to Forensic Psychiatry and Psychotherapy*. London: Jessica Kingsley.

Parker, T. (1970) *The Frying Pan: A Prison and its Prisoners*. London: Hutchinson.

Parsons, T. (1951) *The Social System*. Glencoe, IL: Free Press.

Patenaude, A. (2004) 'No promises, but I'm willing to listen and tell what I hear: Conducting qualitative research among prison inmates and staff', *Prison Journal* 84 (4) (Supplement): 69S–91S.

Pearson, F. and Lipton, D. (1999) 'A meta-analytic review of the effectiveness of corrections-based treatments for drug abuse', *Prison Journal* 79 (4): 384–410.

Pearson, G. (1993) 'Talking a good fight: Authenticity and distance in the ethnographer's craft', in D. Hobbs and T. May (eds) *Interpreting the Field: Accounts of Ethnography*. Oxford: Oxford University Press.

Pfäfflin, F. and Adshead, G. (eds) (2004) *A Matter of Security: The Application of Attachment Theory to Forensic Psychiatry and Psychotherapy*. London: Jessica Kingsley.

Phares, E.J. (1976) *Locus of Control in Personality*. Morristown, NJ: General Learning Press.

Phoenix Futures (2012) *Our Prison Services: Therapeutic Community*. Available at: www.phoenix-futures.org.uk/our-services/our-prison-services/therapeutic-community/ [accessed 10 March 2012].

Piacentini, L. (2004) *Surviving Russian Prisons: Punishment, Economy and Politics in Transition*. Cullompton: Willan Publishing.

Pickering, I. (1970) 'Foreword', in T. Parker, *The Frying Pan: A Prison and its Prisoners*. London: Hutchinson.

Pilling, J. (1992) 'Back to basics: Relationships in the Prison Service: Eve Saville Memorial Lecture to the Institute for the Study and Treatment of Delinquency', reproduced in *Perspectives on Prison: A Collection of Views on Prison Life and Running Prisons. Supplement to Annual Report of the Prison Service 1991–2*. London: HM Prison Service.

Pithers, W. (1990) 'Relapse prevention with sexual aggressors: A method for maintaining therapeutic gain and enhancing external supervision', in W. Marshall, D.R. Laws and H. Barbaree (eds) *Handbook of Sexual Assault: Issues, Theories and Treatment of the Offender*. New York and London: Plenum.

Polsky, N. (1971) *Hustlers, Beats and Others*. Harmondsworth: Penguin Books.

Pratt, J. (1998) 'Towards the "decivilizing" of punishment?', *Social and Legal Studies* 7 (4): 487–515.

Prendergast, M., Hall, E., Wexler, H., Melnick, G. and Cao, Y. (2004) 'Amity prison-based therapeutic community: 5-Year outcomes', *Prison Journal* 84 (1): 36–60.

Presser, L. (2004) 'Violent offenders, moral selves: Constructing identities and accounts in the research interview', *Social Problems* 51 (1): 82–101.

——(2008) *Been a Heavy Life: Stories of Violent Men*. Urbana: University of Illinois Press.

——(2009) 'The narratives of offenders', *Theoretical Criminology* 13 (2): 177–200.

Prison Commissioners (1927) *Report of the Prison Commissioners for 1926*, Parliamentary Papers Cmnd. 2597. London: Her Majesty's Stationery Office.

Prison Rules (1999) *The Prison Rules 1999*, Statutory Instruments 1999 No. 728. London: Her Majesty's Stationery Office.

Prisons and Probation Ombudsman (2011) *Annual Report 2010–11*. London: Prisons and Probation Ombudsman.

Prochaska, J. and DiClemente, C. (1984) *The Transtheoretical Approach: Crossing Traditional Boundaries of Therapy*. Homewood, IL: Dow Jones Irwin.

Pryor, S. (2001) *The Responsible Prisoner: An Exploration of the Extent to which Imprisonment Removes Responsibility Unnecessarily and an Invitation to Change*. London: Home Office.

——(2004) 'Prison – the un-responsible sentence', *Vista: Perspectives on Probation, Criminal Justice and Civil Renewal* 9 (2): 121–24.

Punch, M. (1986) *The Politics and Ethics of Fieldwork*. Qualitative Research Methods Series, Volume 3. Newbury Park, CA, and London: Sage.

Rapoport, R. (1960) *Community as Doctor: New Perspectives on a Therapeutic Community*. London: Tavistock Publications.

Raynor, P. and Robinson, G. (2005) *Rehabilitation, Crime and Justice*. Basingstoke: Palgrave Macmillan.

Redondo, S., Sanchez-Meca, J. and Garrido, V. (1999) 'The influence of treatment programmes on the recidivism of juvenile and adult offenders: An European meta-analytic review', *Psychology, Crime & Law* 5 (3): 251–78.

Reuss, A. (2000) 'The researcher's tale', in D. Wilson and A. Reuss (eds) *Prison(er) Education: Stories of Change and Transformation*. Winchester: Waterside Press.

Rhodes, L. (2010) '"This can't be real": Continuity at HMP Grendon', in R. Shuker and E. Sullivan (eds) *Grendon and the Emergence of Forensic Therapeutic Communities: Developments in Research and Practice*. Chichester: Wiley-Blackwell.

Rice, M., Harris, G. and Cormier, C. (1992) 'An evaluation of a maximum security therapeutic community for psychopaths and other mentally disordered offenders', *Law and Human Behavior* 16 (4): 399–412.

Rich, P. (2006) *Attachment and Sexual Offending: Understanding and Applying Attachment Theory to the Treatment of Juvenile Sexual Offenders*. Chichester: Wiley.

Riessman, F. (1965) 'The helper therapy principle', *Social Work* 10 (2): 27–32.

——(1990) 'Restructuring help: A human services paradigm for the 1990s', *American Journal* of *Community Psychology* 18 (2): 221–30.

Rivlin, A (2010) 'Suicide and self-injurious behaviours at HMP Grendon', in R. Shuker and E. Sullivan (eds) *Grendon and the Emergence of Forensic Therapeutic Communities: Developments in Research and Practice.* Chichester: Wiley-Blackwell.

Roberts, J. (1997a) 'How to recognise a therapeutic community', *Prison Service Journal* 111: 4–7.

——(1997b) 'History of the therapeutic community', in E. Cullen, L. Jones and R. Woodward (eds) *Therapeutic Communities for Offenders.* Chichester: Wiley.

Robertson, G. and Gunn, J. (1987) 'A ten-year follow-up of men discharged from Grendon prison', *British Journal of Psychiatry* 151 (5): 674–78.

Robinson, G. and Crow, I. (2009) *Offender Rehabilitation: Theory, Research and Practice.* London: Sage.

Rose, N. (1998) 'Governing risky individuals: The role of psychiatry in new regimes of control', *Psychiatry, Psychology and Law* 5 (2): 177–95.

Rotter, J. (1966) 'Generalized expectancies for internal versus external control of reinforcement', *Psychological Monographs* 80 (1, Whole No. 609): 1–28.

Royal College of Psychiatrists (1986) 'Obituary: William John Gray', *Bulletin of the Royal College of Psychiatrists* 10 (5): 125. London: Royal College of Psychiatrists.

——(2008) *The Development of Core Standards and Core Values for Therapeutic Communities: Briefing Paper.* London: Royal College of Psychiatrists' Centre for Quality Improvement.

Rubin, H. and Rubin, I. (2005) *Qualitative Interviewing: The Art of Hearing Data*, 2nd edn. Thousand Oaks, CA: Sage.

Rumgay, J. (2004) 'Scripts for safer survival: Pathways out of female crime', *Howard Journal of Criminal Justice* 43 (4): 405–19.

Rutherford, A. (1993) *Criminal Justice and the Pursuit of Decency.* Oxford: Oxford University Press.

Ryan, R. and Deci, E. (2000) 'Self-determination theory and the facilitation of intrinsic motivation, social development, and well-being', *American Psychologist* 55 (1): 68–78.

Sabo, D. (2001) 'Doing time, doing masculinity: Sports and prison', in D. Sabo, T. Kupers and W. London (eds) *Prison Masculinities.* Philadelphia, PA: Temple University Press.

Sabo, D., Kupers, T. and London, W. (eds) (2001) *Prison Masculinities.* Philadelphia, PA: Temple University Press.

Salekin, R. (2002) 'Psychopathy and clinical pessimism: Clinical lore or clinical reality?', *Clinical Psychology Review* 22 (1): 79–112.

Sampson, A. (1994) *Acts of Abuse: Sex Offenders and the Criminal Justice System.* London: Routledge.

Sampson, R. and Laub, J. (1993) *Crime in the Making: Pathways and Turning Points Through Life.* Cambridge, MA: Harvard University Press.

Sapp, A. and Vaughn, M. (1990) 'The social status of adult and juvenile sex offenders in prison: An analysis of the importation model', *Journal of Police and Criminal Psychology* 6 (2): 2–7.

Schmid, T. and Jones, R. (1991) 'Suspended identity: Identity transformation in a maximum security prison', *Symbolic Interaction* 14 (4): 415–32.

Schwaebe, C. (2005) 'Learning to pass: Sex offenders' strategies for establishing a viable identity in the prison general population', *International Journal of Offender Therapy and Comparative Criminology* 49 (6): 614–25.

Schwartz, J., Lurigio, A. and Slomka, S. (1996) 'The impact of IMPACT: An assessment of the effectiveness of a jail-based treatment program', *Crime and Delinquency* 42 (4): 553–73.

Scottish Home and Health Department (1971) *Report of a Departmental Working Party on the Treatment of Certain Male Long-Term Prisoners and Potentially Violent Prisoners.* Edinburgh: Scottish Home and Health Department.

Scottish Prison Service (1994) *Small Units in the Scottish Prison Service: A Report of the Working Party on Barlinnie Special Unit.* Edinburgh: Scottish Prison Service.

Scully, D. (1990) *Understanding Sexual Violence: A Study of Convicted Rapists.* Boston, MA, and London: Unwin Hyman.

Seidler, V. (1985) 'Fear and intimacy', in A. Metcalfe and M. Humphries (eds) *The Sexuality of Men.* London: Pluto Press.

——(1992) 'Men, sex and relationships', in V. Seidler (ed.) *Men, Sex and Relationships: Writings from Achilles Heel.* London: Routledge.

Selby, M. (1991) 'Grendon – The care of acute psychiatric patients – A pragmatic solution', in J. Reynolds and U. Smartt (eds) (1995) *Prison Policy and Practice: Selected Papers from 35 years of the Prison Service Journal.* HMP Leyhill: Prison Service Journal.

Sennett, R. (2003) *Respect: The Formation of Character in a World of Inequality.* London: Allen Lane.

Shaffir, W. (1991) 'Managing a convincing self-presentation: Some personal reflections on entering the field', in W. Shaffir and R. Stebbins (eds) *Experiencing Fieldwork: An Inside View of Qualitative Research.* Newbury Park, CA: Sage.

Sharp, V. (1975) *Social Control in the Therapeutic Community.* Farnborough: Saxon House and Lexington, MA: Lexington Books.

Shefer, G. (2010a) 'Doing Rehabilitation in the Contemporary Prison: The Case of One-wing Therapeutic Communities'. Unpublished PhD thesis. Institute of Criminology, University of Cambridge.

——(2010b) 'The quality of life of prisoners and staff at HMP Grendon', in R. Shuker and E. Sullivan (eds) *Grendon and the Emergence of Forensic Therapeutic Communities: Developments in Research and Practice.* Chichester: Wiley-Blackwell.

Shine, J. (ed.) (2000) *A Compilation of Grendon Research.* Grendon Underwood: HMP Grendon.

Shine, J. and Newton, M. (2000) 'Damaged, disturbed and dangerous: A profile of receptions to Grendon therapeutic prison 1995–2000', in J. Shine (ed.) *A Compilation of Grendon Research.* Grendon Underwood: HMP Grendon.

Shover, N. (1985) *Ageing Criminals.* Beverly Hills, CA: Sage.

——(1996) *Great Pretenders: Pursuits and Careers of Persistent Thieves.* Boulder, CO, and Oxford: Westview Press.

Shuker, R. (2010) 'Forensic therapeutic communities: A critique of treatment model and evidence base', *Howard Journal of Criminal Justice* 49 (5): 463–77.

Shuker, R. and Jones, D. (2007) 'Assessing risk and need in a prison therapeutic community: An integrative model', in M. Parker (ed.) *Dynamic Security: The Democratic Therapeutic Community in Prison.* London: Jessica Kingsley.

Shuker, R. and Newton, M. (2008) 'Treatment outcome following intervention in a prison-based therapeutic community: A study of the relationship between reduction in criminogenic risk and improved psychological well-being', *British Journal of Forensic Practice* 10 (3): 33–44.

Shuker, R. and Sullivan, E. (eds) (2010) *Grendon and the Emergence of Forensic Therapeutic Communities: Developments in Research and Practice.* Chichester: Wiley-Blackwell.

Sim, J. (1994) 'Tougher than the rest? Men in prison', in T. Newburn and E. Stanko (eds) *Just Boys Doing Business? Men, Masculinities and Crime.* London: Routledge.

——(2009) *Punishment and Prisons: Power and the Carceral State.* London: Sage.

Simon, J. (1998) 'Managing the monstrous: Sex offenders and the new penology', *Psychology, Public Policy, and Law* 1–2: 452–67.

Smart, C. (1976) *Women, Crime and Criminology: A Feminist Critique.* London: Routledge and Kegan Paul.

Smartt, U. (2001) *Grendon Tales: Stories from a Therapeutic Community.* Winchester: Waterside Press.

Smircich, L. (1983) 'Studying organizations as cultures: Organization as a network of meaning', in G. Morgan (ed.) *Beyond Method: Strategies for Social Research.* Beverly Hills, CA: Sage.

Smith, C. (2002) 'Punishment and pleasure: Women, food and the imprisoned body', *Sociological Review* 50 (2): 197–214.

Snyder, C.R. (1994) *The Psychology of Hope: You Can Get There From Here.* New York: Free Press.

——(2002) 'Hope theory: Rainbows in the mind', *Psychological Inquiry* 13 (4): 249–75.

Snyder, C.R., Harris, C., Anderson, J.R., Holleran, S.A., Irving, L.M., Sigmon, S.T. and Harney, P. (1991) 'The will and the ways: Development and validation of an individual-differences measure of hope', *Journal of Personality and Social Psychology* 60 (4): 570–85.

Social Exclusion Unit (2002) *Reducing Re-offending by Ex-Prisoners: Summary of the Social Exclusion Report.* London: Social Exclusion Unit.

Solomon, E. and Edgar, K. (2004) *Having Their Say: The Work of Prisoner Councils.* London: Prison Reform Trust.

Solomon, P. (2004) 'Peer support/peer provided services: Underlying processes, benefits, and critical ingredients', *Psychiatric Rehabilitation Journal* 27 (4): 392–401.

Soothill, K. and Walby, S. (1991) *Sex Crime in the News.* London: Routledge.

Spandler, H. (2006) *Asylum to Action: Paddington Day Hospital, Therapeutic Communities and Beyond.* London: Jessica Kingsley.

Sparks, R. (1994) 'Out of the digger: The Barlinnie Special Unit as prison and escape', *Prison Service Journal* 95: 2–6.

——(2002) 'Out of the "digger": The warrior's honour and the guilty observer', *Ethnography* 3 (4): 556–81.

Sparks, R., Bottoms, A. and Hay, W. (1996) *Prisons and the Problem of Order.* Oxford: Clarendon Press.

Sroufe, L. (1983) 'Infant-caregiver attachment and patterns of adaptation in preschool: The roots of maladaptation and competence', in M. Perlmutter (ed.) *Minnesota Symposia on Child Psychology* 16: 41–81. Hillsdale, NJ: Erlbaum.

Stanley, L. and Wise, S. (1983) *Breaking Out: Feminist Consciousness and Feminist Research.* London: Routledge and Kegan Paul.

Stanton, A. and Schwartz, M. (1954) *The Mental Hospital.* New York: Basic Books.

Steele, J. (2002) *The Bird that Never Flew.* Edinburgh: Mainstream.

Stephen, I. (1988) 'The Barlinnie Special Unit: A penal experiment', in S. Backett, J. McNeill and A. Yellowlees (eds) *Imprisonment Today: Current Issues in the Prison Debate.* Basingstoke: Macmillan.

Stevens, A. (2010) 'Introducing forensic democratic therapeutic communities', in R. Shuker and E. Sullivan (eds) *Grendon and the Emergence of Forensic Therapeutic Communities: Developments in Research and Practice*. Chichester: Wiley-Blackwell.

——(2011) '"A very decent nick": Ethical treatment in prison-based democratic therapeutic communities', *Journal of Forensic Psychology Practice* 11 (2): 124–50.

——(2012) '"I am the person now I was always meant to be": Identity reconstruction and narrative reframing in therapeutic community prisons', *Criminology and Criminal Justice*. Pre-published 9 January 2012 DOI: 10.1177/1748895811432958.

——(forthcoming) 'Prisoners' motivations for therapeutic community treatment: In search of a "different" approach to offender rehabilitation', *Probation Journal*.

Stewart, C. and Parker, M. (2007) 'Send: The women's democratic therapeutic community in prison', in M. Parker (ed.) *Dynamic Security: The Democratic Therapeutic Community in Prison*. London: Jessica Kingsley.

Strauss, A. (1987) *Qualitative Analysis for Social Scientists*. Cambridge: Cambridge University Press.

Strauss, A. and Corbin, J. (1998) *Basics of Qualitative Research: Techniques and Procedures for Developing Grounded Theory*, 2nd edn. London: Sage.

Stürup, G. (1968) *Treating the Untreatable: Chronic Criminals at Herstedvester*. Baltimore, MD: Johns Hopkins University Press.

Sugarman, B. (1984) 'Towards a new, common model of the therapeutic community: Structural components, learning processes and outcomes', *International Journal of Therapeutic Communities* 5 (2): 77–98.

Sullivan, E. (2005) 'Reasons for Leaving Grendon: A Study of Drop-Out Rates'. Unpublished internal report. Grendon Underwood: HMP Grendon.

——(2007) '"Seeing beyond the uniform": Positive views of a prison through prisoners' eyes', *Prison Service Journal* 173: 27–33.

Sutherland, E. (1939) *Principles of Criminology*. Philadelphia, PA: Lippincott.

Sykes, G. (1956) 'Men, merchants and toughs: A study of reactions to imprisonment', *Social Problems* 4 (2): 130–38.

——(1958) *The Society of Captives: A Study of a Maximum Security Prison*. Princeton, NJ: Princeton University Press.

——(1995) 'The structural-functional perspective on imprisonment', in T. Blomberg and S. Cohen (eds) *Punishment and Social Control: Essays in Honor of Sheldon L. Messinger*. New York: Aldine de Gruyter.

Sykes, G. and Matza, D. (1957) 'Techniques of neutralization: A theory of delinquency', *American Sociological Review* 22 (6): 664–70.

Sykes, G. and Messinger, S. (1960) 'The inmate social system', in R. Cloward (ed.) *Theoretical Studies in Social Organization of the Prison*. New York: Social Science Research Council.

Szasz, T. (1961) *The Myth of Mental Illness: Foundations of a Theory of Personal Conduct*. New York: Dell.

Tait, S. (2008) 'Care and the prison officer: Beyond "turnkeys" and "care bears"', *The Prison Service Journal* 180: 3–11.

——(2011) 'A typology of prison officer approaches to care', *European Journal of Criminology* 8 (6): 440–54.

Tajfel, H. (1982) *Social Identity and Intergroup Relations*. Cambridge: Cambridge University Press.

Taylor, R. (2000) *A Seven Year Reconviction Study of HMP Grendon Therapeutic Community.* Home Office Research Findings No. 115. London: Home Office Research, Development and Statistics Directorate.

Terry, K. and Mitchell, E. (2001) 'Motivation and sex offender treatment efficacy: Leading a horse to water *and* making it drink?', *International Journal of Offender Therapy and Comparative Criminology* 45 (6): 663–72.

Thomas, C. (1977) 'Theoretical perspectives on prisonization: A comparison of the importation model and deprivation models', *Journal of Criminal Law and Criminology* 68 (1): 135–45.

Thomas-Peter, B. (2006) 'The modern context of psychology in corrections: Influence, limitations and values of "what works"', in G. Towl (ed.) *Psychological Research in Prisons.* Oxford: British Psychological Society and Blackwell Publishing.

Thornton, D., Mann, R., Bowers, L., Sheriff, N. and White, T. (1996) 'Sex offenders in a therapeutic community', in J. Shine (ed.) (2000) *A Compilation of Grendon Research.* Grendon Underwood: HMP Grendon.

Thurston, R. (1996) 'Are you sitting comfortably? Men's storytelling, masculinities, prison culture and violence', in M. Mac an Ghaill (ed.) *Understanding Masculinities: Social Relations and Cultural Arenas.* Buckingham: Open University Press.

Toch, H. (1997) *Corrections: A Humanistic Approach.* New York: Harrow and Heston.

——(1998) 'Hypermasculinity and prison violence', in L. Bowker (ed.) *Masculinities and Violence.* Thousand Oaks, CA, and London: Sage.

——(2000) 'Altruistic activity as correctional treatment', *International Journal of Offender Therapy and Comparative Criminology* 44 (3): 270–78.

——(2006) 'Is there a future for humane imprisonment?', in D. Jones (ed.) *Humane Prisons.* Abingdon: Radcliffe.

Tolson, A. (1977) *The Limits of Masculinity.* London: Tavistock Publications.

Tronto, J. (1993) *Moral Boundaries: A Political Argument for an Ethic of Care.* New York: Routledge.

Tyler, T. (1990) *Why People Obey the Law.* New Haven, CT: Yale University Press.

Uggen, C., Manza, J. and Behrens, A. (2004) 'Less than the average citizen: Stigma, role transition and the civic reintegration of convicted felons', in S. Maruna and R. Immarigeon (eds) *After Crime and Punishment: Pathways to Offender Reintegration.* Cullompton: Willan Publishing.

User Voice (2010) *The Power Inside: The Role of Prison Councils.* London: User Voice.

Valentine, G. and Longstaff, B. (1998) 'Doing porridge: Food and social relations in a male prison', *Journal of Material Culture* 3 (2): 131–52.

Vandevelde, S., Broekaert, E., Yates, R. and Kooyman, M. (2004) 'The development of the therapeutic community in correctional establishments: A comparative retrospective account of the "democratic" Maxwell Jones TC and the hierarchical concept-based TC in prison', *International Journal of Social Psychiatry* 50 (1): 66–79.

van Maanen, J. (1991) 'Playing back the tape: Early days in the field', in W. Shaffir and R. Stebbins (eds) *Experiencing Fieldwork: An Inside View of Qualitative Research.* Newbury Park, CA: Sage.

Veysey, B., Christian, J. and Martinez, D. (eds) (2009) *How Offenders Transform their Lives.* Cullompton: Willan Publishing.

Vidich, A. (1955) 'Participant observation and the collection and interpretation of data', *American Journal of Sociology* 60 (4): 354–60.

Ward, T. and Brown, M. (2004) 'The good lives model and conceptual issues in offender rehabilitation', *Psychology, Crime & Law* 10 (3): 243–57.

Ward, T. and Keenan, T. (1999) 'Child molesters' implicit theories', *Journal of Interpersonal Violence* 14 (8): 821–38.

Ward, T. and Maruna, S. (2007) *Rehabilitation*. London and New York: Routledge.

Ward, T., Hudson, S., Marshall, W. and Siegert, R. (1995) 'Attachment style and intimacy deficits in sexual offenders: A theoretical framework', *Sexual Abuse: A Journal of Research and Treatment* 7 (4): 317–35.

Ward, T., Mann, R. and Gannon, T. (2007) 'The good lives model of offender rehabilitation: Clinical implications', *Aggression and Violent Behavior* 12 (1): 87–107.

Ware, J., Frost, A. and Hoy, A. (2010) 'A review of the use of therapeutic communities with sexual offenders', *International Journal of Offender Therapy and Comparative Criminology* 54 (5): 721–42.

Warr, M. (1998) 'Life-course transitions and desistance from crime', *Criminology* 36 (2): 183–216.

——(2002) *Companions in Crime: The Social Aspects of Criminal Conduct*. Cambridge: Cambridge University Press.

Warren, F. (1994) 'What do we mean by a "therapeutic community" for offenders? Commentary on papers by Harris *et al.* and Cullen', *Therapeutic Communities: The International Journal for Therapeutic and Supportive Organizations* 15 (4): 312–18.

West, C. and Zimmerman, D. (1987) 'Doing gender', *Gender and Society* 1 (2): 125–51.

Wexler, H. (1997) 'Therapeutic communities in American prisons', in E. Cullen, L. Jones and R. Woodward (eds) *Therapeutic Communities for Offenders*. Chichester: Wiley.

Wexler, H., Falkin, G. and Lipton, D. (1990) 'Outcome evaluation of a prison therapeutic community for substance abuse treatment', *Criminal Justice and Behavior* 17 (1): 71–92.

Wexler, H., de Leon, G., Thomas, G., Kressel, D. and Peters, J. (1999) 'The Amity prison TC evaluation: Reincarceration outcomes', *Criminal Justice and Behavior* 26 (2): 147–67.

Whatmore, P. (1987) 'Barlinnie Special Unit: An insider's view', in A. Bottoms and R. Light (eds) *Problems of Long-term Imprisonment*. London: Gower.

Whitehead, A. (2005) 'Man to man violence: How masculinity may work as a dynamic risk factor', *Howard Journal of Criminal Justice* 44 (4): 411–22.

Whiteley, S. (2004) 'The evolution of the therapeutic community', *Psychiatric Quarterly* 75 (3): 233–48.

Whyte, W. Foote (1981) *Street Corner Society: The Social Structure of an Italian Slum*, 3rd edn. Chicago, IL: University of Chicago Press.

——(1984) *Learning from the Field: A Guide from Experience*. London: Sage.

Widdowfield, R. (2000) 'The place of emotions in academic research', *Area* 32 (2): 199–208.

Williams Saunders, J. (ed.) (2001) *Life within Hidden Worlds: Psychotherapy in Prisons*. London: Karnac.

Wilson, D. and McCabe, S. (2002) 'How HMP Grendon "works" in the words of those undergoing therapy', *Howard Journal of Criminal Justice* 41 (2): 279–91.

Winfree, L.T., Newbold, G. and Tubb, S.H. (2002) 'Prisoner perspectives on inmate culture in New Mexico and New Zealand: A descriptive case study', *Prison Journal* 82 (2): 213–33.

Winlow, S. (2001) *Badfellas: Crime, Tradition and New Masculinities*. Oxford: Berg.

Wood, T. (2007) '"We used to make a football out of a goat head": Working with young offenders in a prison therapeutic community', in M. Parker (ed.) *Dynamic Security: The Democratic Therapeutic Community in Prison*. London: Jessica Kingsley.

Woodward, R. (1999) 'The prison communities: Therapy within a custodial setting', in P. Campling and R. Haigh (eds) *Therapeutic Communities: Past, Present and Future.* London: Jessica Kingsley.

Woodward, R. and Hodkin, G. (1996) 'Another British first: Gartree's therapeutic community for lifers', *Prison Service Journal* 103: 47–50.

Woolf, H. (1991) *Prison Disturbances April 1990: Report of an Inquiry by the Rt Hon Lord Justice Woolf (Parts I and II) and His Honour Judge Stephen Tumim (Part II)*, Cmnd. 1456. London: Her Majesty's Stationery Office.

Wortley, R. (2002) *Situational Prison Control: Crime Prevention in Correctional Institutions.* Cambridge: Cambridge University Press.

Wright, K. (1991) 'A study of individual, environmental, and interactive effects in explaining adjustment to prison', *Justice Quarterly* 8 (2): 217–42.

Yablonsky, L. (1965) 'Experiences with the criminal community', in A. Gouldner and S. Miller (eds) *Applied Sociology: Opportunities and Problems.* New York: The Free Press and London: Collier-Macmillan.

Yalom, I. (1980) *Existential Psychotherapy.* New York: Basic Books.

——(1995) *The Theory and Practice of Group Psychotherapy*, 4th edn. New York: Basic Books.

Young, E. and Lee, R. (1996) 'Fieldworker feelings as data: "Emotion work" and "feeling rules" in the first person accounts of sociological fieldwork', in V. James and J. Gabe (eds) *Health and the Sociology of Emotions.* Oxford: Blackwell.

Zhang, S., Roberts, R. and McCollister, K. (2011) 'Therapeutic community in a California prison: Treatment outcomes after 5 years', *Crime & Delinquency* 57 (1): 82–101.

Index

Page numbers followed by 'n' indicate notes. TC is used throughout as an abbreviation for therapeutic community.